THE BIRTHPANGS OF PROTESTANT ENGLAND

The Birthpangs of Protestant England

Religious and Cultural Change in
the Sixteenth and Seventeenth Centuries

*The Third Anstey Memorial Lectures in
the University of Kent at Canterbury
12–15 May 1986*

Patrick Collinson

*Regius Professor of Modern History
University of Cambridge*

First published 1988 by
MACMILLAN PRESS LTD
Houndmills, Basingstoke, Hampshire RG21 2XS
and London
Companies and representatives
throughout the world

ISBN 0–333–43971–6 (hardcover)
ISBN 0–333–54307–6 (paperback)

A catalogue record for this book is available
from the British Library.

11   10   9   8   7   6   5   4   3
03   02   01   00   99   98   97   96   95

Printed in Great Britain by
Antony Rowe Ltd,
Chippenham, Wiltshire

To Geoff Dickens,
who both led and pointed the way,
this book is dedicated with affection
and great respect

Contents

Preface and Acknowledgements

The *birthpangs* of Protestant England should be distinguished from earlier, preparative stages in the life-cycle: impregnation, conception, gestation. A study of these themes would reach back into the religious culture of the fifteenth and early sixteenth centuries. But if I were to be asked when Protestant England was born I would answer, with greater conviction than I could have mustered even a few years ago: after the accession of Elizabeth I, some considerable time after. It is only with the 1570s that the historically minded insomniac goes to sleep counting Catholics rather than Protestants, since only then did they begin to find themselves in a minority situation. I would even be prepared to assert, crudely and flatly, that the Reformation was something which happened in the reigns of Elizabeth and James I. Before that everything was preparative, embryonic. Protestantism was present, but as a kind of sub-culture, like Catholicism later.

How often we have been told, even by proponents of 'slow Reformation', that some areas of the east and south-east, particularly Essex and Kent, were precociously protestant at an early date, so that it could be said of those counties at least, and perhaps only of those, what Sir Geoffrey Elton wrote of England as a whole in 1553: that it was closer to being a protestant country than anything else. Yet in 1598 a man of Kent living in Essex, Thomas Stoughton, recorded this potted history of his own experience:

> Myself, as young as I am, did know the time long sithence the happy reign of her Majesty when we in Kent was most accounted, and also was indeed, the most popish place of all that country. But sithence it hath pleased God to send unto them the ministry of his Word, popery hath there vanished as the mist before the Sun: and now I think it is less noted for popery than any other place, especially any place which hath not had the Word, or that hath had it. Yea, few places are more forward than that in true profession of our religion.[1]

Although this observer's chronology and geography (or at least his syntax) are uncertain he seems to be saying that even Kent was more catholic than otherwise until perhaps the 1570s, when (and there is independent and more objective evidence for this) protestant preaching became more widely and securely established in the Kentish parishes. What he does not tell us is that the build-up of effective protestant evangelism of that decade found itself contending not so much with Catholicism, which Professor Peter Clark has called a paper tiger, as with a way of life and especially a pursuit of pastimes and pleasures which had lived happily alongside the old religion but found that it could not put up with the new. It was minstrels more than mass-priests who proved to be the enemy.[2]

The war against the minstrels and the Sunday dances, symbols and examples of Elizabethan popular culture, represented some of the cultural reverberations of the Protestant Reformation which are the subject of this book. It will be obvious that by no means have I offered to deal with all its reverberations. Those excluded include the subjects on which attention has been focused in much of the earlier literature: the Reformation and the production and distribution of wealth, the Reformation and political ideology and methodology, the Reformation and learning, including scientific learning. The explanation for the rather arbitrary and selective treatment which the subject receives in this little book is that it originated in the self-indulgence of a short course of guest lectures in which I was free to choose my subject and to bore my audience to my heart's content on matters which happened to interest me at the time.

To return to the metaphor of the title: the book was born in the invitation to deliver the third series of Roger Anstey Memorial Lectures in the University of Kent at Canterbury, where from 1976 until 1984 I was Professor of History, in unworthy succession to the founding father of the subject in Canterbury, the late and much lamented Leland Lyons. To have been invited back to give these lectures so soon after departing for Sheffield was a very special courtesy and compliment on the part of recent colleagues, and in particular of three members of the History Board who are most concerned with the Anstey Lectures: David Birmingham, Christine Bolt and Bruce Webster. They deserve my special thanks for the opportunity which this invitation gave to develop my thinking about what Ernst Troeltsch called the 'side-influences' of the Reformation. But many other members of that close-knit and friendly academic community are also to be thanked for the warmth of their reception – not least the Master of Eliot College where the lectures were given, Shirley Barlow.

The invitation from Canterbury hoisted me on my own petard since before leaving the University of Kent I had played some part in setting up this lecture series as a fitting memorial to Roger Anstey, first Professor of Modern History at Canterbury, who like Leland Lyons had died prematurely, in harness and at the height of his very considerable powers. It was right that I should have done so, since Roger Anstey taught me as an undergraduate at Cambridge, remained a friend and in due course encouraged me to tear up the roots I had begun to put down in Australia and to exchange the University of Sydney for the University of Kent.

Professor Terence Ranger, like Roger Anstey an Africanist, asked me why I of all people was giving the Anstey Lectures, and on such an unsuitable subject as the English Reformation. The answer was that these lectures are supposed to reflect Roger's wide interests as a historian, and whereas his particular learning and expertise lay in the history of Africa and in the story of the Atlantic Slave Trade and its suppression (subjects relevant to the first and second series of lectures, given respectively by John Iliffe and Seymour Drescher) he had a more general concern, as a devout historian, with what is generally called the religious factor, but which Roger would have preferred to identify less clinically and more theologically as the question of God in History. I explained to Terry Ranger that Roger and I were not in total agreement about this matter. He believed that God's revelation of himself and his purposes was apparent and progressive, that things could be seen to be getting better. The triumph of Christian enlightenment in the ending of the detestable slave trade between West Africa and the Americas was a case in point. When we talked about these things I took a gloomier view, one of proximate pessimism and only a very ultimate and remote optimism. I must say that nothing which has happened in the world in the eight years since Roger left it has changed my outlook in this respect. 'You mean', said Terry, who turned out to be still listening, 'that all God's fingers are thumbs.' Just so, I answered, that is how it looks from where I stand. But Roger Anstey, his spirit as well as his mind, what he *was* no less than what he did, make it easier to stand and take what has to come with that modicum of serenity which is required to retain sanity. I am glad to have the chance to say this to Rosalind, Charles and Louise, in affectionate memory of their parents, Roger and Avril, but not only to them.

The second chapter of the book was not part of the Anstey series but originated as another memorial lecture, delivered in Canterbury at the Urban Studies Centre in February 1986. This was the second

John Hayes Memorial Lecture, honouring the late John Hayes, head of history at Christchurch College Canterbury and a man of many parts whose historical and contemporary interests focused on the physical and social composition of towns. John was another good friend and close neighbour whose living presence I miss. I am grateful to the organisers of this event and especially to John's widow Peggy Hayes and to Caroline Simpson and Kenneth Pinnock for what was done on that occasion; and not least for consenting to the incorporation of the lecture in an expanded version in this book. The circumstances of its conception explain the choice of illustrative evidence from Canterbury, wherever possible.

This book could not have been brought to the press without the stimulation and encouragement freely given by many friends who share my enthusiasm for the subject and the period. Many of these collaborators have been thanked on previous occasions, but particular tribute is due in this Preface to present colleagues at Sheffield, including Anthony Fletcher (about to leave us for Durham), Mark Greengrass, Mick Hattaway, Michael Leslie and Sandy Lyle. Next I should name John King of Bates College, Maine. It was at the Huntington Library, where I was privileged to hold an Andrew C. Mellon Fellowship in 1984, and while occupying the office next door, that John played a very considerable part in the engendering of this work. My affectionate thanks are due to the Huntington, to its former Director, Bob Middlekauff, to many others on the staff, and to the many resident and visiting scholars who created the intellectual environment for a renewal of inventiveness. Above all I wish to recall the friendship of the late Professor Bill Ringler, the great man who inhabited the office across the hall, allowed me to use his telephone and was never too great to answer the most naive of questions about Elizabethan verse.

Chapter 3 is mortgaged to scholars who will be well enough known to students of family history. They include my old Canterbury colleague Andrew Butcher and his gifted pupil Diana O'Hara. Chapter 4 was long in the womb and went through some earlier incarnations, as lectures and seminar papers delivered in Oxford, at the Huntington Library, at Harvard, at the Folger Shakespeare Library and elsewhere. An earlier version has appeared in print as a Stenton Memorial Lecture, delivered at the University of Reading in November 1985.[3] The Folger seminar sat under the benign presidency of Willie Lamont of Sussex and proved a critical and stimulating experience of great value. Michael Biddiss and Ralph Houlbrooke of Reading were very helpful in connection with the Stenton Lecture. Many of the ideas scattered through this book first turned up in Special Subject seminars at the University of Kent, which were concerned with 'The Making of Protestant England'. My Sheffield Special Subject, 'Catholics, Lollards and Protestants', promises to be no less fruitful. One's historical enjoyment and perception would be even blunter than it is without the help of one's students, undergraduate and postgraduate alike.

This is my first experience of the house of Macmillan and like other Macmillan authors I have been expertly assisted in the necessary practicalities, especially by Pauline Snelson.

Patrick Collinson
Sheffield

FURTHER ACKNOWLEDGEMENTS

I am grateful to Sir Keith Thomas for his careful reading of this book, which led to a number of corrections of points of detail. I also take this opportunity to pay tribute to my many new colleagues and postgraduate students who have done so much to extend my thinking on the matters dealt with in this little volume. Rather than attempting to include so many new insights in its pages I have decided to let them stand, fossil-like, as a kind of memorial of where I stood before October 1988.

Patrick Collinson
Trinity College
Cambridge

1 The Protestant Nation

'Our present task is to examine the peculiar characteristics of the English and the special circumstances from which these derive.' Those are not my words. No English observer can be so detached and no historian ought to stand so far back from his canvas as to be able even to envisage such a task. Roger Anstey, for all his breadth of vision, would not have dreamed of anything so foolish. It is a German scholar (Levin L. Schücking, *The Puritan Family*) who is writing, in 1929, and who is struck by the English character as 'a very special . . . character . . . sharply distinguished from its counterpart on the European mainland', and which he assumes to be a protestant, or puritan character. Nevertheless while this book is not about the peculiarity of the English protestant character it may occasionally suggest why it should have been *thought*, and not only by foreigners, that it was a certain 'very special character'.

The subject of this first chapter is national self-consciousness, a self-consciousness often directly attributed to the Protestant Reformation. We shall try to determine how far that attribution is correct. It was in 1500, well before any change in the national religion could have been discerned, that the Venetian ambassador diagnosed in the English advanced symptoms of ethnocentricity: 'The English are great lovers of themselves, and of everything belonging to them; they think that there are no other men than themselves, and no other world but England; and whenever they see a handsome foreigner they say that "he looks like an Englishman" and that "it is a great pity that he should not be an Englishman".' This rather Gilbertian pleasantry seems to have been a commonplace among foreign observers. The Scottish Parisian intellectual John Major, writing in 1520, reported that if the English abroad happened upon a man of parts and spirit they would say "'tis pity he's not an Englishman'.[1] The Protestant Reformation was *thought* to have made a great difference to national self-esteem, not least by those who were themselves caught up in it; and that fact, an illusion though it may have been, is important in itself. Whether the Reformation really made such a large difference, to the nation or to the local community, or to the family, is another question.

Herbert Butterfield dismissed both Renaissance and Reformation as mere 'internal displacements' in the civilisation of traditional

1

Europe, their geographical equivalent being more like the Urals than the Himalayas, one might say. The critical transition to modernity did not lie in these events or processes, but came later. That was how it appeared from where Butterfield stood, there being no single vantage point from which the past is to be viewed and placed in perspective. But from where most Britons now find themselves the Reformation must seem even more remote and irrelevant to any current concerns. In reporting a recent agreement between Roman Catholic and Anglican theologians on the matter of 'justification', whether by faith only or by faith and works, the British Broadcasting Corporation had to assume even in a programme intended for churchgoers ('Sunday', 7 September 1986) that its listeners would have no familiarity with the issue and would not know why it was once important. Only in Ulster do such things still matter; and who wants to be reminded of that?

At the beginning of this century, when political life in Germany (and to some extent in this country) was still ordered along confessional lines, it was meaningful to conduct a debate about the Reformation and Modernity or, to quote the title of a little book by Ernst Troeltsch, *Protestantism and Progress*. Troeltsch made it a general rule that 'the relation of a religious system to civilization is always very complicated' – and Max Weber did not dissent. So it was evident to Troeltsch that Protestantism could not be supposed to have paved the way directly for the modern world. On the contrary it amounted, at least at first, to a revival and reinforcement of the 'authoritatively imposed Church-civilization' of the Middle Ages. Subsequently its influence was felt in 'indirect and unconsciously produced effects', 'accidental side-influences'. Both Weber's still famous essay on *The Protestant Ethic and the Spirit of Capitalism* and R.H. Tawney's once very famous book *Religion and the Rise of Capitalism* dealt, in very different ways, with the supposed side-influences of Protestantism, even with what might nowadays be called contraflows: specifically with respect to economic organisation and motivation.

Was the sense of nationality, nationalism even, another Reformation side-influence? Troeltsch thought not, and attributed this sentiment to two 'completely modern' forces: democracy and romanticism. However Christopher Hill, writing as recently as 1985, suggests that the intense religiosity of the Reformation, expressed in the single-minded devotion of the nation to a God who was assumed to be no less devoted to his people, effected the transition from the medieval kind of traditional and personalised fealty to the monarch to the modern conformity to the will of the impersonal state. This was to attribute to God himself that elusive quality in political responses and connections which Weber called 'charisma' and saw as transitional between traditional and legal-rational systems; and who could be more charismatic than the Almighty? 'Loyalty to God was the mediating term between loyalty to the person of the King and loyalty to the abstraction of the state.'[2] That looks like a proposition still worth investigation.

I

On the day that war broke out my father heard a London preacher declare that if Hitler were to win he would tear up his Bible (no doubt as strong men occasionally rip up telephone directories). My father was so offended that he resolved never to darken the doors of that church again. The preacher's rhetorical figure and my father's adverse reaction to it are typical of the intricate relationship which the Protestant Reformation established, not so much between church and state (which it both simplified and complicated), or between religion and politics (which was and still is a can of worms), as between God and the Nation; and this is a relationship to which we have scant access except in the rhetoric of the publicist and preacher, in whose mouth it was occasional, opportunistic and even manipulative, playing upon minds, emotions and consciences which may well have been confused but are in any case closed to the historian. Prebendary Colin Kerr of St Paul's Portman Square would not really have torn up his Bible if Germany had successfully invaded England in 1940. He said what he said to make the point that Hitler would not, could not, win. God would not let him. (But my Quaker father was offended, nevertheless, by the sheer presumptuousness of what he said.) Similarly, when seventeenth-century preachers threatened that God was about to desert the nation – 'as sure as God is God, God is going from England' – it is doubtful whether they really meant it. It was a way not only of dramatising the moral danger in which the country stood but also of underlining the special and ultimately secure relationship obtaining between God and at least some of his people. God would not really go from England. Would he?

Well, perhaps. In the Old Testament prophecy of Hosea God pronounces a terrible sentence upon Israel.[3] 'Then said God, call his name Lo-ammi, for ye are not my people and I will not be your God.' Commenting on this text, on which numerous English preachers would presently expound, John Calvin said that this was 'a final disowning of Israel . . . For God here abolishes, in a manner, the covenant he made with the holy fathers, so that the people would cease to have any pre-eminence over other nations . . . And then God wholly disinherited them'. But note Calvin's 'in a manner'. The great reformer seems to read the text as God's ultimate stratagem in a last-ditch effort to save a people whose disease was not so much incurable as 'almost incurable'. For, as English preachers would insist, all God's threatenings are conditional, 'to fall upon us if we repent not of our sins'. And so we come to Thomas Hooker, talking about God going from England on the eve of his own departure from Chelmsford, first for Holland and, later, for New England, where his destiny was to lay the foundations of Connecticut, a state of the Union. Hooker played cat and mouse with the very last English congregation he was ever to address: 'Shall I tell you what God told me? Nay, I must tell you on pain of my life . . . What if I should tell you what God told me yesternight, that he would destroy England and lay it waste . . . Well, look to it, for God is going, and if he do go, then our glory goes also.' But then, a moment or two later, he asked: 'How may we keep the Lord? It would be worth our labor.'[4]

If the reader is already lost in this little thicket of minor prophecy let him take refuge in a simple statement of three words, words invoked more often than any others to encapsulate what is said to be the protestant perception of God's special dealings with the English nation: GOD IS ENGLISH. They appeared in *An harborowe for faithfull and trewe subiectes*, a book written in 1559 by John Aylmer, some time a tutor of royal and semi-royal personages (much beloved by Lady Jane Grey), a recent protestant exile and a future bishop of London. 'God is English' is a marginal note, pungently summarising the rhetoric of the text: 'Play not the milk sops . . . Show your selves true Englishmen in readiness, courage and boldness: and be ashamed to be the last. Fear neither French nor Scot. For first, you have God and all his army of angels on your side.' 'God is English' still has the capacity to shock as well as to amuse, although it was not an original proposition but a commonplace, an aphorism affirming that England was what a Caroline preacher later called 'the peculiar place of God'. Latimer pronounced: 'Verily God hath shewed himself God of England, or rather the English God'. Lyly proclaimed in *Euphues and his England*: 'The living God is only the English God'. And even the sober Archbishop Matthew Parker could remark: 'Where Almighty God is so much English as he is . . .'[5]

In our enlightened age of ecumenical internationalism these sentiments are quoted in the lecture room to provoke a faint laugh from a jaded audience. It *was* a joke, or half a joke, in the sixteenth century, just as it raised a smile in the fourteenth century to say 'now the pope has become French, Jesus has become English'. This referred to a gold coin of Edward III which showed on one face the king standing in a ship, sword in hand, and on the other the text: 'But Jesus, passing through the midst of them, went his way'. But to say that something was a joke is not to say that it was not serious. If it really was the case that England was thought to be God's peculiar place, not just *an* elect nation but *the* elect nation, and if that idea was born out of the experience of the Protestant Reformation and its immediate consequences, then we have unearthed in protestant religious consciousness a root, perhaps even the taproot, of English imperialism.

From the taproot sprang a luxuriant growth which came to its literary climax in Milton's *Areopagitica* where the polemicist asked: 'Why else was this Nation chos'n before any other, that out of her as out of *Sion* should be proclaim'd and sounded forth the first tidings and trumpet of Reformation to all Europe?' – it being ever God's manner to reveal himself 'first to his Englishmen'. Elsewhere Milton wrote of England's 'precedence of teaching other nations how to live'. Was it this conviction which made mentally and morally feasible the acquisition of a global empire? The great F.W. Maitland, writing at a time when more than half the world was still coloured bright red or pink on the map, seems to have thought so. Commenting in *The Cambridge Modern History* on the enormity of events in 1559 and 1560, when the Reformation was gained in Scotland and regained in England, Maitland wrote that what was in the making was 'a new nation, a British nation'. 'The creed of unborn millions in undiscovered lands was being decided.' Addressing himself to the Commissioners of the Virginia Company in 1615, the London preacher Thomas Cooper suggested that the reason why the Gospel had been restored to the English nation was so that England might in her turn propagate it to 'our posterity and brethren, the nations far and near'. It was to this end that the precious seed had been watered with the blood of the Marian martyrs and cherished with the sunshine of the Elizabethan peace, so that 'the rude and savage nations', Ireland and Virginia, might receive 'this blessed light', making 'an inviolable league between those nations and our colonies': of which an early token was the newly baptised princess Pocohantos, 'lately married unto Jesus Christ and become one with you in the household of faith'.[6]

Even someone who took the religious factor as seriously as Professor Roger Anstey would not have accepted the Miltonic vision of England's destiny as sufficient explanation for the British Empire. Quite apart from more material factors we are dealing with only one of several forms of national and historical consciousness. John Pocock reminds us that a cleric, a lawyer and a herald of arms will each recall a different historical past. When the Elizabethan map-maker John Speed wrote of his love for 'this our native land', 'the very Eden of Europe', his inspiration was not that of the theologian or preacher. 'Nation' itself is a symbolic rather than a real entity, attracting to itself various myths suggestive of a common past which may or may not bear relation to the real, or institutional, past.[7]

However, religious myths have often made the most critical contribution to the nation as an idea. This is manifestly the case with the Armenians, the Ethiopians and above all the Jews. And it has recently been argued that in its earliest beginnings the unity and coherence of the English nation in its occupation of this island, which is already a fact in the pages of Bede, and under that name of 'English' rather than the more likely 'Saxon', owed something to Pope Gregory the Great's continued enjoyment of his celebrated pun, 'non Angli sed Angeli'. 'England' was born because successive archbishops of Canterbury, notably Theodore, projected the papal vision of the ideal essence of England before God. For, says Patrick Wormald, 'nations are made not just by conquest and political manoeuvre but by shared ideals'.[8]

Clearly, to start an account of the divinely ordained singularity of the English race at the Reformation is to start about nine hundred years too late. And if we want to trace the more immediate origins of the notion that God is English then the proper place to begin seems to be not the mid-sixteenth century but the mid-fourteenth, and the improbable successes of England in the earlier encounters of the Hundred Years' War. For it was then, in the age which produced Chaucer, when poets, politicians and preachers began to utter in English, that many of the mental attributes of the 'Protestant Nation' originated. It has been shown that the religious symbolism of incipient nationalism was deliberately borrowed from France, where it had been contrived as an ideology to correct centrifugal and divisive forces: something not called for by the more cohesive polity of medieval England, except in unusual wartime conditions. The first Avignon Pope, Clement V, had assured Philip the Fair that the French nation was 'like the people of Israel', 'a peculiar people'. So in 1377 the English Chancellor followed suit, pronouncing in the presence of the young Richard II that 'Israel is understood to be the heritage of God, as is England'. England's victories could be explained in no other way. But defeat had followed these improbable triumphs, and Bishop Thomas Brinton, like any Elizabethan or Jacobean preacher, was soon warning his hearers that 'God who was accustomed to being English will abandon us'. So it appears that Aylmer's slogan 'God is English', his appeal to the true Englishman to thank God daily that he had been born English and not as a French peasant, was not the voice of a new and protestant nationalism but an old rallying cry, uttered a matter of weeks before the Treaty of Cateau-Cambrésis ended what might be called the two hundred years' war between two ancient enemies.[9]

Long before the Protestant Reformation, and for as long after it, the idea that England was like Israel of old, God's preferred and privileged people, was always accessible, and in wartime it regularly received a particular application from the pulpit. In 1756, at the outbreak of the Seven Years' War, a preacher asked rhetorical questions which could have been posed, almost word for word, four centuries earlier: 'Do not we succeed the Jews? . . . Are not we a chosen generation, a peculiar people, as were they?' So when the felicitous Jacobean preacher Thomas Adams declared that '*Israel* and *England*, though they lie in a divers climate, may be said right *Parallels*: not so unfit in *Cosmographical* as fit in *Theological* comparison', he was merely giving a distinctively baroque expression to a commonplace inherited from the past and consigned to the future.[10]

II

At this point one may well ask whether there is anything of interest to be said by a sixteenth- and seventeenth-century historian about the *Protestant Nation* as such. There is. And it is more interesting than the naive and chauvinistic triumphalism of 'God is English', seeping through the pages of A.L. Rowse to add bright colours to the two-dimensional conventions of romanticised Tudor history. The Protestant Reformation extended and intensified the religious sense of English nationhood, according to Christopher Hill sublimating and idealising vulgar Elizabethan nationalism. But it also inhibited and confused that sense, turning it inward and ultimately converting it into a disturbing and divisive as much as a uniting force.

We shall deal later with the inhibition and the confusion, but first

the intensification. Behind the all too well-worn texts (Shakespeare's
'this blessed plot – this England', Queen Elizabeth's own 'the heart
and stomach of a king, and a king of England too') there are
numerous less familiar sources in the religious vein which are
remarkable for the intensity of their patriotic self-consciousness. 'Oh
England! England!', or 'Alas England', are constant refrains. The
first-generation Protestant Thomas Becon was stirred by Henry VIII's
invasion of France in 1543 (the expedition which launched and
sank the Mary Rose) to exclaim how every nation 'is led even of
nature with such an unspeakable loving affection toward his country'.
He even quotes Horace's text with, for us, its 1914 resonance: '*Dulce
et decorum est pro patria mori*', and he rhapsodises over 'England,
England, mine own native country . . .' Two eventful generations
later the Banbury preacher William Whateley (called 'the roaring boy
of Banbury') exulted: 'Ah England! Gods Signet, Gods Jewel, which
he hath fostered as tenderly and adorned as graciously as ever he did
Judea, England, the one only Nation, almost, that doth openly and
solely profess the true Religion of God!'[11]

And here the reader must excuse a little in-fighting. Among
historians of seventeenth-century England there has been a running
debate about the relative strength of provincial and national loyalties.
For a time Professor Alan Everitt of the Department of Local History
at Leicester made it a doctrine that whereas the senses of national
community and county community were both gathering strength in
this period, the stronger of the two sentiments was located in the
county community. England was an informal federation of counties,
and when a man spoke of his country he meant not England but, for
example, Kent, and probably either East Kent or West Kent, for the
frontier of the Medway separated two distinct communities, two
'countries'. More recently the fluid ambiguity of the term 'country'
has been acknowledged. It could and did mean various things, and
this was not so much a source of confusion as something positively
exploited in political rhetoric, as the speaker moved imperceptibly
from local to national issues.[12] But the protestant pulpit knew nothing
of these ambiguities, had never heard of the county community. To
the preacher 'my country' invariably meant England: realm, commonwealth, nation, people. The reason is obvious. The Bible, to
which he was riveted, knew nothing of counties: it knew only of a
nation, Israel, and of a city, Jerusalem. The classical authors, who
were another source of inspiration, also wrote of a transcendent
rather than a deliberately localised patriotism. So protestant learning
and pulpit oratory were powerful forces making for the transcen-

dence of more limited loyalties, and for attracting the minds and emotions of the hearers towards identification with the national community.

How is this intensification of religiously inspired national feeling to be explained? Henry VIII and Elizabeth are, of course, a large part of the answer in their assertion of an almost unreserved regal authority and dignity, hedged about with divinity. The king, in Tyndale's words, was 'in the room of God and representing God'; the royal supremacy was not merely a constitutional principle but an ideology, graphically expressed on the engraved title-page of Henry VIII's Great Bible, where the monarch is seen handing out the Scriptures to his subjects, clerical and lay, male and female, who respond with shouts of 'Vivat Rex', 'God Save the King'. Under Elizabeth the royal arms in every parish church literally usurped the place of honour hitherto reserved for the crucifix; the official sermons or homilies of the newly nationalised Church of England asserted that rebellion is worse than the worst government of the worst prince; Elizabeth, the apotheosis of Tudor monarchy, the crown of godly womanhood and the best of all conceivable princes, represented a paradox of the kind which the Bible delights in, her strength made perfect in weakness. She was described by a court chaplain as 'the peerless Queen of the World' and by a preacher at Canterbury as the corner-stone which the builders had rejected, which was to identify her with King David and even with Christ himself. Much of this was Accession Day rhetoric: 'Adore November's sacred seventeenth day!' But that 17 November should be considered the holiest date in the calendar was itself telling.[13]

All this we could take for granted, had some medievalists not doubted how much novelty there was in the royal supremacy and in the Henrician reconstitution of church and state. Long before he thought of breaking with Rome Henry VIII had changed his coronation oath to read that he would maintain the rights and liberties not of 'Holy Church' but of 'the holy Church of England'. The iconography with which the protestant monarchy of Elizabeth I was projected incorporated much late medieval symbolic language and has been called 'a reincarnation of the iconography of late medieval queens'. At the Council of Constance which convened in 1415 (the year of Agincourt!) the English delegation had strongly asserted the claims of the English church and nation, 'the famous and undoubted English nation', and had greeted French attacks on these pretensions with 'whistles and groans'. And what was the first of their claims? Why, that England had never left the obedience of the Roman Church.[14]

But now the king, in matters divine no less than secular, was, in Tyndale's words, to 'give accounts but to God only'. And the initial, legislative repudiation of the papal nexus steadily widened in its implications until anti-catholicism, founded on the formal proposition that the Pope is none other than Antichrist, became the sheet-anchor of England's nationhood. The prince's pre-eminence and splendid isola-ation on earth was matched in Heaven by God's unrivalled sovereignty. No more saints. If God was 'mere English', the English now had no god but God.

While investing the monarch with reflected divinity the Reforma-tion charged with moral significance all other authorities and political duties, all normative structures of the social order: magistracy, cer-tainly, but also the household and its head. In Elizabethan England moralistic discourse was pervasive, extending far beyond what might be considered a suitably religious context. An almanac of 1564 (the most popular and ephemeral of early printed literature) forecast a wet autumn and added: 'Therefore sleep no longer in sin but awake, awake, for it is high time'. And it was England which was to awake, for the nation itself acquired a highly personalised ideal and moral character which enabled it to be apostrophised – Oh England! – and held to moral account.

An almost sufficient explanation for that was the exploration of the Bible, now more or less freely if patchily available in the accessible and singularly authentic vernacular of Tyndale and the other trans-lators. This was a collection of texts of which the protestant preachers could soon assume, at least on the part of that minority of the population which came within the sound of their voices, a sophisti-cated and resourceful knowledge, and of the Old Testament as much as of the New – perhaps especially of the Old Testament. So it was that the Israel of the Old Testament became a familiar paradigm for England, Jerusalem for London. Every biblical type and figure of God's people was now applied to England, *ad nauseam*. England was a vineyard, a vine (but bringing forth wild grapes), a lodge in a garden of cucumbers. The Christ who wept but once over Jerusalem was forever weeping over London. Everything was turned to account. St Paul had expressed reluctance to leave Corinth. So when a bishop of London was translated to York he told his London flock: 'The city is like, the people are like, my departure from you is like'.[15] These people were living, in a sense, in the pages of the Bible. Theirs was a mode of discovering a shared identity which was indirect and is somewhat mysterious to us, but it was as meaningful as those other processes of England's self-discovery which involved chroniclers, antiquarians, topographers, surveyors and map-makers. Personal identity, we are told by developmental psychologists, emerges through a process of successive crises which effect degrees of detachment from parental ties leading to the achievement of personal autonomy. In the case of the nation we may observe a reverse process: an increasingly intimate involvement with God, cemented in the bonds of a covenant made between him and his people.

For political and social purposes the covenant was the most protean and formative of all biblical principles. In a late Elizabethan sermon a Bristol preacher declared: 'Blessed is Israel, because the Lord is their God, and blessed is England, because the Lord is their God'. That was to go beyond a merely rhetorical commonplace, Thomas Adams's 'right parallels'. It was to allege two equally covenanted nations, virtually fused in one in the single bond sealed between God and his covenanted people.[16]

These discoveries were not made in a vacuum but in the context of the threatening international situation in which England was caught up from the mid-sixteenth century onwards, and which differed from all earlier international crises in that its character was more ideological than dynastic, and as much an internal as external source of perceived danger, involving plots, subversion and the threat of terrorism. A process of ideological politicisation can be traced from the unpopular Spanish marriage of Mary, and from the excessive Spanish-style repression of heresy carried out in her name. A broadsheet published before the burnings had even begun invited God to 'defend thy elect people of England from the hands and force of thy enemies, the papists'. Thereafter Protestantism, originally suspect as a foreign importation, began to be identified with the national interest, Catholicism with all that threatened that interest. Apparently the gunpowder plotters of 1605 imagined that they were doing something patriotic, but their motivation would have seemed to contemporaries as incomprehensibly suspect as that of the Baader Meinhof Gang in our own century. As Professor David Loades has remarked of the cementing of the alliance of Protestantism and patriotism in the long hot summer of Elizabeth's reign: 'Nothing succeeds like success'.[17]

III

So why suggest that protestant religiosity inhibited and confused the sense of England as special and divinely elect? Before engaging with that question we must first introduce into the discussion, and not before time, the large figure of John Foxe and his truly monumental 'Book of Martyrs'. For an account of the Protestant Nation without Foxe is indeed *Hamlet* without the Prince. But Foxe is himself a complicating factor.

Foxe's Book of Martyrs, more properly *Actes and monuments of these latter and perilous dayes touching matters of the Church*, began life as a modest but tendentious historical essay on recent ecclesiastical history, that is an account of events since the time of Wyclif. But it grew through successive editions (1563, 1570, 1583, 1587) into a work of universal scope and stupendous length, twice as long as the Bible but treated as a kind of appendix to the Bible, a 'book of credit, next to the Book of God' and, like Scripture, read systematically or 'throughly'. In the 1620s it was said of a certain Exeter worthy that in this way he had read the Bible 'ten times over', but the Book of Martyrs only 'seven times over'. Families used it to record births and other notable events, as they would use the Bible.[18]

Following certain leads given by the ex-Carmelite John Bale, a more precocious, original and scholarly writer, Foxe made of fifteen hundred years of church history a coherent and meaningful plot, its ground bass the unrelenting warfare between the false church, visible, commanding and apparently flourishing, and the true church, depressed almost out of sight, a 'secret multitude of true professors'. This struggle consisted of aggressive persecution on the one hand and patient suffering on the other, the one a sure sign of error (for 'they shall not hurt nor destroy in all my holy mountain'), the other of truth. This was an account of history which we call apocalyptic, and it was apocalyptic in a double sense. The notion that truth, far from being extinguished by persecution, vindicates itself in suffering, derived from the apocryphal and intertestamental literature of which the Apocalypse of St John, or the Book of Revelation, was a late example. And from these same prophetic and almost cabbalistic sources, extending back to the Book of Daniel, Foxe, like so many other speculative theologians hooked on prophecy, derived the principles, including mathematical principles, with which to read into history a meaningful pattern and even a programme. Thus Foxe speculated on the Millennium, a notion derived from Revelation of a thousand-year epoch in which the force of evil would be restrained, allowing the Church of God a measure of peace and prosperity; and on the figure of Antichrist, named as such only in the Johannine epistles but easily connected with other figures and types to be found in the Apocalypse, including the Beast, the Dragon and the Woman, the Whore of Babylon. By the time that Foxe wrote, and certainly by the period in which he was so widely read, it was more or less consensual among English Protestants that the Roman papacy was to be identified with Antichrist, the Roman Church with 'Babylon' or 'Babel'.

The historical scenario on which Foxe eventually settled, after some false starts, associated the Millennium with the conversion of Constantine in the fourth century and identified it with the Peace of the Church which followed. But it envisaged Satan struggling free from his chains long before the literal completion of the thousand years, a process demonstrated in the regressive degeneration of the Church from the truth and in the escalating claims of successive popes to earthly domination, accompanied by intensified persecution of God's saints. Repression of the truth and faithful witness to it both reached a climactic period at the end of the millennial age with the emergence in England of John Wyclif and in Bohemia of Jan Hus, who was burned by the Council of Constance. Of Wyclif, Foxe wrote: 'What time there seemed in a manner to be no one little spark of pure doctrine left or remaining, this foresaid Wyclif by God's providence sprang and rose up, through whom the Lord would first waken and raise up again the world'. Thereafter persecution had not relented and Foxe's account of it, especially in England, progressively thickened as his narrative approached more recent times, culminating in hundreds of pages of documentation, eye-witness description and polemical journalism devoted to the Marian burnings, arousing public excitement by the naming of persecutors still living and victims whose children and grandchildren were proud to be 'of the stock of the martyrs'. William Whateley of Banbury would mention to his father-in-law in 1623 'that great happiness which God hath bestowed upon you, in that you are the son of a father whom only the death of his persecutors and of Queen Mary . . . did hinder from being crowned with the most honourable crown of Martyrdom' – 'as Master *Fox* hath set down'.[19]

While Foxe continued to engage in the immense labour of extending his book, going weekly to his publisher John Day on Monday mornings, persecution continued unabated on the Continent, reaching its grisly climax in France in 1572 in the St Bartholomew massacres. However in England the peace of the Church had been restored by Elizabeth, a second Constantine but herself a near-martyr in the reign of her sister; and it was Foxe who turned that story into an abiding legend, to be reworked for years to come by ballad writers and dramatists. *If you know not me*, ran the title of one of these plays, *you know nobody*. Constantine himself had been a kind of Englishman, or so Foxe believed, being the son of a British princess and proclaimed emperor on British soil.

So much for Foxe's book. What about its effect on the national consciousness? In 1963 the American literary scholar William Haller published an elegant and persuasive study, *Foxe's Book of Martyrs and the Elect Nation*. This argued that Foxe was the principal architect of the conviction that the English were a people 'set apart from all others', an explanation in himself for Milton's famous obsession about 'God's Englishmen'. Haller was all too persuasive and excessively influential. He was primarily a Milton scholar and so began his investigation of Foxe on the basis of Milton's rather extreme statement that if Wyclif and Hus had not been silenced there would have been no need for Luther and Calvin: 'the glory . . . had been completely ours'. There is of course no way of knowing how many readers of Foxe derived from their reading a sense that England was not merely *an* elect nation but *the* elect nation. However it was not the lesson which Foxe intended to teach.

In representing the Book of Martyrs as a lens which brought into sharp focus England and its divinely appointed reformers and godly monarchs, while blurring the landscape to either side, Haller was responsible for some distortion and he made altogether too much of the attention naturally and properly paid to things English by an English author, mindful of his English readers. If Foxe celebrated Wyclif, he praised above all the German Luther whom 'the Lord did ordain and appoint . . . to be the principal organ and minister under him, to reform and re-edify again the desolate ruins of his religion'. That Luther was known to the English religious public as an edifying spiritual writer was very largely due to Foxe, who was active in promoting editions of some of the great reformer's most affecting writings. In *Acts and Monuments* Foxe's subject was not so much England as the Church, to which he attributed a universal and mystical identity, the whole body of the elect scattered over the face of the earth. In a huge Latin commentary on the Apocalypse on which he was labouring in his last and declining years, and which Haller evidently found it possible not to read, there were no apocalyptic references to England as a nation but an explicit denial that the Church was limited to any single country. And far from envisaging a glorious terrestrial future for the English Church under its new Constantine and her successors (still less the British Empire)

Foxe evidently expected the imminent return of Christ and the end of all things, since he wrote towards the end of what he believed to be the final three hundred years of history, which had begun in 1294.[20]

Other Elizabethan Protestants had less confidence than Foxe that the rationale and ultimate destiny of history could be deciphered from the cabbalistic mysteries of biblical and apocalyptic arithmetic. Although they knew that history had a beginning and believed that it would have an end, they seem to have shared with the twentieth century the conviction that all the ages in between have been, in a sense, 'equidistant from eternity', sharing a common significance. In effect they were working their own variations on St Augustine, for Augustinian all these philosophies of history were. William Harrison was an Essex country parson who had dealings with Raphael Holinshed and others of his circle, and he wrote a famous *Description of England* – more national self-consciousness. The *Description* seems to have been written almost without method and is apparently bereft of any philosophy of history. But Dr Glyn Parry has now shown that Harrison thought more penetratingly and expansively even than Foxe on the meaning of the past, incorporating his ideas into a grandly conceived 'Great English Chronology' and other 'Reflections'. In Harrison's scheme the conflict between Cain and Abel, personifying the principles of falsity and truth, or 'Gentilism' at war with Israel, 'the line of the right wise', had continued ever since the beginning and still raged, not only between Protestant England and its popish enemies but also within the Elizabethan Church itself. Consequently Harrison was less disposed than Foxe to recognise Constantinian figures as instruments of divine providence, or the earthly dispensations over which they ruled as 'true', and even more suspicious than Foxe of the sense of false security which such potentially 'triumphalist' notions might encourage. Far from attributing to 'Constantinian' England any special role in a divine historical plan, Harrison seems to have regarded his country's history as teaching the same lessons which the devout of other nations ought equally to learn from their own historians.[21]

Since most of us belong to a particular nation and look out at the world from a certain vantage point, ethnocentricity will creep in, even through the back door. A Puritan of Bury St Edmunds appeared to be critical of his country, certainly of his queen, when he caused to be inscribed below the Royal Arms in his parish church the words from the Book of Revelation: 'Because thou art lukewarm, and neither cold nor hot, I will spue thee out of my mouth'. He was hanged for his pains. The offensive words were first uttered by the Holy Spirit to the angel of the Church of the Laodiceans and they were later applied to the Church of England by the post-Foxeian apocalyptic writer Thomas Brightman.[22] Yet there is more than a hint in Revelation that if only Laodicea will deny its wealth and acknowledge its true poverty and wretchedness it will become truly rich and perhaps the brightest star in the ecclesiastical firmament. Why was the Spirit so harsh in its criticism of Laodicea? 'As many as I love, I rebuke and chasten: be zealous therefore, and repent' (Revelation 3:19).

But even in Foxe any ethnocentric enthusiasm for what he admittedly called, in a striking phrase, 'this my-country Church of England' was tempered by the sense that the Church achieved its truest identity above nationality and beyond history, as a mystical entity. All English Protestants, Foxe included, were internationalists, conscious of their common identity with the other Reformed churches of Europe. Although this is to compare the incomparable, their international sense was probably more acute, and certainly no weaker, than the sense of the English nation at the Council of Constance. In the very same breath in which he prayed for victory in Henry VIII's last campaign Thomas Becon had expressed an equal concern for 'the Christian public weal', which was not England but more or less equivalent to Christendom. The continual wars vexing foreign parts ought, wrote Becon, 'to move any true English heart to have pity and compassion upon the christian brothers, dwell they never so far from us, seeing that we be knit together in one faith'. In Mary's days the English protestant leadership had found safety in continental exile. Under Elizabeth they returned the compliment by receiving the refugees of the French and Dutch troubles, religious solidarity transcending traditional xenophobia. In Canterbury protestant Walloons made up more than a third of the population, as did the protestant Dutch in Norwich. Even in the late twentieth century no British city has a higher proportion of immigrants in its population. William Bradshaw wrote: 'Touching the word *foreign*, those Churches being all of the same household of faith that we are, they are not aptly called foreign'. Calvinism functioned both in the mind and to some extent in the practice of voluntary aid and relief as an international organisation in a manner which anticipated some aspects of our own century's history. Geneva was its Moscow, the Netherlands and in the 1620s the Palatinate its Spain, battle grounds for opposed ideologies, inviting the active intervention of sympathisers from other parts of Europe.[23]

Paradoxically it was the great hope placed in England by continental Protestants at the time of the Thirty Years' War which served to foster the millenarian idea that England had a manifest destiny as an elect and (to use the American phrase) redeemer nation. On the eve of that war a London preacher told his audience that 'this little island', 'this angle of the world', had been 'the sanctuary of all the christian world'. 'Have not all the neighbour nations taken hold of the skirts of an Englishman?' Some years later the same man thought it a 'wonderful mercy' that England not only enjoyed peace, 'environed round about with such tempestuous seas', but was able out of its abundance to entertain and relieve its distressed neighbours.[24] It was Milton's bitter disappointment at England's subsequent failure to fulfil this promise and play its proper part which fuelled, as a negative reaction, his sense of England's 'precedence'. 'How should it come to pass?' he wrote in 1641, at the height of the reaction against Archbishop Laud's crypto-catholic isolationism, 'that England having had this grace and honour from God to be the first . . . should now be the last? . . . We are no better than a Schism from all the Reformation.' So Protestantism complicated the religious sense of nationhood even while it intensified it.

IV

It would be pointless to deny that that sense was heightened by the Elizabethan experience of living dangerously, which was in a general sense an apocalyptic experience, since the source of danger was located in the papacy and the papacy was identified with Antichrist. But apocalyptic ideologies in the more developed and formal sense, involving the construction of elaborate philosophies of history, have been exaggerated as a source of national self-consciousness. Modern intellectual historians are fascinated by these ideas, but we cannot assume that even the regular reader of Foxe shared such interests, at least until the Civil War stimulated the taste of the religious public for the exotic and obscure in biblical prophecy. Much more persuasive was what we may call the ordinary prophetic mode of religious discourse, of which much less has been made in recent scholarship. This was a perception of God's relation to history which was not at all historical in any progressive sense, since it presented Israel and England, or Israel and the Church as if contemporaries, *sub specie aeternitatis*. The very fact that the early protestant preachers re-invented the critical role of the biblical prophets was in itself important. So Becon in his *Invective Against Swearing* quotes Isaiah with relish: 'Cry, cease not'. He is echoed by a Jacobean preacher, similarly inspired: 'Cry aloud . . . and outcry the crying sins of England'.[25] As these words imply, the prophetic mode required that the preacher address his hearers not as individuals, nor as a congregation, but as standing for or representing the nation. The appeal also envisaged an active, willing response. Apocalyptic utterance pointed to divine intervention; prophetic discourse spoke of what a nation could do to help itself.

But if prophetic preaching intensified the nation's sense of its own identity, it also sought to subdue it and drive it inwards, for by its very nature prophetic discourse was anything but triumphalist. It was castigatory, almost never congratulatory, feeding on catastrophe or threatened catastrophe. England was compared to Israel in its disobedience, Israel under judgment: rarely to Israel in its prosperity, except when prosperity was denounced as spiritually hazardous and the cause of national apostasy. The argument (such as it was) never varied, so that one marvels at the resilience of minds and consciences which must have been exposed to it on so many occasions. Like Israel, England had been uniquely favoured. God had not dealt so with any nation. As one writer put it: 'You are at this day, and long have been, the astonishment and wonderment of all the world'. Another spoke of the English *now* God's people, as the Israelites were *then* God's people. But the identification consisted in the scale and enormity of the nation's sins, for like Israel England had been faithless, careless, unthankful. 'We seem to have entered into a contention with the Almighty, whether he shall be more merciful or we more sinful'. That was why England had suffered God's repeated warnings and why, if repentance did not come in time, worse plagues were like to follow. It is always the land, the whole land, which is threatened, an inevitable deduction from the entire corpus of Old Testament prophecy. A Jacobean preacher spoke vividly of every man under his vine and fig tree 'from *Kent* to *Kentyre*, from the *South of England* to the *North of Scotland*', all at peace but all under judgment.[26]

The only variation is in the nature of the sins denounced. And it is to be noted that *sins* are the target, rarely institutions. This was preaching which assumed and underwrote the social and political order, offering no challenge to it. There may have been a perceptible shift from the 'social' sins complained of in Edward's days, in a word 'covetousness', to the 'moral' and personal offences which exercised the Jacobean pulpit: drunkenness, whoredom, Sabbath violation, swearing. Some would see this as indicative of a significant change, from a bias towards the poor to a measure of prejudice against them, as the new religion ceased to be new and became more closely associated with the social order and with the interest of social control. However moral and personal sins, which in any case were by no means confined to the poor, had been denounced from the early days of the Reformation, not to look to earlier times still. And it would be a mistake to regard such offences as occurring in some privatised area of moral and sub-criminal behaviour, a 'soft' and uncontroversial area for the preacher to penetrate and exploit. So it may be in a liberal society like the twentieth-century United States. But in the perception of thoroughly illiberal Elizabethan England these were matters of lively public concern. To indulge such sins was to expose the entire community to divine retribution; to complain of them was to court extreme unpopularity as a 'busy controller'.

Among other offences, swearing, what the author of *Englands summons* called 'this infernal dialect and language of the Devil', was considered the most dangerous sin of all because, like some sinister cloud of nuclear fall-out, it threatened the whole nation which tolerated it in its streets. So after the sharp earthquake which struck the south-east of England on 6 April 1580 the pulpits had a field-day against national apostasy. And not only the pulpits. An opportunistic and mostly scientific treatise on the cause of earthquakes, published within a week of the event, concluded: 'Surely it cannot be without the special finger of God'. It was as if God should have nodded his head to all the sermons preached in the last twenty-one years. Others dramatised those lost years. 'The Lord hath come to his fig tree of England not three but almost twenty-three years, and behold, yet he findeth little fruit.' A Coventry chronicler recorded the earthquake and added, with a nice sense of irony: 'This year was a disease all the land over, called speedy repentance'. On 11 November 1618 the appearance of the phenomenon we know as Halley's Comet induced a similar effect. It was the 'stately tongue of Heaven ... that prodigious star', God's lecture in the sky; its likely effect was 'Death, Drought, Dearth, Winds, Wonders, Wars'.[27]

As the distance in time separating the preacher and his congregation from Elizabeth's restoration of the Gospel increased, so the growing contrast between God's mercy and the nation's indifference offered ever greater rhetorical scope:

Oh the oaths and blasphemy in our Nation! O, the contempt of Gods word and gospel in our Nation! O, the pride and idleness in our Nation! O, the drunkenness, whoredom and filthiness in our Nation! If Rome or Constantinople abounded with swearing and cursing, who could look for better there? If France and Italy were full of whoredom, who could expect other in those corners of popish darkness? But England, Ah England! Gods Signet, Gods Jewel . . . I say England aboundeth in all these sins. What shall we say or do? Whither shall we turn ourselves . . . What? Swearing in England? Cursing in England?[28]

V

And so we return to all those sermons on Hosea, the text where we began. 'Then said God . . . ye are not my people, and I will not be your God . . . The Lord hath a controversy with the inhabitants of the land.' Taking account only of those which found their way into print, sermons or courses of sermons on this prophetic scripture were preached in 1609, 1612, 1613, 1616, 1617 – and so on. Hosea Chapter 4 was a favourite springboard for a Paul's Cross sermon, for this was a national pulpit, the nearest thing that the age offered to broadcasting. And presently Thomas Hooker's flock in Chelmsford would be assured, on the basis of a text in Jeremiah supplemented by information directly vouchsafed to the preacher, that 'as sure as God is God, God is going from England'.[29]

Here was a great contradiction and some confusion. The more the Gospel had been preached, the more persuasive the preacher and the more unmistakable the signals of warning and mercy (1588 and the Armada, 1603 and the plague, 1605 and the Gunpowder Treason), the more obdurate was the nation's indifference, or so it seemed. Things were worse and not better. But the confusion was potentially deeper than that. For if so much of the nation so consistently rejected God, in what sense could it be said to be his people at all? But could a nation which God had chosen reject him? And would God, could God, abandon a nation which he had once taken to himself? The evidence was perhaps discouraging to the thesis that God ever had chosen England. But was the sentence pronounced by Hosea against Israel a final sentence? And who or what was Israel: the entire nation, or only a faithful remnant within the nation? At this point the doctrine that God is English foundered on the contradictions between the principle and claims of the all-inclusive national Church, and the religious self-awareness of the godly people, the virtuoso minority whose practice of religion was prodigious. In fact more was involved in that shipwreck than Aylmer's blithe motto. It was the English Reformation and the Reformed English Church itself which struck this reef of contradiction, and we call the resultant disaster the English Civil War.

The difficulty in which the religious public, and especially the prodigiously religious public, now found itself was both existential and exegetical, as preachers wrestled with difficult texts, or exploited the ambiguities the texts contained, for immediate pastoral advantage. Viewed simply in terms of the observable situation, there was a problem in that the status of Christian and Protestant which was attributed by law and by courtesy to the entire population was in practice actively appropriated and enjoyed only by some, probably a minority of the whole. That faithful, godly, 'conscionable' minority, fortified by the conviction that among its members were God's own elect children, distanced itself mentally and to varying extents in social practice from the 'reprobate', 'carnal' majority. And yet their preachers continued, as public officers and spokesmen of a national and established Church, to exhort the whole population, entire parishes, to repentance, even while they administered the sacraments, in effect, to all and sundry. George Widley was insistent: 'Every hill is Sion, every river is Jordan, every country Jewry, every city Jerusalem'. 'All must be compelled unto the true religion.'[30]

The exegetical difficulty consisted quite simply in the fact that 'Israel' served as a paradigm both for the Church, as a mystical and universal society, and more literally for the English nation (and other nations), often represented as if it stood in the same relation to God as the Jewish nation of old. And to confuse the matter still more the nation was also the Church, a local and visible expression of the universal company of the faithful and bearing a certain problematical relation to that wider and invisible company.

It might have been less troublesome if the preachers had identified England (or London) with Nineveh, since Nineveh, metropolis of the Assyrians, was a gentile city which had nevertheless responded with alacrity to the preaching of the prophet Jonah. Nineveh consequently prefigured the gathering into the Church of the nations, of which England was one. Christ himself had used the example of its repentance to shame his Jewish contemporaries. But English preachers made only occasional and incidental use of this story, for example to make the point that if Nineveh repented in three days after a single sermon, one might reasonably expect more success after twenty years of incessant preaching in London. There were understandable reasons why England did not want to identify either itself with Assyria, a ferociously ungodly world-imperial power, or its monarchy with Sennacherib. But the main reason why the English nation was given a Jewish rather than gentile identity was theological. Significantly it was a Lutheran (anticipating 'Arminian' doctrine) who taught that Jonah's preaching in Nineveh demonstrated that God would not have one nation or people, but all men to be saved.[31] The Calvinism which dominated the English Church after the mid-sixteenth century retreated from universalism. By stressing and elaborating the doctrine of exclusive election and the correlative principle of covenant, Calvinism tended to restrict the divine plan of salvation to a single nation or people, Israel.

But what was Israel? And when in Hosea God threatened to cast Israel aside and yet to save Judah, or his children, what did this signify for protestant Englishmen? Whom did he intend to destroy, whom to redeem? And when God spoke of destruction, did he really mean it? Would the faithful few rescue the rest, or on the contrary would the corrupt nation pull down to destruction even the godly remnant within it? And what was destruction? Were the preachers talking about temporal judgments, the famines, plagues and wars which had been visited upon Israel, and which were the only judgments which could be experienced by entire nations? These would befall just and unjust. No one could escape, however godly. A preacher who taught otherwise, that those who died of the plague in London in 1604 were deficient in faith, spent the next two years in prison for the dangerous infamy of his doctrine.[32] Or did judgment mean hellfire, which Elizabethan and Jacobean preachers seldom mentioned? And what was it to be saved? To be preserved from invasion and conquest, as England had been in 1588, or to be assured of ultimate security beyond the grave, the salvation procured through Christ for his elect of which pious English Calvinists spoke with keen expectation when writing their wills and preparing themselves for death?

Attempts have been made to read consistency and coherence into English protestant discourse on these perplexing themes, but they have not been very successful. Making use of a distinction which by the early seventeenth century was standard, between the covenant of works made by God with Adam and ratified by Moses with the Jews, and the covenant of grace binding God to his elect children in Christ, it has been suggested that the argument of the fullest English exposition of Hosea, by John Downame, was that God had a covenant of works with the English nation which was distinct from his covenant of grace with the elect within all nations. But since man could not fulfil the terms of that covenant its eventual outcome could only be judgment and death upon the nation, leaving the elect to be saved not by their good works but through a free covenant of grace, available only to them. However, whether or not this was Downame's meaning, it was far from constituting the consistent message of English protestant divinity.[33]

Preaching in 1593 to a congregation of businessmen drawn from the largest trading towns in the country, the famous William Perkins tackled the most chillingly apocalyptic and threatening of all the minor prophets, Zephaniah, who addressed Israel as 'O nation, not worthy to be loved'. In rehearsing the English nation's long apostasy ('ignorance after five and thirty years' preaching is counted no sin, . . . vain and customable swearing, mocking of religion and the professors thereof no sin') Perkins put the question: 'And is Israel only a nation not worthy to be beloved? Nay, I may cry out with as good a cause, O England, a nation not worthy to be beloved.' For God had poured out the same mercies and far greater upon us, and his kindness had been requited with an even greater measure of unkindness. But who was 'us'? Perkins at first seemed to be calling for repentance from the nation which had been so favoured. 'So may England prevent God's judgments.' But as he warmed to his theme this began to look less certain. The manner of God's judgment was expounded in the terms of Zephaniah's metaphor of the winnowing of so many heaps of corn, representing the 'several nations'. But these heaps, 'that is the particular churches', were full of hypocrites which God's powerful fan would winnow out. One of God's fans, or winds, blew after this life, finally separating the wicked from the elect. Another was the word preached, separating those it saved from the reprobate it merely condemned, leaving them without excuse. The third was the fan of immediate, temporal judgment: 'the wind of his wrath'. This was evidently equivalent to the 'natural' disasters of famine, plague and war. Now the English Church was 'doubtless' God's cornfield, 'a good heap of God's corn'. Those who taught otherwise, the Separatists, Perkins dismissed with scorn. But 'alas, the pure wheat, how thin it is scattered!' God would have to winnow hard to find it. 'He will not cease to blow all the chaff to hell to find out those few corns of wheat, to lay them up in heaven, so that out of question, England being so full of chaff must look to be winnowed.'[34]

The conclusion seemed to be that the godly, 'us', were to search their own hearts, fanning themselves, if they wished to avoid a share in the dire fate of national judgment. For as another preacher put it, the effect of repentance by a 'competent number' might be to tie the hands of God, at least for a time.[35] Then indeed, said Perkins, the 'glorious prosperity of England' might continue 'from generation to generation'. But if judgment could not be averted and this kingdom, 'this glorious nation', were to be brought to 'some miserable ruin', that would be God's way of sifting the corn from the chaff. So, by the end of his sermon, it appeared that Perkins was preaching to the converted, appealing realistically enough to his hearers, not to those beyond the sound of his voice and indifferent to it. 'Let us all be Noahs, Daniels and Jobs in our generations. If we do thus, then when judgment come we shall either turn them away from our nation, or at the least we shall deliver our own souls.' A London preacher envisaged the future with the same ambivalence: 'Either the Church visible shall recover its former glory and beauty, or at least the elect shall hereby be bettered and furnished to perfection'.[36]

It would be wrong to classify such doctrine as the voice of an extreme and sectarian puritan fringe. Thomas Jackson, prebendary of Canterbury and lecturer in the cathedral, was a successful Jacobean preacher and although he was a disciple and even a convert of Perkins he was too much of an establishment figure, too ambivalent in his churchmanship, to be usefully identified as a Puritan. Indeed he openly censured 'schismatics', both the Separatists and 'others that make a division' with their pleas for 'parity, the mother of confusion and anarchy'. It was typical of such a lifelong 'moderate' that he should not know which side to choose at the outbreak of the Civil War. Yet in his Canterbury sermons *Judah must into captivitie* (1622) he was every bit as drastic in his judgmental, prophetic preaching as Perkins. His text was Jeremiah 7:16, 'Therefore, pray not for this people, neither lift up cry nor prayer for them, neither make intercession to me: for I will not hear thee'. Jeremiah was actually forbidden to prevent Judah's impending calamity by his preaching. Admittedly many of God's threatenings were conditional. But this, like the destruction of Sodom, would prove to be an absolute sentence. 'The Lord grew to be resolute.' But until that moment when the godly would share in the generality of God's destructive temporal judgment they stood in the gate, proclaiming God's message and, they hoped, turning away his wrath (Jeremiah 7:2). Like Perkins and Cooper, Jackson taught that even if the godly eventually shared in the forthcoming catastrophe, they would at least save their own souls.

'How ever things go, it shall be well with the just . . . Pray, pray, pray, you shall at the least deliver your own souls.'[37]

It has been said that some preachers 'practised the craft of suspense'.[38] The Kentish corn merchant who travelled back to Canterbury after hearing Perkins at Stourbridge Fair was perhaps impressed, even persuaded, by the metaphor of the goodly heap of corn which, like the New Testament parables, was close to his own experience. He knew what to do about his own soul, and perhaps what to hope for for himself and for those like him. But as to the prospects for his neighbours and his country (Kent and the nation) he may have been troubled and confused. Apparently the best means to perpetuate the peace and prosperity of England was for godly persons like himself to draw apart, like Noah in an earlier day of impending wrath. Should he begin to build an ark in his own backyard, to join in some little separated conventicle, rather than continue to sit with his ungodly neighbours in his familiar seat in his parish church? No, for that would be to deny that England was 'a good heap of God's corn'. But it was a heap in which he was made to feel increasingly uncomfortable, the chaff as it were getting between his collar and his neck and up his nose. Forty years later his son would ask himself whether Noah's ark was not located on some distant Ararat in America. John White, the 'patriarch' of Dorchester and a great promoter of the New England enterprise, put the question in 1629 and circulated it widely: 'All other churches of Europe being brought to desolation, it cannot be but that the like judgment is coming to us, and who knoweth but that God hath prepared this place for a refuge for many whom he meaneth to save in the general destruction?' Thomas Shepard, an Essex minister, 'saw the Lord departing from England when Mr Hooker and Mr Cotton were gone'.[39]

And so the idea of the elect nation, God's Israel, once a means of consolidating the Protestant Nation, now threatened to distract and divide it. Foxe had written of God placing 'us Englishmen here in one commonwealth, also in one Church, as in one ship together'. That sense of being in the same boat had been strengthened by the long Elizabethan crisis. In 1586, the year of the Babington Plot, even the notion that God's people was a small remnant was deployed as an argument for national unity in adversity. In a book called *A mirror for the multitude* the patriotic publicist John Norden warned against the spiritual danger of agreeing with the many on the broad way that leads to destruction, which was 'both weak and wicked'. 'Take heed therefore, be warned, let not custom or the multitude make you fain to follow their folly.' It was commonly the case that 'the most part' were alienated from the truth. Only 'the lesser number' were true servants of the living God. 'From the beginning, the Church of God hath been from the least part of the world, the least part of every country and kingdom, the least part of every city, yea the least part of every congregation.' With other, puritan, writers this theme would have been explored with critical introversion, to condemn the false and hypocritical religion of the mass of nominally protestant Englishmen. This indeed served as a sub-text even for Norden, who used some of his space to complain of 'dissembling Christians', 'key-cold or neuters'. 'Let us not deceive or flatter ourselves with a foolish conceit of being Christians when in deed our conversation differeth far from the doctrine of Christ.'

But in the main thrust of his argument Norden was extrovert, identifying 'the little flock of true Christians' with the embattled protestant nation, 'little England'; the impious multitude with its enemies, and in effect with the swaggering pride of international popery, 'the brags, boastings and thundering vaunts of *Senacherib* of Rome'. With England cast as the diminutive hero, Norden embarked on a spirited rehearsal of the story of David and Goliath:

> There was no comparison between the great *Golyah* and little *David* to the eyes of those that saw them both march towardes the combat. For natural reason could not have judged the victory to go with *David* for that, that in respect of his stature and person, there was no more equality than between a little mouse and a great elephant, and as their persons and strengths were far unlike, so were their weapons and external instruments of war, for the strong man had far the greater odds, for he was armed for the purpose with spear and shield, and poor *David* was naked, only a sling in his hand, wherewith (yet such was God's providence) with a stone he killed this huge and mighty monster, who vaunting of his own strength, blasphemed the God of Heaven, in whose miraculous death the power of GOD and his hatred against man's trust and confidence in the strength of flesh and blood was showed: to the comfort of the godly and confusion of the wicked.

'Thus may we, little Israel of England, say If the Lord had not been on our side when men rose up against us, they had swallowed us up quick.' This was written two years before the Armada sailed. But already it was forseen that the 'mighty monarch of Spain' that 'seemeth to rule' was himself overruled.[40]

This was rousing, patriotic and uniting. But in the increasingly divisive religious discourse of the ensuing decades, the ungodly multitude was represented as the bulk of the English nation itself, the faithful remnant as Perkins's 'few corns of wheat' in a heap of chaff. Thomas Cooper reminded his London congregation that Christ had spoken of a 'little flock'. 'Oh how vain is their conceit, that dream all shall be saved ... The number of his chosen is a little flock in comparison of the *cast-aways*.'[41] In November 1640 the Kentish Member of Parliament Sir Edward Dering was exhorted by a zealous correspondent to 'fight it out against the Goliaths of these times'. These 'Goliaths' were no longer a foreign enemy, the Spaniards, but the bishops of the Church of England.[42]

The notion that England was united in godliness, a truly protestant nation, had always been somewhat specious. Quite apart from that other considerable minority of popish recusants who stayed away from their parish churches and were debarred from active participation in the affairs of the commonwealth, a body shading into an immeasurable but certainly substantial number of so-called 'church papists', one can only assume that most Englishmen were carried along more or less passively by the public mood of protestant embattlement, making no active contribution to it. The Elizabethan régime was narrowly based and unrepresentative (more so than the entrenched 'majority' in modern Ulster) and even if it claimed a kind of mass support as part of its legitimation it was not in reality indebted to the masses for very much.

By the end of the century preachers like Perkins were abandoning all pretence. Perkins, who died in 1602, did not presume to know when God's wind would blow, or from which direction, or what form it would take. He did not know that it would blow a hurricane forty years later, in civil war. But a generation later the sense of apprehension was more sharply focused. When people asked the Suffolk minister John Carter whether they were to expect popery again, he would reply: 'You shall not need to fear fire and faggot any more: but such dreadful divisions will be amongst God's people and professors as will equalize the greatest persecutions.'[43] It was an accurate prophecy, perhaps because it was recorded some time after the prophesied events had happened. And by that time the forms had begun to assume shape and substance not of one Protestant Nation but of two, or at least of a permanently divided nation.

2 The Protestant Town

If this chapter, like a sermon, required a text, it could be supplied from Psalm 122: 'Jerusalem is built as a city that is at unity in itself' (in the words of the English Psalter) or (as the Geneva Bible [1560] has it) 'that is compact together in itself'. The force of the original Hebrew depicts the crowded, even slumlike character of the city, as if it were the 'Great Wen' of London of which King James I and William Cobbett in their generations complained, or some human catastrophe of the modern Third World. It is indicative of the positive evaluation of civic life in early modern Europe that the translators and exegetes of Psalm 122 altered this meaning to celebrate the city as embodying a dreamlike model of human society in a state of perfection, while implying that the condition of realising such perfection was the moral resource of principled consensus.

Not only this text but also the frequent attention paid in Scripture to Jerusalem, the embodiment of the people of Israel in an especially intensified and apprehensible form, encouraged townspeople, who were in any case disposed to take themselves seriously, to suppose that their own civic community was possessed of ideal and admirable qualities. *This* town, *our* city, is to be compared, even identified, with God's own metropolis of Jerusalem. So it was with many a town and city in Reformation Europe. Medieval towns and the social groups and divisions which they contained shared many patrons. In Canterbury St Thomas competed with St George. There were implied ideological distinctions between the proud prelate who had died defending the liberties of the Church against the Crown and England's ghostly champion who had secured victories for her kings in the field. One could choose between one and another idealised personification of the city's identity. Or perhaps the choice would be made for the citizen, by the parish in which he was born and baptised or the fraternity to which he was committed in membership. But now there was but one patron, God.

Like other ideas and institutions explored in this book, the idealised identification of the city – almost any city – with Jerusalem was not a totally novel consequence of the Protestant Reformation. When King Richard II was reconciled with the city of London in 1392 the

28

accompanying pageantry proclaimed that it was with a new manifestation of Jerusalem that this successor (or impersonator) of Jesus Christ came to terms. A late fifteenth-century town clerk of Bristol, Robert Ricart, drew a map of his city which represented it as 'the navel of the world', a cross within a circle, representing a heavenly Jerusalem divided into four quarters defined by its four principal streets: a little model of the world. (Would Ricart have been as scandalised as orthodox Christians of the 1650s when the Quaker James Nayler made his 'blasphemous' entry into Bristol, seated like Christ on Palm Sunday on a donkey, a parody of such civic traditions?) The saints who served as patrons of the medieval civic community represented it in heavenly intercessions which imparted to the social body a holy distinction, making it a 'microcosm of the world' in its harmonious wholeness. But this wholeness was – or should have been – greatly enhanced by the substitution of a single God for a whole panoply of proprietary saints. For the city now stood before God, the one, as a seamless whole, containing no rival loyalties to various sub-deities, no rival jurisdictions, no religious liberties or enclaves which were no-go areas for the civic authorities. 'Now the command of the Mayor and his brethren was efficacious in every quarter of the city, and every inhabitant, burgess or stranger, was equally subject to their rule.'[1]

And for God there was only one city, Jerusalem. Even if a passing interest was taken in Nineveh, this was not so much for Nineveh's sake as to teach Jerusalem a lesson, through the fable of the prophet Jonah. In the New Testament God's Apostle, St Paul, travelled the length of the Eastern Mediterranean, but when he communicated by letter with the cities which he had visited it was to the Christians in the cities, not to the cities themselves, that he wrote. As strangers and pilgrims Christians had here no continuing city. And when in the Book of Revelation St John the Divine wrote to the seven churches which were in Asia they were located in famous cities, but it was not to the cities that he conveyed the message of the Spirit. There was only one Jerusalem. But now there were many Christian cities for which Jerusalem stood as model and paradigm, and for Englishmen Jerusalem was naturally London. Delivering his first sermon as Bishop of London at the great open-air preaching place of Paul's Cross, Edwin Sandys exclaimed: 'Our Lord and Saviour Jesus Christ, ... casting his eyes toward the city of Jerusalem, bewailed the lamentable estate thereof, and that with tears. The like effect ... I find in myself, beholding this Jerusalem of ours, this famous city.'

Another preacher in the same place echoed the bishop: 'Our Saviour Christ, if he were here, should be moved to weep over England as he hath wept over Jerusalem'. In fact it was to become a vulgar commonplace. A ballad-monger joins in:

> O London, London, Jerusalem I may thee call,
> For why? thy conversation agreeth thereto now:
> They would take no warning before the plague did fall
> And at this present day O LONDON no more dost thou.

A Jacobean preacher coming out of Kent to a prominent London pulpit spoke of the city as 'the very ark of the presence of God, above all other places of this land'. 'Oh London, London, excellent things are spoken of thee, thou city of God.'[2]

If London was Jerusalem, Canterbury, according to the Jacobean preacher James Cleland, was Sychar, the Judean city where the patriarch Jacob (in his very name the precursor of King James) had sunk a famous well, and where Jesus converted the Samaritan woman. For Archbishop Abbot 'on his second coming into Kent' had made a well, or conduit, in Canterbury, a city 'builded in the sweetest air, between two little hills, . . . in the best place of the chiefest shire of this country, even in Canterbury, the Metropolis or Head Town of Kent, if not of all England'.[3]

Thither, we read elsewhere in the Psalms, the tribes go up. So a related theme was that of the city set on a hill, either Jerusalem as the crown of the hill country of Judea, or that city of which Jesus spoke in Matthew 5:14, 'A city that is set on a hill cannot be hid'. Colchester in the 1550s was so regarded: 'The ancient and famous city of Colchester . . . became like unto the city upon a hill; or a candle upon a candlestick'. Colchester is indeed sited on a steep hill, which may have made the identification more plausible. And so was Rye, in Sussex. A hundred years after Colchester had discovered itself in the Gospel, Rye's inhabitants were told (in 1652): 'You are as a city set on an hill, labour to hold forth an holy life, lest it be said what do you more than others?' But Gloucester too, for all its level, riverain topography, was equally identified with the biblical motif, as were several towns of the West Riding of Yorkshire and, most famously of all, Boston in Massachusetts.[4] Boston's several hills numbered something less than seven, which was an undesirable number, suggesting another city altogether: Rome, successor to the biblical Babylon, or Babel.

These paradigms served to reinforce civic identity and to foster a sense of civic pride. But as explored by any preacher less flagrantly flattering than Cleland they also nourished a critical mood of moral responsibility, in the spirit of the text which teaches that from those to whom much has been given, much shall be required. Judgment was pronounced in the manner of those Old Testament prophets (the words are Jeremiah's) who had uttered *against* the city, in the name of the Lord: 'For Jerusalem's sake I will not hold my peace'. Even the flatterer Cleland, remembering that 'harlot' Jerusalem and 'bloody Nineveh', not to speak of Mahomet at Constantinople and Antichrist at Rome, thought that 'the great sins' ordinarily had their origin in the city, 'from hence derived to the country'. Londoners were warned that God had not dealt so favourably with any city, Jerusalem only excepted, and no city so sinful. If God had not spared Jerusalem, his own, but had suffered it to be repeatedly devastated, its inhabitants put to the sword or carried into exile, why should he turn a deaf ear to the crying sins of London? However to prophesy in this sense against Jerusalem was not the same thing as for Jonah to prophesy against Nineveh in the hope of converting and redeeming that great but heathen city; still less to preach against Babylon, which was the antitype of Jerusalem, inherently corrupt, utterly irredeemable. Babylon's fate was already sealed and certain. Elizabethans took comfort from the reverberating reiteration of God's sentence: 'Babylon, which is Rome, is fallen, according to the prophecy of this angel. *She is fallen*, saith the angel, *she is fallen*' (Revelation 14:8).[5]

To return to Psalm 122, Jerusalem is here described as a city the principles of whose foundation and construction embody civic harmony and wholeness: 'that is at unity in itself', or 'compact together in itself'. The Geneva Bible supplies this marginal comment: 'By the artificial joining and beauty of the houses, he meaneth the concord and love that was between the citizens'. That was the great urban myth of late medieval Europe which the sixteenth century, and especially the Protestant Reformation among other considerable changes of that century, hardened and somewhat stridently reinforced – even as it dealt a death-blow to the actuality of that unity, by dividing along lines of formal religious division communities which were previously at least nominally at one, and perhaps by distracting them in other ways. For the alteration in religion was accompanied by and interacted with other social changes which tended to accentuate the distance between classes, while making it more difficult for those distances to be bridged and for tensions to be expressed, contained and surmounted by ceremonies and rituals.

So there is a paradox at the heart of this subject. In the history of English towns, according to a prevalent ideology, a series of events, or a process, which we call the Reformation was ostensibly a means of promoting such social success and wholeness as had never been known before, while on the national scale it affirmed the unitary and uniting authority of the one godly prince over the godly common-wealth of England, the type or paradigm of which was Israel. But in truth the immediate effect was separation and confusion. The con-tradiction is acknowledged in one of the official Homilies of the post-Reformation Church, 'A Sermon Against Contention and Brawling', which complains of 'these words of contention which be now almost in every man's mouth – "He is a Pharisee, he is a Gospeller, he is of the new sort, he is of the old faith, he is a new-broached brother, he is a good catholic father, he is a papist, he is an heretic." O how the Church is divided! O how the cities be cut and mangled! O how the coat of Christ that was without seam is all to rent and torn!' And so it was in Canterbury in 1543. The old-fashioned complained of the new-fashioned as 'newfangles' and assailed them as 'you fellows of the new trickery, that go up and down with your testaments in your hands!' Soon such people would be stigmatised as 'Puritans'. They gave as good as they got, denouncing religious conservatives as 'pope-holy knaves'.[6] The Homily com-ments: 'They be unworthy to live in a Commonwealth, the which do as much as lieth in them, with brawling and scolding, to disturb the quietness and peace of the same'. Was such 'brawling and scolding' really new, or did it now break out on an unprecedented scale? The Homily seems to confront an unprecedented threat to the harmony which the parish was supposed to embody. Had unity ever been demanded more stridently and peremptorily in printed and spoken word? Never.

II

'The Reformation in the English Towns' makes a modest, low-profile, Hobbitish sort of subject by comparison with the altogether grander theme of 'The Reformation in the Imperial German Cities', just as those English towns were themselves small-scale Toytowns and Trumptons when compared with Nuremberg, Augsburg, Cologne or Erfurt, the German Rome. Italian visitors reported that in all England there was only one town worthy of the name: London, which in the sixteenth century was busily doubling its population every fifty years, from 50 000 in 1500 to 100 000 in 1550 and 200 000 by the end of the century. This was a prodigious phenomenon, more start-ling for the sixteenth century, which had known nothing like it, than for our own. No provincial town before 1600 had as many as 20 000 inhabitants and only ten had more than 7000. In Europe there were forty-two cities with populations exceeding 40 000, in England none, London excepted. Out of 600 or 700 English towns, fully 500 were so small as to prompt the modern mind to question what it was about these little places – Abingdon, Burford, Congleton, Dunster, Evesham, Faversham, Godmanchester, Harwich – which was distinc-tively *urban*. Only about a hundred would today rank as towns at all, most of them places of 2000 to 4000 inhabitants. Exeter was the fifth city of the kingdom, yet the area enclosed by its walls measured just 93 acres. We are dealing with a time when Canterbury, with about 4000 inhabitants, was seventh in ranking order of English towns in terms of its tax yield, and when the population of Sandwich was perhaps 2000 and that of Faversham no more than 1000.[7]

Unlike Germany's prouder cities, English towns were lacking in political clout. To be sure they were represented, even over-represented, in Parliament, where 'burgesses' greatly outnumbered knights of the shire. But for the most part these so-called burgesses were not bona-fide townsmen, but carpet-bagging gentry who owed their seats among other favourable factors to the patronage of the territorial magnates who were the equivalents of Trollope's Duke of Omnium, and who were able to find their own expenses, thus saving the money of the constituencies which they represented. The minority of genuine burgesses at Westminster must have felt increas-ingly out of place in the gentlemen's club which the House of Commons had become, their speeches unremarked by parliamentary diarists. And the town which dared to refuse its patron the nomina-tion of at least one of its representatives risked a stern rebuke such as the corporation of Denbigh received from the Elizabethan Earl of Leicester: 'Be ye well assured never to look for any friendship or favour at my hands in any of your affairs hereafter'. Sir John Gray told the civic fathers of Leicester: 'If you are able to cross me in one thing, I can requite your town with twenty'.[8] Consequently towns were eager to curry favour with tactful gifts of sugar loaves or tuns of claret, as well as with political favours. In 1568, when seventeen killer whales swam up the Orwell to Ipswich and stranded, they were at once cut up and the massive chunks of reeking flesh despatched on carts to those courtiers and noblemen to whom the town was in any way beholden. It was the thought which counted.[9]

So far the argument has tended to confirm the bald and discouraging statement by the lawyer, politician and political theorist Sir Thomas Smith that 'generally in the shires' citizens and burgesses were 'of no account'. However this was not the whole story of the politics of town and country in Tudor England. The goodwill of a town was worth cultivating, whatever Smith might snobbishly say. Not even the wealthiest and most 'worshipful' town would quarrel with its neighbouring gentry, if conflict could be avoided. And even the poorest and most contemptible could be jealous in defence of its liberties and resourceful in the use of the law to that end. Ipswich regularly retained two attorneys in the London courts, one of whom advised the bailiffs: 'You have no walls nor bulwarks, no gates by strength to defend your town, but your town standeth and resteth to be defended by the maintenance, preserving and well keeping of your liberties, franchises and customs'.

Diarmaid MacCulloch has shown that in East Anglia these guardians of a town's material interests were under increasing threat as the sixteenth century progressed. For in many a Suffolk town the gentry were now the enemy, or at least the irritant, within the gates. With the dissolution of the monastic houses much desirable urban property had passed into the hands of new proprietors, and the new owners laid claim to the legal privileges and powers of the former monastic inmates. In early Elizabethan Ipswich one such interloper, Peter Withipoll, was busily constructing the prestigious mansion of Christchurch House on the site of the former priory of the Holy Trinity. His continual provocation of the town led to a series of law suits, including the inevitable set-piece confrontation in Star Chamber. Ipswich could afford to fight Withipoll and had to, since he threatened to purchase the fee-farm of the town, 'for then he should rule'. But the legal battle between little Beccles and the gentry family of Rede over the management of the town common of Beccles Fen lasted for fifty costly years and ended, insofar as such things ever do end, in victory for the townspeople. So, apparently, ended all these disputes, through sheer importunity and persistence, but in the case of Beccles this was not without the assistance of other, more powerful county gentry. Elsewhere, at Faversham in Kent, the differences between the town and the new owner of Faversham Abbey, Thomas Arden, had a quicker, neater conclusion. Arden was murdered, and the crime was later the subject of a sensational Elizabethan drama.[10]

This was one not inconsiderable consequence of the secularising process of the Reformation for many towns. But for the dissolution of the monasteries, Arden would not have made himself so fatally unpopular in Faversham and the inhabitants of Ipswich would not have had their newly-paved streets ruined by the water escaping from Peter Withipoll's hydraulic experiments with the fishponds of Christ-church Park. But how important otherwise was the Protestant Reformation in the historical timescape of the early modern English town? The history of the German Reformation has been dominated by the cities, and the history of the cities by the Reformation. Recently there has been some reaction against the paramountcy traditionally accorded to religion in describing the civic politics and life of the world of Wagner's *Mastersingers of Nuremberg*, that is if religion can be considered to be a more or less independent, irreduc-ible factor. Erfurt, where Martin Luther was educated, was a com-munity coping with an excess of economic problems and political difficulties, as local trades and industries contracted and even col-lapsed, and as the city conducted both a foreign war against the centralising regional government and a civil war between its own competing classes and factions. The religious issues posed by the Lutheran preachers proved to be just one more worm in a can of wriggling worms, another spoke of the wheel rather than the hub. It would be a mistake to write the history of sixteenth-century Erfurt as if it simply consisted of the reception of the Protestant Reformation.[11]

By contrast the history of the early modern English town, which has been made a popular subject in social and regional history by such distinguished historians as Peter Clark, Paul Slack and Charles Phythian-Adams, not to speak of the interest of the Open University, has suffered from a reverse tendency. The religious upheaval of the Reformation receives due mention but in the integration of the subject it remains peripheral, one topic among several. The reason seems to be that social history is commonly understood as the application of economics to every aspect of communal, shared exis-tence: thus the dominant theme in the literature is *urban decay*, the fact that in the sixteenth century the majority of ancient, well-established urban settlements found themselves stuck in a long-standing economic bind of declining industry, receding commerce and demographic contraction. These factors are assumed to have been at the root of everything else discussible which was happening to urban politics, religion and culture, in themselves explaining, or going far towards explaining, the Reformation itself. Professor Clark looks

instinctively in this direction to account for the fact that early
seventeenth-century Gloucester was puritan in religion and fought
against the king in the Civil War.[12]

Admittedly urban decay has not been invented by economic historians and vaguely Marxist social analysts. It was as much a fact then
as it is, on a vastly greater scale, now, in what were once Britain's
major manufacturing centres. In the sixteenth century textiles had
moved to the countryside as surely as electronics have now migrated
to the vales of Berkshire or to the slopes of South Cambridgeshire.
In the towns, as wealth dwindled, it became progressively more
difficult to maintain urban amenities and even urban government.
The traditional and costly trappings were neglected (as in Professor
Phythian-Adams's Coventry) and it was no longer easy to persuade
individuals of the appropriate status to assume the expensive burdens
of civic office. This was not universally the case but it was the
experience of Canterbury, where it was said in 1523 that 'divers
aldermen and commoners . . . of late have departed out of the said
city to the utter undoing of the same'.[13]

But this was neither the whole story of sixteenth-century towns nor
even, necessarily, the bedrock to which all other events and circumstances can be reduced. It will somewhat redress the historiographical
balance if we insist that the Reformation was much more than a
side-show: that it was as central to the urban history of the period as
religious change has traditionally been to the national history of
England under the Tudors.

III

The Reformation can be discussed as something which affected the
towns, being in its widest sense a profound and extensive revolution
altering much for ever. We shall come to that. But before we consider
what the Reformation did for the towns, it is proper to ask what the
towns did for the Reformation. Was it the towns which converted a
reluctant countryside and turned seventeenth-century England into a
(largely) protestant nation?

The answer is a guarded yes. It would be wrong to call the
Reformation an urban phenomenon and leave it at that. By the same
token it would not be sufficient to call it a revolution of youth, or an
episode in female assertion and emancipation, although both these
social dimensions of the movement attract attention. The secularising
operations of the Reformation greatly increased the ecclesiastical

patronage of the landed gentry and this, together with the wealth and general desirability of many of the parishes which the gentry now controlled, meant that, as members of the governing class were attracted to the new religion, so protestant preachers fresh from university were 'planted' more or less randomly in rural locations, where there was not necessarily any general desire to have them. So it was that John Bland, a fiery and quarrelsome ex-monk from the far north-west, found himself in Adisham, a deeply rural parish of East Kent, where he soon had more enemies than friends (which helped in due course to bring him to the stake). However he made it the base for an effective roving apostolate which took him to many other places, including the small towns of the region.[14]

But in many towns there was a protestant constituency, the nucleus of an audience for John Bland and his ilk. This was often small at first, but sufficient to create cells and a following for the new tendency, which was caustically critical of the old ways, in the tradition of the long-established Lollard heresy. It attacked pilgrimage, confession, the Mass itself, and sustained itself by bible-reading, at first quietly and unobtrusively in conventicles, but presently noisily and with deliberate provocation at the west end of the church. So it was in the Canterbury parish of Northgate, a poor quarter but with a few richer inhabitants, where John Toftes, a lawyer and 'common maintainer, supporter and harbourer of persons accused of heresies', openly in church and with a loud voice read the Bible in English to an audience consisting of his wife, his son and daughter-in-law, and the parish midwife – and this was at the height of the late Henrician religious reaction, when bible-reading was restricted and a conservative code of religious practice enforced under the Act of Six Articles. This practice remained an emotive symbol of something like religious insurrection for the quarter-century it took to win the main struggle of the initial Reformation. At Deal a group of laymen which included a thirty-two year old soldier from a neighbouring garrison were 'discouraged' by the parson from reading the Scripture amongst themselves in English, 'saying . . . you ought not to read it, it doth pass your capacity'. At Rye the protestant faction was conspicuous by the 1530s, bound by close ties of friendship, kinship and marriage, a group in the ascendant in the economy and politics of the port town. At Colchester it was said that 'this town is a harbourer of heretics and ever was'. Yet it was not until the 1540s that Protestantism made any real headway in Colchester and Protestants were still a minority sub-culture even at the end of Edward's reign.[15]

Mrs Toftes of Northgate, Canterbury, declared that church images were 'devils and idols' and boasted that her daughter could 'piss as good holy water as the priests could make any'. And Christopher Levins, another prosperous parishioner and the town clerk, pulled down the images in the churches of St Mary's Northgate and St Peter's and burned in his own house the bones of St Blaise which had been brought to Canterbury early in the tenth century, the earliest of its relics, and under whose shrine Becket had died. But twenty years later, in early Elizabethan days, with Protestantism legally but barely established, willing adherence to a religion of bible-reading and sermons was still an acquired taste in Canterbury, and a taste which few seem to have acquired. When three neighbours went to hear a sermon on a certain Sunday afternoon and later retired to the Fleur de Lys to drink a pot of beer, the rest of the company in the bar asked them: 'Where have you been you three good husbands, not at the sermon I trust?'[16]

But before long some East Anglian towns, Colchester, Ipswich and soon Bury St Edmunds, became organised centres of early and precocious reform, supporting protestant plays and printing presses as well as bible-reading and Sunday afternoon sermons. Colchester in the years of the Marian reaction and persecution was not only a city set on a hill but a Mecca whither, we are told, people resorted for the comfort of their consciences 'and repairing to the common inns, had by night their Christian exercises' – leading A.G. Dickens to remark that if the Battle of Waterloo was won on the playing fields of Eton, the English Reformation was secured in the pubs of Colchester.[17]

London was the most important of original protestant centres. As early as the 1530s the social spectrum of the unorthodox was wide, extending from the Whitechapel bricklayer who preached regularly in his garden and was said to have declared Scripture as well as if he had studied at the universities to members of the city's merchant aristocracy, the Mercers and Merchant Adventurers and, conspicuously, their wives and daughters. In so far as the Reformation Parliament, which from 1529 followed a governmental lead in attacks on ecclesiastical interests, was motivated by real rather than synthetic anticlericalism, this seems to have been the anticlericalism of London's merchant princes and lawyers. The familiar homespun preaching of Hugh Latimer, bitterly critical of the church hierarchy, was heard by five or six thousand at a time. It was said: 'Latimer many blameth and as many doth allow'. So London, if not yet a protestant city, was more or less evenly divided for and against religious change, which in itself indicates some measure of mass support for reform.[18]

At Bristol there was a preaching contest between Latimer and an unreconstructed preaching friar of the old school called Hubberdyne, 'a great strayer about the realm in all quarters' whose sermons consisted of 'tales and fables, dialogues and dreams' enlivened by hops, leaps and other histrionic gestures. This caused some excitement, until Hubberdyne's antics broke the floor of the pulpit and caused gangrenous injuries to which the defender of catholic orthodoxy presently succumbed, leaving the churchwardens to plead that they had built their pulpit for preaching, not for dancing.[19]

Although Latimer was said to have 'sorely infected' Bristol, the 'good catholic people' of the town deplored his doctrine. It would be a mistake to suppose that a majority of the population either in London or in provincial towns consisted of enthusiastic protestant converts and critics of the old church. If the Canterbury parish of St Mary's Northgate contained the fiercely iconoclastic Toftes family, it was also frequented by more conventional parishioners who reacted to thunderstorms by rushing to church to fetch the holy water which Mrs Toftes despised, casting it about their houses to drive away evil spirits and devils. Not far away, in the village of Herne, the parish sexton thought that the Devil had no power to come near holy water, holy bread or hallowed bells. But he had heard his elders say that whenever a rumbling was heard in church that presaged a death. And, sure enough, when he slept in the church one Christmastime and heard thunder he was able to assure the curate 'that there should be a corpse shortly' – which for him was presumably good news, since a grave would have to be dug.[20] These were some of the old ways in religion. In Canterbury there were still, in the 1540s, plenty of conservative priests to tell their people that Protestants were like the man who, hopelessly lost, was told: 'You be clear out of the way and must turn back again where you left'. Many had not turned aside. In Elizabethan Hull 'certain disordered persons' maintained the old and 'popish' custom of ringing the church bells on the night of All Saints Day, until the mayor and a posse descended on the church to disperse them.[21]

Much recent research suggests that the bulk of the population was conventionally but also actively pious in orthodox religious practice for as long as it was legal and feasible to be orthodox: that is, until the Reformation was made official. Popular anticlericalism may have been a paper tiger. When Henry VIII swung the Church back to a conservatively defined Catholicism in the early 1540s, the city authorities in London clamped down on the hardcore protestant population, those who despised holy bread and holy water, read the Bible in church and were anticlerical and iconoclastic. This led to the arrest and temporary detention of five hundred people, less than one per cent of the population.[22]

There is much that is unbalanced in Professor J.J. Scarisbrick's book *The Reformation and the English People*. Yet it is hard to disagree with its second sentence: 'On the whole, English men and women did not want the Reformation and most of them were slow to accept it when it came'. He must mean 'most' English men and women for Protestants did exist and should not be discounted. However all historians, Scarisbrick not excluded, remain puzzled about the readiness with which these 'most' people abandoned religious habits which seem to have been meaningful and dear to them, simply at the behest of the government. Late medieval Catholicism has been called a cult celebrated by the living on behalf of the dead. No religious exhortation was commoner than that inscribed on innumerable funerary brasses: 'Pray for my soul and for all Christian souls'. If you really did believe that your grandmother was suffering in purgatory and that prayers and masses could shorten and alleviate her pains, you might be expected to have made more of a fuss when it became impractical and (in effect) illegal to pay for this service. A modern parallel might be the enforced closure, without compensation, of all hospices for the terminally ill, with the proceeds used to give members of the Cabinet a hefty pay rise.[23]

Such questions have to be lived with and cannot easily be resolved. As the alteration of religion became official and general it was more often than not the towns which became centres of more than a merely formal and nominal Protestantism and centres of regional evangelism. In the early Elizabethan decades Leicester, Norwich, Kings Lynn, Northampton, Hull all assumed the role of cities set on their respective hills. A generation later the West Riding joined in. In 1538 an early northern Protestant had complained that 'Rotheram, Doncaster, Pontefract, Wakefield, Leeds, Bradford, Halifax, Manchester and many others have not one faithful pastor . . . Newcastle and the country round is also destitute of good pastors.' Within a hundred years (and it took almost that long) all these towns became famous protestant preaching centres, and Newcastle had transformed the civilisation of its hinterland in Durham and Northumberland, indeed had introduced into that region for the first time what the Elizabethans could recognise as civilisation.[24]

How had it happened? Not by accident, or by osmosis. Urban

parishes were typically small and poorly endowed. In Ipswich and Colchester few could support even a humdrum curate without supplementation. So well-qualified graduate preachers would not appear on the scene as a matter of course, and without special efforts to attract them. Conversely, where the Church was still powerful and wealthily entrenched, towns and especially cathedral cities could remain bastions of religious conservatism far into the new age. This was conspicuously true of York, where there were six hundred priests at the time of the Reformation (six to eight per cent of the city's entire population!) and where religion of a traditional kind still enjoyed the active and generous support of the merchant class. A year after the first protestant Prayer Book came into use in 1549 a vicar choral of the Minster made a traditionally catholic will in which he bequeathed his soul to God, 'our blessed Lady and to all the celestial company of Heaven'. Six months after the Elizabethan Settlement a York canon declared boldly that he was 'pretending [that is to say, claiming] to die in the catholic faith, desiring all saints to pray for me'. Some years later still no objection was made to entering in the archbishop's register the will of a parish priest who bequeathed his soul to 'our blessed Lady, Saint Mary, and to all the holy company of Heaven'. When radical change came it grew not from the roots but by imposition from above, with the arrival on the scene of earnest reformers as a Dean of York (Matthew Hutton, 1567), an Archbishop (Edmund Grindal, 1570) and a Lord President of the Council in the North (the Earl of Huntingdon, 1572).[25] Canterbury, too, remained somewhat backward in religion, the sort of town where a backlash in favour of traditional ways was possible as late as 1647, when a riot in support of Christmas helped to usher in the second Civil War.

But in so far as leading townsmen were sympathetic to the new religion, they and the more powerful members of the new protestant ascendancy moved heaven and earth to get a preaching ministry established, for this was the favoured instrument of conversion and also the principal amenity to which a progressive town could now aspire. The Earl of Huntingdon told the Bishop of Chester: 'I do all I can to get good preachers planted in the market towns of this country'. Archbishops Grindal and Hutton and, later still, arch-bishop Tobie Mathew co-operated enthusiastically in this enterprise.

How was the 'planting' done? As far as was feasible a parochial structure well designed for the singing of many masses and for baptising and burying within a few steps of people's doors was overhauled to provide for a learned preaching ministry. This involved the 'rationalisation' or pooling of resources. Corporations acquired the patronage of livings, small and scarcely viable parishes were amalgamated and livings were topped up with semi-voluntary contributions or, as in the case of Ipswich, by a local tax which required the backing of a special Act of Parliament. Lincoln's twenty-four parishes became nine, Stamford's eleven six. Scarcely more than half York's parish churches of 1500 were still in consecrated use in 1600. But such efforts were not always successful, or sufficient. Exeter failed in its parliamentary campaign to turn its many small parishes and unsuitable church fabrics into a single, barn-like building to accommodate sermons for the whole town. But fortunately in this city a new building was not necessary, as one already existed in the shape of the cathedral. Above all, the Church in the towns was hamstrung, and disproportionately, by the alienation or 'impropriation' of the bulk of its tithe revenues, a problem so extensive and fundamental as to require general legislative remedies which that side of the nineteenth century were beyond the capacity of the English political and legal system.[26] In these intractable circumstances the solution was often the appointment of a non-parochial clergyman, a figure of standing and commanding influence, often styled 'lecturer' but also called the 'common', 'ordinary' or 'public' preacher of the town.

The cities of protestant Europe were first in creating this role, elevating clerics whose place in the pre-Reformation ecclesiastical firmament would have been humble indeed into the exalted position of effective bishop or 'antistes' of these compact republics. So it was that in Strasbourg Martin Bucer, an ex-religious in charge of a poor suburban parish, became more potent than the ecclesiastical patricians of the cathedral chapter, and that in Zürich Huldreich Zwingli invested the hitherto lowly calling of 'people's priest' at the Grossmünster with a transcendent significance. It was the intellectual power and pulpit fluency of Bucer, Zwingli and other reformers which secured their charismatical ascendancy, for it was their sermons which brought salvation to whole cities. But such luminaries were much more than preachers of sermons, mere 'media' figures. Zwingli was soon hailed as 'bishop of the Fatherland', and from Bucer's household in Strasbourg the Italian reformer Peter Martyr Vermigli reported that at last he had seen with his own eyes the kind of primitive episcopacy described in the pastoral letters of the New Testament. 'This is the office of a pastor, this is that bishop-like dignity described by Paul in the Epistles unto Timothy and Titus.'[27]

The more modest setting of the provincial English town was imitative of this example and of these arrangements. John More, curate of the little Norwich parish of St Andrew's, came to be regarded as the 'Apostle of Norwich', John White in early seventeenth-century Dorset as the 'patriarch' of Dorchester. Such figures cultivated lengthy beards as symbols of their *gravitas*, and to make visible the recreation of the Old Testament prophetic role. Some vaguely scholarly memory of the original conditions within which and over which bishops had presided in primitive times in the many little cities of the Mediterranean world, reinforced by a contemporary sense of provincial political realities, commended to sixteenth-century Protestantism the model of a town sufficient unto itself and answerable for itself in religion as much as in other respects. The authority of a diocesan, living remotely in the country, visiting occasionally and burdened with innumerable distracting responsibilities, seemed by contrast unappealing and anomalous. So when Ipswich conducted its long and for some years mainly fruitless search for the ideal town preacher it was looking not for a mere lecturer but for a spiritual and pastorally gifted religious leader, capable of visiting the sick, comforting 'afflicted consciences' and defending true religion against its enemies and detractors.[28]

Not least among these functions was that of supporting and suitably exhorting the secular government of the town: ministry in close and confident association with magistracy. When dedicating to his employers, the corporation of Yarmouth, his own published catechism (itself serving as a standard of local orthodoxy) the town preacher Bartimaeus Andrews (and how much more authority he wielded as 'Bartimaeus' than as simple 'John Andrews'!) reminded these worthies of their solemn promise 'at my first entry amongst you' to promote God's glory. John Calvin had extracted a similar undertaking on arriving in Geneva. Andrews went on:

> You must know that the burthen of this people lieth upon your shoulders, and that their eyes look at you, as those by whose example the people either perish and fall or are preserved and stayed up, for the fall and uprising of many dependenth upon your public persons . . . Be you presidents in godly and sober example to this great people.[29]

To secure a man who could utter such words of reproving exhortation with credible conviction East Anglian towns were prepared to spend time, effort and money. In 1578 Yarmouth offered a yearly salary of £30 to a preacher of their choice 'if he will come hither'. Five years later its efforts to attract another promising man involved journeys to Cambridge, to the diocesan bishop and to the candidate himself. It was soon after this that one of the bailiffs travelled to the borders of Essex, fifty miles to the south, to persuade the ministers of the Vale of Dedham to release Bartimaeus Andrews from his country parish in order for him to assume the spiritual burden of Yarmouth. One of the Dedham ministers remarked that to remove Andrews from his pastorate would be like plucking out an eye. Mr Mayham of Yarmouth replied: 'Sir, if you cast out your eye you will give me leave to take it up'. In the words of Samuel Ward, the most celebrated of the town preachers of Ipswich, magistracy and ministry were 'principal lights', 'these two optic pieces' by which the whole body politic was enlightened.[30]

Andrews was offered, and accepted, a yearly salary of £50, substantially more than his rural living had been worth, at least on paper. At Ipswich the wages of the common preacher rose from £20 to £50 and then to £113, money enough for two preachers, in spite of difficulty in raising these sums from a partly apathetic citizenry. At last, when Jacobean Ipswich found its ideal in Samuel Ward, it was prepared to reward him with a stipend of £100 and a house worth £120. Was any officer of the town recompensed more handsomely? Towns fought relentlessly to prevent their patriarchs and apostles being taken from them, either by more attractive offers from elsewhere or by bishops jealous of their reputation or troubled by their Puritanism. Sensible, not to say negligent, bishops of Norwich left Ward, 'the glory of Ipswich', well alone. To attempt to eject the likes of Ward meant immediate trouble for themselves; to do nothing meant, at worst, future embarrassment for their successors.[31]

This was not the only model or the sole means by which a preaching ministry was securely established in provincial towns. Actual circumstances depended upon local conditions, which were variable. Where incumbents were 'topped up' to bring their income to levels acceptable to professional men it would be difficult to say whether those so maintained should be styled vicar, curate or lecturer. In Boston the corporation owned the living, in Rye part of the living, and in each case the principal clergyman of the place was more the employee of the town than owner of a parson's freehold. Most corporations were less prosperous than Ipswich or Yarmouth, and it could be argued that the presence of competent preachers supported by the tithe income of country parishes within riding distance of the local market town rendered it unnecessary to tax the townspeople for the wherewithal to secure regular sermons. Since the country clergy were bound to come to town in any case for their necessary occasions, why not prevail upon them to preach before returning to their parishes? This was part of the rationale of setting up in the early Elizabethan Church the institutions known somewhat mysteriously as 'prophesyings', which were both festivals and schools of preaching. Typically held in market towns, and enjoyed by sermon addicts from both town and country, prophesyings brought together the clergy of the district, learned and unlearned, preachers and non-preachers, in regular 'exercises' and became one of those institutions which constantly mediated between two somewhat distinct but not separate worlds.[32]

These occasions differed from a simple 'exercise' of preaching in that as many as three sermons were delivered in turn from the same text and the preaching was followed by 'conference' among the assembled clergy, perhaps extending to the exercise of mutual discipline on a more or less presbyterian plan. Because such arrangements pointed to a church structure in many ways different from that assumed within diocesan episcopacy, and perhaps also on account of the somewhat exotic name of 'prophesying', these institutions attracted hostile attention, not least from Queen Elizabeth herself. In 1577 the queen directly ordered their suppression, after Archbishop Grindal of Canterbury had declined to transmit an order to this effect.

However the official cessation of prophesying made little difference to what was by now a settled pattern of provincial religious life, and one which was destined to outlive both the Tudors and their immediate Stuart successors. In scores, perhaps even hundreds, of market towns it was a regular habit for the country clergy to come together monthly, fortnightly or weekly, in what came to be known as a 'combination', each to take his turn in the 'exercise' or 'combination lecture'. The auditory formed a microcosm of seventeenth-century English society, representing as it did the ministers themselves, sitting in a body in their black gowns, the local gentry and the townspeople, from the mayor, bailiffs and other officers downwards. The eighty-five towns where it can be shown that combination lectures were regularly kept in the early seventeenth century included, in Norfolk, Diss, Fakenham, Hingham, King's Lynn, North Walsham, Wighton, Wiveton and Wymondham; in Cheshire, Bowden, Budworth, Congleton, Frodsham, Ince, Knutsford, Macclesfield, Motteram, Nantwich, Northwich, Tarporley and Tarvin. But it may be that if all the evidence were available to us it would be found that a shorter and more revealing list could be made of market towns where there were no regular lectures and where the authorities took no interest in preaching and made no provision for it.[33]

Everyone was supposed to benefit. At least, all right-minded and orderly persons benefited. Market town lectures both directly assisted in the promotion of civil order and symbolised the kind of order desired, so that they were popular with the protestant magistracy as a kind of polar opposite to the disorder associated with alehouses and other places of evil repute. Apart from sharing in such aspirations the clergy enjoyed the congenial and learned society of their brethren and, in addition to the general benefit of sociable collegiality, sought their own professional advancement by regularly exposing their talents to the critical appraisal of the religious public of the district. As argued in Norfolk, the advantages of combination lecturing included 'advancement to the clergymen, when their gifts shall be known', and 'increase of love and acquaintance amongst preachers'. It is significant that after the lecture at Winwick in Lancashire the secular notables dined together in one ordinary or public eating house, the ministers at another, 'every man accompanying his acquaintance and so making as it were a whole chain of many links'.

But the rank and file of the laity, 'private Christians', were also said to gain: most obviously from the ready availability of religious instruction and inspiration. At Bury St Edmunds it was said: 'Your townsmen of Bury are such diligent hearers of the Word on the Monday exercise that they may easily be singled out from other men'. But there was also profit in a more literal sense in the stimulus which the regular lecture gave to the business of the market and to the general secular interests of the town. 'Benefit also to the inhabitants for their market by concourse of people', it was noted in Norfolk, where an unsympathetic ecclesiastic sourly complained that 'not a market, or a bowling green or an ordinary' could stand without a lecture. The cost to the town was, by convention, the price of the dinner consumed by the assembled clergy, or more often only the gallon or two of wine required to wash it down, the ministers paying modestly for a subsidised meal. An Oxford scholar and future bishop undertaking a rustic ride during the Long Vacation remarked satirically on his reception at puritan Banbury: we had the usual preacher's wages – 'thanks and wine'.

So 'prophesying' and the 'combination lecture' expressed the reciprocity of town and countryside in early modern England. As we have seen, most municipal corporations were neither powerful nor impressive, but their significance lay in the very fact that they did not inhabit a sharply differentiated world. As Thomas Hardy wrote of nineteenth-century but still pre-industrial Casterbridge (Dorchester), it was the *complement* of rural society, not its opposite. (Yet socially speaking, as we learn from George Eliot's Middlemarch [Coventry], they were very different worlds. The reader of the novel who knows both the neighbouring gentry and the urban bourgeoisie has an advantage over the characters themselves, and especially over the gentlefolk who are literally unable to recognise the wives and families of even the richest townspeople.) It was in town that those with spending power, gentry and yeomanry, made most of their purchases, not only of market staples like corn and livestock, but of a vast miscellany of consumer goods. When Sir Nathaniel Bacon's man went from the north Norfolk coastal village of Stiffkey to Norwich he returned with 'nails, soap, currants, bellows, white lead', as well as 'three ounces of sugar candy for my mistress'. The mercer's shop in late Elizabethan Cranbrook (Kent) was crammed with several hundred pounds' worth of gloves, ribbons, silk buttons, drinking glasses, playing cards and, as Professor W.G. Hoskins wrote of a similar establishment in Exeter, 'Heaven knows what else'. It was a great age of penny numbers.[34]

One went to town to consult lawyers, physicians and astrologers. It was in town that local government had its seat and juries assembled for sessions and assizes. Inns for travellers (and for a great variety of other purposes, from auction sales to cockfights) were mainly located in town centres. One third of all the inns in Yorkshire were situated in the city of York. Schooling was on the increase, and schools of any reputation were to be found in towns. Shakespeare, Marlowe and Nashe were all products of grammar schools in provincial towns and owed their school places to their bourgeois origins. The entertainments provided by travelling players, wild beast shows and itinerant musicians were also something to be sampled in town. With all these activities (except 'unlawful', even 'filthy' entertainment) protestant religion was very much at home, whilst making its own distinctive contribution to the rhythmical patterns of urban life. The boys of the town grammar school were set to take notes at the sermons as a routine exercise. The more accomplished note-takers seem to have been responsible for the published versions which have come down to us. At Bury St Edmunds the full draconic severity of puritan discipline was exacted against fornicators and other offenders as a public *auto de fe* on Monday mornings, as people came from the weekly lecture and prepared to do their marketing and shopping.

The history of provincial England in the later seventeenth and eighteenth centuries consists (from one point of view) of the ever closer integration of town and country as the late medieval retreat from town (a prudent response to plague and other unhealthy conditions, as well as to business failure) was now reversed. The country gentry began to make more use of urban facilities and were joined by the growing ranks of pseudo- or semi-gentry, and by the more or less professional people who began to flesh out the upper levels of town society. The architectural symbol of this social and cultural transformation was the assembly rooms. In early eighteenth-century Kent even New Romney, with only 500 inhabitants, boasted assembly rooms; so did Lamberhurst, a village of 750 people. Towns, and especially country towns, were becoming the desirable focal points of provincial existence as never before.[35]

The Reformation contributed significantly to the impression that town was a good place to be, even to stay. In 1591 a schoolmaster with hopes of preferment in Colchester informed its 'Senate': 'To be seated in a healthsome place where there is an ordinary publicke sanctifyed ministry is one special point, and not the least to be regarded'.[36] What made Colchester so 'healthsome' all of a sudden? Most towns still killed off their inhabitants at a faster rate than they could reproduce themselves. In 1579 plague carried away a third of the entire population of Norwich, a natural holocaust still hard to imagine, even in the terrible twentieth century. Deaths from plague in Norwich were on the same scale less than a generation later, in 1603–4, and in the intervening years a mortality rate of ten per cent was attributable to plague in the periods 1584–5 and 1589–92.[37]

But it was the poor, and poor immigrants, who died in disproportionate numbers of this particular, terrible cause. (In 1558–9 the great outbreak of 'influenza', if that is what it was, was less choosy and in Norwich killed the city recorder and ten aldermen.) The wealthy could leave at times of danger. Moreover, although doctors were not of much use in such emergencies it may have been thought that they could help and the supposed healthiness of towns may have been attributed to the presence of physicians of good reputation. As for Colchester, perhaps its principal amenity was the hill on which it does in fact stand, providing some protection against agues and the noxious humours supposed to cause many ailments. A contemporary account of Taunton describes it as 'well and healthily sited'.[38] But the schoolmaster's reference to the 'publicke sanctifyed ministry' was probably already a commonplace. A pseudo-gentleman who took up residence in Gloucester did so 'for his better service of God and for recovery of his wife's health by physic'.[39]

What such facilities represented was 'civility', a quality of life increasingly prized. Of Swaffham in Norfolk it was said in 1608 that the inhabitants were 'more rude than easily will be believed to be of those that have been brought up in more civil places'.[40] Swaffham was not 'civil'. No more was Ireland. But Colchester, or Taunton, or Gloucester were civil places. But what *was* 'civil' about such places in 1600? In 1740 there would be assembly rooms, coffee shops, theatres, the first public libraries, musical events, all the necessities of a polite and cultivated existence. In 1600 there was only religion. This, of course, is to exaggerate. But the exaggeration serves to turn over the coin. What did the Reformation do to or for the English towns?

IV

The difficulty with local or regional history is that everywhere is different, so that the subject by its very nature courts particularism and resists treatment on a general or national scale. Ecclesiastically and religiously, the English towns were very diverse: as diverse as pre-Reformation York, neighbouring Hull or Rye in Sussex. York had its Minster, the richest abbey and the largest hospital north of the Trent, eight other religious houses, no fewer than fifty parish churches and as many as six hundred priests; Hull, an important sea-port and garrison town, had just two churches, neither of them technically a full parish church; Rye was served by just one great parish church. Religion in Hull seems to have consisted of a rather formal and even sterile practice which served to keep the inhabitants in place, rank and order. But Norwich on the eve of the Reformation was still the home of virtuoso religion, 'a religion of considerable richness and variety, a kind of High Church, almost Baroque Christianity'. Its devotees still included religious solitaries and its pious ladies lived in halfway houses between monasticism and lay piety, somewhat like the Dutch *béguinages*.[41]

In some towns and cities the eve of the Reformation witnessed the still exuberant celebration of civic religious ceremony and ritual, including the plays performed on the feast of Corpus Christi and at other seasons. Elsewhere, as at Canterbury and Ipswich, enthusiasm had drained away from these things and pageantry was in decline well before the Reformation. It has been suggested that towns which were relatively free of social tension had no need to spend money on this expensive mode of affirming social values.[42] The reductionist potential of this argument, if pushed too far, is disturbing. Are we to interpret the strength of religious life in the late medieval town as an inverse reflection of the extent of the civic harmony actually prevailing? However there is unlikely to have been any single reason for the intensity or otherwise with which the 'mysteries' were celebrated.

The diversity of towns means that we have to talk in ideal-typical terms of no one town in particular and thus, in a sense, of nowhere, in order to encapsulate what the religious changes of the sixteenth century may have entailed. Religiously speaking they consisted of a vast reduction, simplification and, in modern jargon, rationalisation. The base-line from which 'reformation' began consisted of churches where the masses said or sung at the high altar attracted less attention than the many masses and offerings made at the side altars along the aisles of the nave, the altars of personal and family chantries and of those poor men's chantries which were the religious fraternities. In the Canterbury parish church of St Dunstan there was the Roper chantry chapel, erected above a vault containing the remains of the Ropers, the kinsfolk of Sir Thomas More's daughter, as well as the head supposedly salvaged from the Thames by Margaret Roper which some piously believed (and believe) to be that of More himself. But in this same small parish there were also fraternities of St John, St Anne and the Shaft of the Cross, each with its own rituals and rules, employing and paying its own clergy, conducting its annual general meetings, its processions and feasts. The religious and civic year was punctuated by formal ritual: in Canterbury this included the Corpus Christi processions and pageants of midsummer, the annual celebration of the Translation of the relics of St Thomas à Becket and the St George's Day solemnities in the breezy sunshine of late April, when the saint's image was carried in a procession headed by the mayor, aldermen and their wives. This tradition was hotly debated in the divisive 1540s, when Archbishop Cranmer's commissary asked the curate and churchwarden of St George's church whether they had obeyed their orders in pulling down the image of St George. 'They made answer and said Yes. Have you cut it in pieces? They said No. Then said the Commissary: It is not only the king's majesty's pleasure to have such images abused to be pulled down, but also to be disfigured, and nothing of such images to remain.' Mr Rand the churchwarden protested, pointing out that St George was patron of England. We have no patron but Christ, said Commissary Nevinson, and yet we pull down the Crucifix. 'Then, answered Mr Rand, if you pull down the Crucifix, then pull down all.'

The fear that 'all' would indeed be disfigured and pulled down was a lively apprehension. At Louth in Lincolnshire 'all' included a stupendous tower, 295 feet in total height, including the spire with which it had been capped as recently as 1515, erected at a cost of £305 8s 5d which had been subscribed to the last penny by the townspeople themselves. At the consecration ceremony, which included the installation of a weathercock made from a great bowl which a king of the Scots had left behind on a visit to England, several inhabitants were proud to testify that they had been present to witness the laying of both the first and the last stones of this crowning edifice. It was out of this church, through doors which still exist, that a local priest led his congregation in 1536, exhorting them to follow the cross or soon they would have no cross to follow. What ensued we know as the Lincolnshire Rising and the Pilgrimage of Grace.[43]

The priest of Louth was not wrong in all his predictions. Presently the cross became an emotive symbol for two hostile religious factions. At Colchester in 1541 an iconoclast declared: 'I will do no more reverence to the Cross made in the similitude of the Cross of Christ than I would to the bathhouse'. This was shocking, even to the man of Appledore in Kent who confessed in 1543 that he crept to the Cross on Good Friday 'more for company than for devotion'. With Edward on the throne, crosses began to disappear. In 1548 it was reported from one Kentish parish: 'The image of the cross accustomed to be borne in procession doth not stand in any of the tabernacles at the high altar, since the commandment was declared at Ashford that such things should be taken away'. When 'such things' returned under Mary, Protestants, so far as they dared, voted with their bottoms at procession time. 'Why follow ye not the cross?' asked Richard Baker of Thomasine Ashton, who had sat in her pew while the rest of the parish of Westgate, Canterbury, processed. 'Ye be a heretic, will ye never leave your heresy?'

Just as a string of beads in the hand was a notorious badge of popery, so it is very likely that in the new Elizabethan dispensation crosses were no longer worn as personal adornment, and that cautious people were careful not to cross themselves when they sneezed. Perhaps the crosses were not laboriously hacked out of those many surfaces on city walls where they served the same function as the Victorian notice 'Commit No Nuisance'. That would have been to carry municipal Protestantism too far and to have incurred needless expense – and perhaps nuisance. But the authorities expected free-standing crosses in churchyards, however ancient, to come down, and in 1571 proceedings were taken against the churchwardens of one Yorkshire parish for not 'plucking down' such a cross, and for leaving their roodloft intact. By this late date the great cross or rood which had dominated virtually every church from its high station on the rood beam or 'loft', flanked with images of Mary and John, had mostly disappeared, the demolition having been carried out in most places in 1559–60. At supper in a Kentish parish John Maycot remarked that the roodloft 'went down merrily'. But what had been done was not universally acceptable and in a neighbouring village some that had been 'accusers' in Mary's days were dragged in against their will to witness the act. So Robert Colwell told Maycot: 'Let them take heed that they pull not down more this year than peradventure they shall set up again next year'. It was some few years after this that the suffragan bishop of Dover, Richard Rogers, was 'in a great chaff about the roodloft' in Great Chart church and created a minor sensation in the country by using a traditional catholic oath to one of the leading parishioners in the hearing of the entire congregation: 'By God's Soul'. But Rogers was entitled to feel indignant that the roodloft was still intact at Great Chart as late as 1568, for he had been rector of the parish since the previous year. So the symbol of the cross tracks the uncertain and rancorous progress of the Reformation in English provincial life. At court Queen Elizabeth made her position plain by restoring the crucifix to her royal chapel, thus provoking in Canterbury a rumour that the great rood would soon be replaced in the cathedral, and pushing the newly-appointed protestant bishops to the brink of resignation.[44] Reformation, even official reformation, was more drastic in many of its effects than either Anglican or puritan folklore has led us to suppose.

With the images and crosses went, by degrees (the process was far from complete until the 1570s or 1580s, or even later in some towns), not only solemn religious processions but also a variety of other customary and seasonal 'pastimes' associated with the church calendar, from the Corpus Christi plays of midsummer to the licensed misrule of midwinter. The antiquarian John Stow, an Elizabethan author of distinctly catholic sympathies, wrote a nostalgic account of the 'orders and customs', 'sports and pastimes' of his own native London where, as a boy, he had fetched milk hot from the cow in the fields beside the Tower. For the feast of Christmas every Londoner's home and the parish churches were decked with green. In Lent a twisted tree or 'with' was brought out of the woods and set up in people's houses. In May maypoles were brought in from the country and erected in the streets, with bonfires and stage-plays. Come June and July the vigils and feasts of St John the Baptist, St Peter and St Paul saw houses dressed in summer greenery, flowers and lamps. In the street were lit bonfires (so called because they were *good* fires, creating amity among neighbours, even as the fires purged infection from the air), and the wealthier sort set out tables with plentiful food and drink, inviting neighbours and passers-by to share their good fortune. It sounds too good to be true, and no doubt it was not quite like that. As Keith Thomas has suggested, 'Merrie England' always existed in the past, never in the present. But it existed in the future too. The customs which Stow described were by no means extinct in the London of Samuel Pepys and John Aubrey.[45]

So far as we can tell, such occasions were often rowdy and bawdy. In York the Christmas procession of Yule and Yule's Wife was presently described by a protestant archbishop and other senior clergy as 'a very rude and barbarous custom', 'very undecently and uncomely', and we may well believe it. In late medieval civic ceremony decorous processional order and indecorous disorder were never far apart: indeed they were often juxtaposed. The formal drinking of healths could easily become informal drunkenness. And yet the nuts which Yule scattered as he rode were said to be symbols of 'that most noble Nut, our Saviour's blessed body'. The notion that Christ's humanity could be 'aptly compared to a nut' may be taken as a small symbol of the old religious culture, now under sentence. All these colourful rituals had a positive social purpose: either to affirm the fundamental unity of the civic community, the value of good neighbourhood which Stow held so dear, or (which is not quite the same thing) to provide relatively harmless channels for expressing antagonism in the near-violence of misrule. And in London the seasonal exits to the woods and fields to return with greenery and maypoles perhaps symbolised something even more subliminal: the need to reconcile the teeming, crowded city with the countryside, where the service of God was still sustained in kind through the tithes which were the product of the soil, and where an important annual ritual involved the perambulation of the parish and its resources. In one Kentish parish the little procession took in 'the house of old Mr Gybbes, and had good cheer and dined there as the use was in those days'. 'Those days' were already distant when this was remembered, in 1567. When, in 1568, a cleric of Birchington in Thanet 'brought a faggot out of his chamber' on St Peter's Eve and lit the traditional bonfire this was a punishable offence.[46]

These seasonal rituals were almost all contained in that half of the year which runs from Christmas to Midsummer, and which can be considered a distinctive and extended festive season, set against the relatively industrious second half of the year with its uninterrupted work discipline. Calendarwise the Reformation amounted to the intrusion of the working season into the months traditionally associated with a kind of holy play, in Phythian-Adams's words, 'a triumph of the secular half over its ritualistic counterpart'. For urban society there were no more important consequences of the Reformation than this: indeed there were few events of more importance between the Middle Ages and modern times. It was 'an obliteration of the established rhythm of life itself', no less a piece of secularisation than the conversion of the Black Friars in Canterbury to serve as Thomas Bathurst's cloth works.[47] In York Archbishop Grindal ordered that ministers and churchwardens

> shall not suffer any lords of misrule or summer lords or ladies or any disguised persons or others in Christmas or at May games, or any minstrels, morris dancers or others at rush-bearings or at any other time to come unreverently into any church or chapel or churchyard and there dance or play any unseemly parts, with scoffing jests, wanton gestures, or ribald talk . . .

In many East Anglian parishes the traditional religious drama died its death in the 1560s. In Chelmsford it was in 1576 that the plays were suppressed and the costumes sold 'by the consent of divers of the parishioners'.[48]

The traditional 'mysteries' were put down at about the same time in York, Wakefield, Chester and Coventry, to be replaced with midsummer shows and sports which were without religious associations and were purged of 'unseemly' or merely boisterous elements. At Chester the violent football matches always played on Shrove Tuesday ('Goteddsday') were replaced with running races and horse races, with silver cups for prizes. Here, indeed, one senses the advance of modern times in the form of our own youthful experience. But the dragon, naked boys in nets and devils in feathers of the midsummer show were replaced by the martial figure of a man on horseback in body armour which, contrariwise, looks like a piece of medieval atavism. These reforms were presided over by the aptly named Mayor Henry Hardware, who also 'caused the giants which use to go at Midsummer to be broken, the bull ring at the high cross to be taken up'. 'This mayor was a godly, over-zealous man', remarked a local chronicler.[49]

But if this was a kind of secularisation, it paradoxically involved the *sacralisation* of the town, which now became self-consciously a godly commonwealth, its symbolic and mimetic codes replaced by a literally articulated, didactic religious discipline. In place of the seasonal complexities of the old calendar, the secular and festive half-years, there was now a new rhythm of working days and sabbaths, its keystone a weekly day to be set apart for the learning and performance of religious duties, when not only work but also all forms of play were forbidden. In the 1560s the corporation of Stratford-upon-Avon was preoccupied with such purely secular nuisances or offences between neighbours as pigs being allowed to wander, the dumping of middens on the streets and the pursuit of noxious trades. But by the early 1600s Shakespeare's neighbours were concerned with offences against God: swearing, contempt for God's ministers and God's sabbaths, drunkenness. Stratford had become a little Geneva, resolved, like so many other early modern European communities, to take the Ten Commandments seriously and to live by this divinely inspired code of conduct rather than by merely traditional norms.[50]

Meanwhile the interior of the churches had been devastated, totally remodelled: the old imagery gone and replaced by the royal arms and scriptural texts, principally the Commandments, inscribed on boards. The building was now filled with 'convenient' seating which was not only practical but also symbolic in a new way, since it enabled the society of the town or parish to be arranged in ranking order of dignity and degree. The purpose of church assemblies was now to engage actively, attentively, but in quietly submissive order in a service of spoken prayer interspersed with congregational psalm-singing, and to listen, bible in hand or on lap, to sermons delivered from a physically dominant pulpit.

The new order, presided over by a tight alliance of 'ministry and magistracy', was as much concerned as the old to avoid scandalous disorder and conserve the harmony and wholeness of the town: indeed this was an objective now made more explicit. But the objective was now connected with obedience, disorder with disobedience, that is to say with disobedience to God, sin. Therefore order was to be spelt out in the spoken word and enforced by coercive discipline, not achieved in the charmingly roundabout fashion of 'pastime' and instinctive ritual and carnival. But there was also, in

towns which were subject to the most vigorously ideological protestant influence, a determined, rational and, it must be said, enlightened onslaught on social evils and endemic problems: programmes
of poor relief which were in advance of anything proposed or legis-
lated on a national scale, as in Elizabethan Norwich and Ipswich, or at
Salisbury and Dorchester in about 1630, where brewing was
municipalised and the profits applied to social security.[51]

It would go too far to call these policies and programmes disin-
terested. Everyone had an interest in controlling and if possible
removing the worst symptoms of urban poverty, but those with the
property of the town in their hands had the greater interest. The
grammar school was a notable ornament, but it favoured the sons of
the ruling oligarchies. Whereas the early Reformation, in Canterbury
for example, was associated with the efforts of the middling and
politically disadvantaged elements of society to break into town
government,[52] the middle age of the Reformation was often accompanied by the tightening grip of oligarchies which used religion as a
prime instrument of social control and self-advancement.

V

Protestantism was supposed to recreate that Jerusalem whose outstanding feature, according to the Psalmist, was that it was at unity in
itself. In fact it brought division and accentuated political conflict: to
the kind of contest over public resources and office holding which was
doubtless endemic and may be considered normal it added a more
unusual and transcendent element of religious, moral and cultural
strife. Preaching ministers were often accused by their enemies of
dividing communities which had previously been at peace. In
Elizabethan Hull the preacher Melchior Smith was said to have been
'a great occasion of contention and great strife amongst the inhabitants', having earlier sown discord in Boston and Burton-on-Trent.
Similar charges were laid against the preachers in the market towns of
the Kentish Weald: 'Hath not Minge brought Ashford from being the
quietest town of Kent to be at deadly hatred and bitter division? . . .
Hath not Eelie set Tenterden, his parish, together by the ears, which
before was quiet? What broil and contention hath Fenner made in
Cranbrook!'[53]

Such complaints were more polemical than factual. Modern historians should not too readily assume (as they sometimes do) that the

parishes most exposed to puritan preaching and discipline were necessarily the most faction-ridden, or that towns characterised by the relaxed values of 'good fellowship' were always quiet and orderly. But some credibility is given to the charge that fiery Protestantism was divisively aggressive by the fact that the preachers complained of did not always simply deny it. Melchior Smith would not admit to provoking dissension in Hull deliberately but he conceded that offence might be a consequence of preaching frankly against popery and heresy and 'beating down' the 'wicked vices reigning in these evil days among this sinful and adulterous generation'. If this was to offend, the prophets and apostles were all equally to blame; 'yea, and Christ himself, at whose preaching there was as much dissension as at any man's'. On the other hand Smith insisted that with enemies like the people of Boston he had no need of friends, for they had treated him with extraordinary kindness and generosity: 'Their love was such towards him that willingly they would hear none preach but him'. And it is very likely that no town was more united than the town which was united in the enjoyment of the Gospel.

Alas, there seem to have been few such towns! At Maldon in Essex there were, in the 1580s, two ministers. Both were preachers, indeed they competed in unseemly fashion for occupancy of the same pulpit. But they preached different doctrines, or at least applied their doctrine differently and had widely different notions of how the town should get along. George Gifford gathered his friends and disciples into domestic conventicles and wrote books explaining that the proper way not only to preserve the peace and harmony of the community but also to ward off the wiles of the Devil, perceived by the simple as witchcraft, was for every man to search and try his own heart and conscience. To live 'conscionably' would be to live amicably. But Robert Palmer, his rival, drummed up custom in a bowling alley in which he himself had an interest ('a great sort or swarm of men') and spent so much time playing cards in the New Inn that (according to his enemies) 'he cannot set down'. Gifford wrote caustically about such clerics and their followers who thought time spent on the alebench a 'godly way' to promote love and fellowship among neighbours. Rival factions took shape behind these two recipes for civic harmony.[54]

Both factions consisted of Protestants, or would have claimed to be protestant. In Gifford's dialogue *The countrie divinitie* the character of 'Atheos' asks: Why do you speak to me of the pope? 'I would that he and his popery were buried in the dunghill.' But, outside the ranks of office-holders and sometimes no longer in their seats in church to which their status as rate-payers would have admitted them, there were those 'pope-holy knaves', the surviving or newly converted Catholics. Perhaps there were not very many of them, especially in the towns, where there were fewer than in the great country houses of the recusant gentry and in the villages of their tenants. Often they disguised their true beliefs and motives and as 'church papists' avoided outright recusancy. In Stratford-upon-Avon in the 1590s Shakespeare's father stayed away from church, pleading his embarrassment as a debtor who was liable to be attached or arrested if he appeared in such a public place. Was that the real reason?[55]

Such uncertainties bred suspicion. In Elizabethan Thetford, a town said to be divided between 'a side of godly and honest men' and 'an other part . . . frowardly inclined', the 'froward', that is to say religiously conservative, maintained control of the town at a time when much of East Anglia was passing into the control of staunchly protestant magistrates. Indeed it was the newly dominant puritan gentry of West Suffolk who were responsible for this prejudicial analysis of Thetford society, in a report to the Privy Council. The mayor, it was said, stayed away from the sermons offered by visiting preachers (Thetford had no resident preacher), and of his colleagues in the corporation one was said to keep in his house 'relics of the pope', another seemed 'rather papist than otherwise' for he too disliked sermons, while yet another seemed 'of no good religion' for if he were he would not sit drinking and gaming at service time. Another prominent townsman was of indeterminate religion, 'but he hath a brother there, a notable papist'. Very few of the city fathers of mid-Elizabethan Thetford could sign their names. In every way they were resistant to 'civility' on the godly pattern.[56] But as a new breed of magistrate came to the fore in towns subject to regular and systematic protestant indoctrination they, like the preachers, proved divisive influences: in Chester, in Banbury, in Exeter, and in a score of West Country towns where Professor David Underdown has found that 'cultural conflict' 'raged' in the early years of the seventeenth century.[57] To these cases we shall return in the final chapter.

Here we may end on a more positive if speculative note, taking a more distant view with the aid of a metaphorical hour-glass. Late medieval culture, inextricably involved with religion as it was in the matrix of the English provincial town, was a rich, tumultuous, irrepressible animal: the fat upper half of our hour-glass. Late seventeenth- and eighteenth-century town life acquired a new richness, solemnity and style as notable public buildings were erected and the gentry and pseudo-gentry proceeded to make it their own. The festive, ritual scene revived and there was much frank enjoyment of the good things which the town had to offer. Dr Borsay writes of 'the formidable variety' of public rituals and ceremonies which flourished in this later period, civic, élite and popular. Once again such activities served to express and motivate feelings of authority and consensus, but were also vehicles of barely suppressed social conflict.[58] But now it all happened on somewhat altered terms. Popular culture was condoned, even encouraged, by the élite for its value as a safety-valve, while the élite in its own no less elaborate rituals expressed 'profound disengagement' from traditional, unsophisticated culture. The English town had discovered not just 'civility' but civilisation, high society and social class. This was the lower half of the hour-glass. In between there was a narrow neck, through which the sand fell finely but with considerable force: the Protestant Reformation, which destroyed so much and limited and restricted what was left, but which acted as a kind of midwife for the future.

3 The Protestant Family

I

Early modern minds, fascinated by supposedly significant 'correspondences', constantly drew parallels between political and domestic institutions: the macrocosm of state, church and city resembling the microcosm of the family. The family or household (the terms were virtually synonymous) was 'a small commonwealth', 'a little church'. What was meant was more than a telling analogy. It was believed, for example by the mid-Tudor statesman Sir Thomas Smith, that complex social and political structures had their origins in the family, which contained 'the first and most natural beginning and source of cities, towns, nations, kingdoms and of all civil societies'.[1] The Fifth (in catholic arithmetic Fourth) Commandment, 'Honour thy father and thy mother', was universally construed to extend far beyond its immediate frame of reference to define the ground of all social and political being, articulating what the title of a Jacobean book called *The doctrine of superioritie and of subiection* (Robert Prick, 1609). This was no fantasy. In an age of personal and dynastic monarchy, politics really was a family affair. How else to explain the Italian Wars or the War of the Spanish Succession? Or, for that matter, *King Lear*?

Conversely the authority of fathers in families and domestic arrangements generally were matters discussed and justified in political terms. William Vaughan wrote: 'Every man's a king in his own house'. There was, or ought to have been, a perfect congruence of domestic governance and the government of the commonwealth. This was an assumption entertained on a European scale, Jean Bodin holding that 'all will be well with the commonwealth where families are properly regulated'. A variation on this theme was to define the household as the nursery of both church and state, in John Downame's words 'the seminary of the Church and Common-wealth . . . wherein children and servants are fitted for the public assemblies'. So Clarendon took it more or less for granted that the Civil War must have accompanied a change for the worse domestically, young women conversing without circumspection or modesty, children forgetting their manners. Whether he had any evidence for this I do not know, and he may not have felt that any was needed. Dr Susan Amussen writes: 'Political theory assumed the family, household manuals assumed politics'.[2]

So, if there were no other difference between the family then and now, we can register this: that early modern families were not areas of privacy (as Locke began to define the family in the late seventeenth century) but the bricks or molecules of which the commonwealth was composed, and were thus public institutions in themselves. It was not so much individuals as households which were publicly acknowledged and represented, for example in the seating allocated in parish churches and even in the principles underlying parliamentary representation. Even the Levellers, the supposed radicals of the English Revolution, proposed to extend the franchise no further than to the heads of independent households, who were assumed to 'cover' all those others, wives, children, apprentices and servants, who slept under the same roof and had no need of separate political recognition. That would have been to limit the vote in early seventeenth-century Sheffield to just 260 persons out of a total population of 2207.[3]

Consequently the internal affairs of families were a matter of legitimate interest to others: neighbours, the parish, even the state. Against such domestic incongruities as wives beating husbands (often assumed to be cuckolds) or a gross difference of age between marriage partners the village expressed its disapproval in the street theatre of 'rough music' or with mocking rhymes and songs. When a Kentish priest, sitting naked in bed at ten o'clock at night, received a cup of drink from a woman and then put out the candle 'very suspiciously', half the parish was there, at the church stile, to witness the fact. A Faversham man encountering a neighbour in the churchyard early in the morning and being told that she was there to observe the suspicious company-keeping of John Tylsey and Jennings's wife, told her: 'Goodwife Fynn, if I were as you are I would meddle no further therein but let them alone'. But Mrs Fynn shouted back at him: 'Shall I suffer the arrant whore to undo her husband?'[4]

Official intervention of a kind which is now justified only in extreme circumstances was then routine. The constable was empowered to make forcible entry if he had cause to suspect that the crime (as much as sin) of fornication was being committed inside a house. Justices of the Peace were to cause the constable to arrest 'all night walkers', especially those haunting suspected brothels or using 'suspicious company' at night time. The Kentish justice William Lambarde wrote that he 'liked well' the opinion that if information was given to a constable that a man and woman were committing adultery or fornication, he should 'take company with him' and, finding them in the act, carry both parties to prison. So it was that in the Canterbury parish of Northgate on New Year's Eve 1561 rumours of 'ill rule' in Thomas Calcott's house, involving Mrs Calcott's step-son, caused the constable to join one Robert Betts in a raid. They searched the bedchamber, which was empty, but 'the bed of the said Alice Calcott lay so as it was evident by the print in the bed that two persons had been there lying'. Thomas Harrison and his wife, standing at their chamber window to observe 'what was there to do in the street', saw it all happen and spotted a man brought out of the house about midnight.[5]

This may explain the fact, at first sight contradictory, that English men and women of the sixteenth and seventeenth centuries seem to have been more jealous and touchy than ourselves in defence of their own small pieces of private space. Writing of their fourteenth-century ancestors, Dr Barbara Hanawalt suggests that privacy was 'almost an obsession'. Gossiping and unwarranted spying were serious offences.[6] One way and another the family enjoyed a high profile, which is a boon for the historian since it provides a wealth of contemporary discussion of all kinds and at many levels, as well as a copious record from the church courts of matters which would not now come to any court at all. None of these sources, however, provides us with a straightforward account of the matter.

II

As a topic, then, the Protestant Family follows logically enough on the heels of the Protestant Nation and the Protestant Town. In the past it would have been easy to play a historian's version of the correspondences game. Just as the Reformation elevated the authority of the state and enhanced the dignity of magistracy, arousing a heightened national and civic consciousness, so it gave rise to the family in its modern form and strengthened its nearly exclusive claims upon individuals. If the Reformation consolidated monarchy, it riveted home patriarchy. Tyndale had said that the king was 'in the room of God'. A century later another author taught that 'parents and masters of families are in God's stead to their children and servants'.[7] The general moralisation of political obligations was mirrored in the family, where duties were no longer simply contractual but owed in conscience to God who had established the ground-rules of domestic relations, literally on tablets of stone. But, as if to offset the potential repression of unalleviated patriarchy, Protestantism, especially in its pronounced puritan form, deepened the emotional quality of family life, enriching relations between spouses, parents and children. These sentiments were the domestic equivalent of patriotism. So we might say that the Reformation aroused both political self-consciousness and familial self-consciousness. And so we could go on, or would once have gone on. Unfortunately we shall find that this promising balloon is now in some danger of being pricked.

As with the Protestant Nation important issues are at stake, involving the understanding of some fundamental processes at work in British history. National self-consciousness contributed not only to English nationalism but also to British imperialism – although that is a proposition rather than a fact and one that we cannot pursue for more than a few decades without encountering complications. In the case of familial self-consciousness we may be dealing with something more momentous still: the processes which favoured the precocious emergence in this country of capitalism and other attributes of advanced economic development. It was an assumption of early Marxist thought, reflected in the Communist Manifesto of 1848, that the family in its restricted, elementary form of parents and children was a bourgeois institution, enjoying a close affinity to the capitalist mode of production and distribution of goods. Indeed the necessary conditions for such a family – the family, as we might now say, of the cornflake packet – existed only among the bourgeoisie. Marriage in pre-capitalist societies was assumed in nineteenth-century social theory, Marxist or otherwise, to have concerned extended kinship groups and the consolidation and transmission of property which belonged, in effect, to the group. Conservation was the prime purpose of monogamy. But bourgeois marriage was characterised by individualism and the free market choice of the couple themselves, the currency in this market being attraction and love, which were themselves commodities. Hitherto coupling by simple attraction or for sensual gratification had been a privilege confined to the propertyless proletariat and was naturally and intrinsically non-monogamous.

In *The Origin of the Family, Private Property and the State* (recently described as a text 'not really equal to the weight of deference that has been loaded upon it')[8] Friedrich Engels argued that marriage as we have known it ('a conjugal partnership of leaden boredom, known as "domestic bliss"') was a product of the needs of early capitalism. This was to locate its origins in the sixteenth and seventeenth centuries, and to make changes in sentiment dependent upon developments in distributive economics. Max Weber, while sharing a sense of the affinity of the acquisitive and romantic impulses, dealt with the matter less dogmatically and more subtly. Love, or sexual attraction, was the most non-rational of all human impulses, leading not infrequently to incongruous unions, yet it became a dynamic element in the rationality of the capitalist system, perhaps because the urge to accumulate wealth for its own sake was equally irrational and yet equally lay at the heart of capitalist rationality. This was close to that other argument of affinity and latency: that the religious ethic of Calvinism, which on the face of it had nothing to do with the making of money, made money nevertheless. Just as Weber opened up the possibility that the protestant ethic was not so much a consequence of the spirit of capitalism as its cause (and given the reserve built into Weber's philosophy of causation the case cannot be stated more positively than that), so Engels's theory was close to being turned on its head, with the nuclear family and individualistic love-marriage seen as social arrangements which helped capitalism and industrialisation to come about but which themselves had other, non-material, causes.

Was the Protestant Reformation such a cause, or at least a major contributory factor in what Edward Shorter called *The Making of the Modern Family*? And did the family in its turn create capitalism? In his brilliant collection of essays *Society and Puritanism in Pre-Revolutionary England* (1966) Christopher Hill does not exactly say so. More like Weber than like Marx or Engels, he keeps the options open. But having first described 'the spiritualisation of the household', as fathers assumed the role of priests and families became little hothouses of intensified religious experience, Hill suggests that these developments, which he locates somewhere between the fourteenth and the seventeenth centuries, were effectively confined to 'the industrious sort', skilled tradesmen, artisans and petty entrepreneurs, which was to suggest the simultaneous development of the household, or of a certain kind of household, as a unit of both economic and religious production. Compulsory communities, embodying communal ties and the principle of hierarchy, were breaking up and giving way to voluntary communities, characterised by acquisitive and competitive, but also a kind of romantic, individualism. The natural religion of these communities, itself represented (dubiously, in my opinion) as intrinsically individualistic, was Protestantism. Although Hill's Marxism is modified in a Weberian direction his understanding seems to be that economic processes were at the root of these tendencies, which religion merely facilitated. However he finds no difficulty in describing the household, more or less simultaneously and with equal validity, in religious and economic terms, so avoiding vulgar material reductionism.

III

The proposition that the modern family as described by Hill and many others was essentially protestant (one recalls the suggestion the President Kennedy was a Presbyterian whether he knew and acknowledged it or not) requires us to pay some attention to the inventor of Protestantism, although Martin Luther's views on marriage, like some of his other ideas, were idiosyncratic and not transmitted in anything like their original form to the ongoing protestant tradition.[9]

Luther insisted, with a peculiarly biological intensity, on the absolute necessity of marriage as the fulfilment of the first commandment ever given to man and, as it were, encoded in his nature: 'Be fruitful and multiply'. When his own wife, Katherine von Bora, found herself pregnant he wrote: 'My Katie is fulfilling Genesis 1:28'. He told another correspondent: 'I have noticed that you would like to marry, or rather are forced to do so by God himself, who gave you a nature requiring it'. Marriage was presented as a universal and nearly inescapable vocation, and a devastating polemic was directed against the religious vows leading to a celibate life as presumptuous and unnatural. In respect of nuns, this was 'liberation theology'.[10] Luther rhapsodised over the harsh realities of the married state, pulling no punches about the bitterness and drudgery which it entailed but insisting that in the light of Christian faith these humble and distasteful duties were 'adorned with divine approval'. 'God with all his angels and creatures is smiling, not because that father is washing nappies, but because he is doing it in Christian faith.'

Protestant historians have seen in these texts a watershed between a pre-Reformation, negative appraisal of marriage as an unfortunate necessity for the avoidance of fornication and the perpetuation of the species, and the total endorsement and enjoyment of marriage by Protestants. To be sure Luther himself, once a monk and in a sense always a monk, carried an unresolved tension within himself between old and new attitudes. He wrote that 'intercourse is never without sin' (and of course nothing in this life was without sin – *simul justus, simul peccator*) and he marvelled that God could bring any good out of this evil. 'When I consider marriage, only the flesh seems to be there. Yet my father must have slept with my mother and made love to her, and they were nevertheless godly people.' All the prophets and patriarchs had done likewise. This was a different attitude to the physical side of marriage from that held by Calvin, not to speak of Edmund Spenser and Sir Philip Sidney or of the 'undefiled bed' over which Milton later rhapsodised. For Calvinists marriage as a remedy for sin could not itself be a sin. Post-Lutheran protestant teaching, represented by the Strasbourg reformer Martin Bucer and revived by Milton, attached such appreciative value to the enjoyment of marriage as to envisage the necessity of divorce where pleasure and love had manifestly evaporated. This was a concept not remote from today's legal principle of the objectively verifiable breakdown of a marriage. However the force of convention was too great for a radical doctrine of divorce to take root in the law and social practice of protestant societies. An English author who allowed it was obliged to beat a humiliating retreat in a subsequent publication.[11]

Luther's own marriage, contracted to an ex-nun primarily to bear public witness to his convictions on the subject and out of filial respect for his father's desires, not out of love, established one of the earliest and the most celebrated of the clerical hearths of the Reformation era. Thanks to the conversation copiously recorded at their table, we have a more intimate knowledge of the married life of the Luthers than of any other couple of the sixteenth century. It was a good match, founded on different but complementary talents, on two equally strong but compatible temperaments, and on the trading of sex-specific jokes and insults. A feminist might remark on Frau Luther's remarkable tolerance of Luther's gratuitous chauvinism as the only thing which held the couple together. On one occasion Luther argued facetiously in favour of polygamy, on the grounds that a woman can only bear once in a year, while a man can beget many children. Katie said: 'For shame! Before I put up with this I'd rather go back to the convent and leave you and all our children.' But feminists would do well not to repeat the mistake of the Jesuit Hartmann Grisar in misunderstanding the beneficent thrust of such conversational sallies. It was also not irrelevant to the solidarity of the Luther marriage that Katie was Martin's social superior, a *von* Bora, and possessed of her own property, which she managed not unsuccessfully as a farmer rather than as a farmer's wife. All this enabled Luther to write: 'There is no sweeter union than that in a good marriage. Nor is there any death more bitter than that which separates a married couple. Only the death of children comes close to this.'

It is more likely that these remarkable sources show us a typical and successful marriage in late medieval Germany than that they chronicled the first beginnings of a new institution called protestant marriage, or the origins of that companionate form of marriage of which Professor Lawrence Stone found little trace in England before the eighteenth century. (But was he looking in the right places?) The only original feature of the Luther household was that the husband and father was a preacher. From the early years of the Protestant Reformation a married ministry became the norm. In the Strasbourg region in 1609 only two out of seventy-one reformed ministers were bachelors, both of them still in their twenties.[12] And in England single clergy were soon the exceptions who proved the rule. The Essex preacher and diarist Richard Rogers marvelled from afar at the 'contentation' of a distinguished colleague in 'a sole and single life', and when his own wife fell dangerously ill he listed first among the consequences of her death 'the fear of marrying again, dangerous as two marriages are'. Nevertheless it was assumed that remarriage would be a necessity.[13]

The marriage of the clergy was the only substantial change in marital practice to have occurred in the sixteenth century, and perhaps the only respect in which the official, magisterial Reformation may be said to have made a social revolution. There was a polarity of public attitudes towards this still unfamiliar practice. The curate of Birchington in Kent was asked by a parishioner: 'Mr Cryar, how chanceth it that you have not a wife?' Mr Cryar deftly countered, asking his interlocutor why he did not have two wives. When he replied that he was not allowed to, the curate said, 'no more may we have one'. Many of the laity would have agreed with Cryar. As late as 1581 in the village of Wye in Kent (a notorious centre of residual Catholicism) William Nightingale and his wife went about saying that 'our ministers, naming them priests, ought to be married to their books and not to their wives'. When a Canterbury alderman of conservative religious views denounced the new clergy as knaves, 'all the many of them', and was told by a bystander that not all priests were knaves, he replied: 'I do not mean priests, I mean ministers'. Elsewhere in the same county it was said (and the words have the ring of a proverb) 'there is never new trick but ministers' wives bring them first of all up', and in Old Romney a song was sung with the refrain 'all priests' wives are drabbles or queens'.[14]

It may be that reluctance to enter into a marriage alliance with the clergy accounts for the high degree of clerical endogamy soon experienced. Almost half the ministers' wives in early seventeenth-century Alsace and one third of those in Kent were daughters of other clergy, and contemporaries spoke significantly of the 'tribe' of the prophets. Naturally Trollope's Mr Quiverfull had many precursors and the children of the clergy rather than the poor of the parish became the first call on limited clerical incomes, which in itself may have helped to fuel a new anticlericalism.[15] But in so far as the reconstructed parish clergy, both protestant and catholic, became in the age of Reformation and Counter-Reformation ideal figures, models of the Christian life, clerical families were supposed to be model families. An Elizabethan bishop and his wife were said to live 'after St Paul's rule', and visitors to the home of the Suffolk preacher John Carter came away saying that 'they had seen *Adam* and *Eve* or some of the *old Patriarchs*'.[16] From this time on generations of clerical marriage partners were to experience the discomfort of living out on a pedestal the stresses of daily life, which they shared with all mankind, as if they were different from the rest of mankind.

IV

In the past, counsel on marital and domestic matters had been dispensed within the pastoral and penitential office by celibate priests. Now advice was given by preachers who were themselves family men, typically in sermons preached at weddings. Most of it was doubtless of a more conventional kind than that reportedly offered by a certain vicar of Halstead in Essex, described by his professional colleagues as 'a very ridiculous preacher', who was given to imparting such homely wisdom as this: 'Now all you young men that lust to be married, be ruled by me. Marry an old hag that hath not a tooth in her head be that she have a peck of money: ye may then gad around the country with whom ye please.'[17]

Most of the 'conduct books' of the late sixteenth and early seventeenth centuries grew out of wedding sermons made by clergymen belonging to the broadly puritan wing of the church. They included two works by Banbury's 'roaring boy' William Whateley, *A bride bush, Or, a direction for married persons* (1623) and *A care-cloth: or, a treatise of the cumbers and troubles of marriage* (1624); John Dod and Robert Cleaver's *A godly form of household government*; and, most famous of all, William Gouge's exhaustive treatment in *Of domestical duties*, with editions in 1620, 1622 and 1634. But the doctrine of these seventeenth-century divines does not differ significantly from an influential treatise by the Swiss reformer Bullinger, translated by Miles Coverdale as *The christian state of matrimony*, which reached nine editions by 1560. These texts have always appeared to provide immediate access to the study of the early modern family and in the past they have been read as if they contained original and even revolutionary views on relations between the sexes, marriage and parenthood. Crowned by the apotheosis of 'conjugal love' celebrated in that transcendent conduct book, *Paradise Lost*, this literary tradition served to establish Puritanism as the most likely source of the family in its modern shape and of the most exalted expression of Christian marriage founded on mutual devotion. In 1897 it was said to be a common observation that 'we owe our English ideal of family life and domestic affection to the teachings of the Puritan party'. More recently Lawrence Stone's *The Family, Sex and Marriage in England* has connected Protestantism, both Anglican and Puritan, with the emergence of what he calls 'the restrictive patriarchal nuclear family' and with further developments towards the conjugal family and the companionate marriage, since it encouraged 'a new emphasis on the home and on domestic virtues'. 'This was perhaps the most far-reaching consequence of the Reformation in England.'[18]

Hitherto it has not been established just how 'far-reaching' such consequences were: how speedily and to what extent this 'new' emphasis (if indeed it was new) converted itself into a general cultural change. Stone's own book, ostensibly magisterial, confines itself to the relatively well-documented aristocracy, on the quite fallacious ground that no direct evidence for the marital and domestic history of the lower orders exists. The normal procedure for historians who have wished to avoid this damaging limitation has been to use the conduct books as a general commentary on social practice and as a control over the more selective evidence of diaries, autobiographies and letters; or conversely to use these more personal documents to test the validity of the conduct books. Only recently has there been any significant exploitation of what might be called prime sources: ecclesiastical court records and especially the copious testimony offered by witnesses in marital suits, usually for breach of contract, and the telling evidence of coroners' inquests into accidental deaths. And hitherto there has been a characteristic neglect by historians of literary evidence, which includes the often valuable evidence of ballads, proverbs and other surviving ephemera. For as the learned John Selden remarked: 'More solid things do not show the complexion of the times so well as ballads and libels [i.e. little books]'.[19]

The major difficulty in extracting a coherent, credible picture of post-Reformation family life from the sources which have been exploited so far is to reconcile an apparent discrepancy both within the conduct books themselves and also between the conduct books and other evidence: between on the one hand a stress on patriarchy amounting to a kind of benevolent despotism; and on the other hand attitudes towards the inferior members of the family (for such we must consider women and children) which encouraged affection and respect for their personal autonomy within a balanced framework of mutual obligation. These we may call hard and soft, or dry and wet, attitudes. The point of maximum friction, where the two lines of opinion and argument ground against each other, was the matter of choosing marriage partners. The conduct books took a hard line on parental consent, if not choice, which was probably no more true to contemporary practice than the equally conservative teaching of the same protestant divines on the lending of money at interest, 'usury'. The cause of this discrepancy seems to have been the intrusion into the sphere of domestic relations of political theory. All protestant writers were disposed to agree, with Milton, that relations between married persons had to do with 'the apt and cheerful conversation of men with women'. But, as we have seen, there was more to marriage than cheerful conversation and in so far as it concerned the order of society and property it was a political matter. Hence the stress on monarchical patriarchy. Yet just as seventeenth-century political philosophy (or sub-philosophical commonplaces) balanced and reconciled royal prerogatives and subjects' rights which were both, in principle, absolute and might seem to be irreconcilable, so the conduct books embody an ameliorating doctrine of balance by matching every obligation on one partner within marriage with a corresponding duty owed by the other. For example Thomas Becon's mid-sixteenth-century catechism 'Offices of all Degrees' couples 'Of the Duty of Husbands to their Wives' with 'Of the Duty of Wives Towards their Husbands', and is careful to ration out the same number of words to each topic.[20]

In this Becon was followed seventy years later by the author of *Of domestical duties*. William Gouge, as minister of the small but fashionable London parish of Blackfriars, preached to a congregation containing a preponderance of wealthy city wives, often swelled by such notable visitors from the country as the godly Herefordshire gentleman Sir Robert Harley and, if she came with him, his remarkable third wife, Brilliana. We are told that such people 'thought not their business [in London] fully ended' until they had heard Gouge preach.[21] This was the public to which the most influential of the conduct books was addressed, in the first instance from the pulpit. In the preface Gouge tells us that to this original version 'much exception was taken', especially to the doctrine that the common goods of a marriage were wholly at the husband's disposal, and to what had been said by Gouge about the 'particular duties' of wives. It was even said that the preacher was 'an hater of women'. Evidently, Gouge suggested, his doctrine came 'too near to the quick and pierceth too deep'. He explained that what a husband could in principle exact from his wife 'in the uttermost extent of that subjection under which God hath put her' was not what in circumstances of ordinary mutuality the good husband would require of the good wife. So in the printed work he retracted nothing of what he had said about those 'particular duties', but he laid out the argument in such a way as to draw visual attention to the perfect balance of duties on either side of the marriage, as well as the typical failings and aberrations of both wives and husbands, 'as they answer each other'. To this end they were 'parallel'd and laid over, one against another'. An appendix contains prayers 'which a husband should use' and the same number 'which a wife should use', with further prayers for parents and children, all equally 'paralleled' and exactly reciprocal. Here was a mighty effort to abandon some attributes of what has been called 'the double standard'. Yet when Gouge's wife died in childbirth she was said to have perished like a soldier on the battlefield or as a preacher in the pulpit, 'performing her office'. One does not have to be a radical feminist to find that analogy contrived and offensive, not at all a true 'parallel'.

Whether the ladies of Blackfriars were pacified we cannot say, but in William Whateley's *Bride bush* there is further evidence of what they might have objected to. The early pages of this extended marriage sermon rhapsodise over love as 'the life and soul of marriage'. Love is 'king of the heart, which in whom it prevaileth, to them is marriage itself'. A married couple must do more and suffer more, each for the other, than for any other in the entire world, bearing with one another's faults and pains. 'Let them be as much in each other's presence as business or their callings will permit. Let them often talk together and be sorry together and be merry together.' They should share, as it were, a joint bank account. 'Betwixt man and wife, all things ought to be common, goods as well as persons . . . They must get in common, and save in common and use in common.'

After listening to what sounds like Barbara Cartland in a Banbury pulpit the reader is startled to come later in the same book to the uncompromising doctrine that the authority of the husband is paramount and absolute: 'It is a model of God's sovereignty and a little map of his great greatness'. All the gracious and kindly benefits which husbands naturally and normally bestow on their wives can, if necessary, be withheld as punishment, the exact analogue of God's judgments'. Whateley is not in favour of wife-beating except in extreme circumstances ('who is not ashamed to strike a woman?') but the rights and wrongs of the issue are discussed, and at length, whereas the question whether wives may ever beat their husbands is not, of course, ever put. One senses the oppressive nutcrackers of indulgence and punishment as they crunch their way into a marriage in Ibsen's *Doll's House*. It must be said that other authors condemned wife-beating more unreservedly, 'silver tongued' Henry Smith asserting that 'her cheeks are made for thy lips, and not for thy fists'. And in Elizabethan Dymchurch a man was prosecuted in the archdeacon's court for inciting other men to beat their wives, saying, when his wife fell out with her gossips, 'neighbour, if you will beat your wife I will beat mine'.[22] That was not defensible. Nevertheless Whateley is in no way deviant from the acceptable teaching of the times when he makes the wife say: 'Mine head is my superior, my better. Unless the wife learn this lesson perfectly, if she have it not without book, . . . there will be nothing betwixt them but wrangling, repining, striving and a continual vying to be equal with him or above him.' Doctrine like this led Edward Shorter to write of 'the Bad Old Days – let us say the sixteenth and seventeenth centuries'.[23]

But evidence of the implementation of this hard line in the real world is hard to come by. We do not find it at the level of the landed gentry: in the surviving letter collections of the seventeenth century the conversational tone is habitually familiar and affectionate. 'Sweet Bass' was how the Norfolk landowner and parliament man Bassingbourne Gawdy was usually addressed by his wife. Even in a marriage which experienced irrevocable and spectacular breakdown it was only slowly that the conventions of extreme affection in correspondence were relaxed and finally abandoned. The letters of George Talbot, sixth Earl of Shrewsbury, to his termagent wife Bess of Hardwick degenerate in their form of address from 'my own sweetheart', 'my jewel', 'my sweetheart' to 'wife'.[24] As for the diaries and autobiographies of the seventeenth century, many of which take us, roughly speaking, into the world of the yeomanry, there is more evidence of comfortable sharing than of what even Milton called 'absolute rule'. So too with the plebeian scene of the broadsheet ballad, admittedly consisting of two-dimensional pasteboard, but erected on consensual assumptions and expectations about married life. Among the truly godly many husbands, it appears, were prone to place their wives on mental pedestals, an attitude not inconsistent with a certain kind of 'chauvinism'. Within hours of her death a Somerset clothier wrote this of his wife:

> My beloved, the joy of all my travails, departed about six of the clock at night . . . This my beloved was full of virtues . . . She was godly of mind, a diligent hearer of the word preached, devout in her secret prayers. I will leave this for truth, her knees were hard with kneeling, she being a tender woman. She loved her house and never delighted in gossiping, no lover of wine . . .[25]

Whateley's patriarchalism seems to have been at variance with what he himself must have known of the reality of marriage in his own circle and perhaps it was consciously reactive to his own experience. If such absolute monarchy existed why did both Whateley and Gouge find it necessary to warn wives not to address their husbands as Tom, Dick or Ned, or with such ridiculous nicknames as 'duck', 'chick', and 'pigsnie'? The Kentish politician Sir Edward Dering addressed his wife as 'My dear and comfortable Numpes'.[26]

The contemporary drama expressed in its own language an often humorous but equally anxious response to the threat of gender inversion. In the late Elizabethan play by Henry Porter *Two angrie women of Abington* (1599) Mr Goursey and Mr Barnes, neighbours quite unable to control their battling wives, ruefully agree: ''Tis but a woman's jar, their tongues are weapons, words their blows of war'. When Mr Barnes boldly but tentatively suggests to Mrs Barnes that she may have been in the wrong – 'in my mind, today you were to blame' – it is almost more than his life is worth: 'She is a strumpet, and thou art no honest man to stand in her defence against thy wife. If I could catch her in my walk now by cock's bones I'll scratch out both

her eyes!'; Mr Barnes: 'Oh God!' Social historians encountering the
thousands of real-life cases of abuse and slander which remain
embedded in the evidence recorded in the church courts – a vast and
still mostly untapped well of street language – are not in agreement
over how they should be interpreted. To some this is evidence of
female ascendancy, verbal at least, of the kind deliciously parodied by
seventeenth-century madrigalists, Purcell included. But to Miranda
Chaytor these cases are so many pathetic demonstrations of the
impotence of a sex whose 'honesty' was all that it had to defend and
something which it could not afford to lose.[27]

V

If the conduct books were the only means by which the Protestant
Reformation impinged upon the status and experience of women we
might judge the result as inconclusive at best. John Bossy, the leading
historian of the post-Reformation catholic community, suggests that
'the average woman of the upper classes might reasonably feel that
the Reformation had not been designed with her in mind'. Married,
she had lost many of the functions which would have been hers in a
catholic household; unmarried, she had lost the chance to become a
nun, which in spite of Luther was for many a positive and attractive
option. The successful practice of the protestant religion required
literate skills which most women lacked. And then there were all
those unacceptable tokens of protestant 'domestic authoritarianism'.
Bossy concludes that there would almost have been no continuing
catholic community without the outstanding leadership offered by
women in the domain of the catholic household, which was primarily
theirs, and perhaps fewer catholic women to make that indispensable
contribution without what he calls 'gentlewomen's dissatisfaction
with the Reformation'.[28]

Since no gentlewoman left on paper a record of her dissatisfaction
expressed in such frankly pragmatic terms this is an inference the
plausibility of which is a matter of judgment. But the inference
certainly ignores the outstanding leadership of women in the protestant community, both in relatively orthodox, mainstream circles and
more adventurously in the radical sects of the mid-seventeenth
century. Women who, by whatever means, 'got religion' easily
cleared the hurdle of literacy, at least in the upper and middle levels
of society. Mrs Gouge, for example, 'did spend much time in reading

English books of divinity, whereof she had a pretty Library'. So it was with the wife of her husband's friend, Sir Robert Harley. Lady Brilliana's brother wrote to Harley: 'In your house the order of things is inverted. You write to me of cheeses and my sister writes about a good scholar.' What was said of Brilliana, that in religion she 'transcended' her husband, might have been said of many of her kind. The greater natural 'propensity' of women to religion, while neither tested nor perhaps testable, was a conventional commonplace which Richard Hooker discussed and attempted to explain in *The Laws of Ecclesiastical Polity*.[29]

One explanation not proposed by Hooker is that the frustrations arising from the subordination of women, exacerbated by the psychological as well as physical consequences of frequent and traumatic child-bearing, led to sublimated outlets in the enthusiastic adoption and support of religious causes. And this was literally an outlet, since the conduct books recommend that like Abraham's wife, 'sage Sara', women should stay within the tent. Whateley says 'he without door, she within; he abroad, she at home', while Henry Smith reminds us that she is a *house*wife.[30] This was no less a commonplace of seventeenth-century popular literature, and one which was heavily underscored by the satirical, music-hall theme of role reversion, *The woman to the plow and the man to the hen-roost*, which David Kunzle has called 'the most ubiquitous motif of all' in contemporary popular culture, a large part of 'the world turned upside down'.[31] But religious partisanship led women quite literally into the streets, to demonstrate support for their favourite preachers or to express contempt for popery and its outward trappings. To go on to the streets was one thing: to go to the stake something beyond anything. Foxe included forty-eight women in his tally of 358 Henrician and Marian martyrs. Women were often prominent in religious petitioning of a 'tumultuous' kind. In the 1580s it was a question in puritan circles whether a woman could lawfully pray, 'having a better gift than her husband'. In more radical groups women later took a leading part in setting up gathered and sectarian congregations and even began to preach.[32]

Protestantism provided another kind of outlet in the spiritually intimate dealings – one is tempted to call them affairs – between women of the leisured classes and certain popular and pastorally gifted divines. This was not a wholly novel development in religious interaction since it perpetuated the dependence of pre-Reformation women upon confessors whom, if possible, they themselves chose for their sympathetic compatibility. But now the relationship was founded on the particular anxieties aroused in women of a certain temperament by the Calvinist doctrine of election, related (or so it seems to this observer) to the physical and social constraints to which they were subjected. 'Hath your husband been unkind unto you?' asks the affecting preacher Edward Dering of Mrs Mary Honeywood. 'Bear it and you shall win him at the last; if not, thank God that you can continue loving and obedient even unto an unkind husband . . . And therefore (good Mistress Honeywood) give not yourself any inordinate affections, to offend God and hurt yourself.' Mrs Honeywood, as the mother of sixteen children and, by the time of her death, the grandmother and great-grandmother of half the gentry of Kent, was the personification of protestant matriarchy, a phenomenon never to be forgotten in discussing patriarchy. Yet she was as sure to be damned as the drinking glass in her hand was to be broken, she told John Foxe as she hurled it to the floor – whereupon there happened a wonder: the glass rebounded entire.[33]

That was an easy cure, but the symptoms of spiritual dread and self-hatred which haunted Mary Honeywood were often so deep-seated and intractable among Puritans that the Northamptonshire parson and paramedical practitioner Richard Napier (who was pre-judiced against Puritans anyway) declined to treat such cases. In the 1620s some of the most gifted spiritual physicians of the age, includ-ing John Dod and Thomas Hooker, later of Connecticut, spent years in an inconclusive attempt to cure the condition of 'desperation' in young Mrs Elizabeth Drake of Esher, a lively soul 'having a full nimble quick sparrow-hawk eye', accidentally rather than naturally melancholy after her first and difficult experience of childbirth. The Scottish reformer John Knox contended strenuously with the equally grievous temptations of his mother-in-law Elizabeth Bowes, whom he addressed as 'dear mother and spouse' and who was the mother of fifteen children. Knox asked Mrs Bowes to 'call to your mind what I did standing by the cupboard in Alnwick' when, he remembered, 'I thought no creature had been tempted as I was', a question arousing the salacious imaginations of later generations. But the temptations which the reformer shared with his 'spouse' (I heard proceed from your mouth the very same words that [God] troubles me with') were, he explained, 'not in the flesh . . . but it was in the spirit: for Satan did continually buffet her, that remission of sins in Christ Jesus apper-tained nothing unto her, by reason of her former idolatry and other iniquities'. When Mrs Bowes declared that she was guilty of all the sins of Sodom and Gomorrah, Knox told her: 'Dear mother, my duty compels me to advertise you that in comparing your sins with the sins of Sodom and Gomorrah ye do not well . . . Ye know not what were the sins of Sodom and Gomorrah.' 'Despair not mother', he assured her, 'your sins are remissable. What! think you that God's goodness, mercy and grace is able to be overcome with your iniquity? Will God, who can not deceive, be a liar, and lose his own glory, because that ye are a sinner?'[34]

Yet Mrs Honeywood and Mrs Bowes were not crushed and obliterated by their despair. Elizabeth Bowes had the courage to stand out as the first Protestant of her sex and class in the whole north-east of England, and to desert her husband, following her unusual son-in-law into the exotic environments of Geneva and Scotland. And Mrs Honeywood, who in her youth had lost her shoes in the mêlée surrounding the burning of the martyr John Bradford, became a legend in her own lifetime and in due course one of Thomas Fuller's 'worthies'. Ronald Knox wrote that 'the history of enthusiasm is largely a history of female emancipation'.[35] But what is emancipation? The active part played by protestant women in religious causes was of a kind called 'collusive': that is to say, far from resisting male dominance as a kind of sublimated feminist assertion, it was acknowledged and allowed for in a world of male-regulated behaviour. These women made no attempt to break the mould or to redefine the ground rules of their existence. If they had done so they would surely have been resisted and probably defeated. To petition, even tumultuously and almost violently, or to engage in certain kinds of enclosure riot, was an activity more safely and appropriately undertaken by women than by men and in any event a means of self-expression conventionally tolerated in their sex.

The question also arises: did gentlewomen or bourgeois housewives *need* emancipation? Emanuel van Meteren remarked on the unusual measure of freedom permitted to the wives of the London merchant class.[36] And Natalie Davis has suggested that the religious involvement of French Calvinist townswomen is not to be understood as a form of female revolution expressing a sense of futility and restriction but as the complement, in a new sphere, of the scope and independence which their lives already enjoyed.[37] Similarly the worm's-eye view afforded by ballads and court records suggests that women were forever out and about, drinking and chatting with their 'gossips', in no way prisoners of their situation.

VI

Children are in danger of being squeezed out of the story, just as they are neither seen nor heard in much documentation of the sixteenth and seventeenth centuries. However, a similar debate over opposing dominance and affection could be mounted in respect of children and child-rearing. But in this case the historian faces a somewhat starker contradiction between the austere severity of the conduct books and what little can be glimpsed of the real world outside these texts.[38]

'What is a child, or to be a child?' asks Thomas Becon in 1550, and we prick up our ears, since according to the French historian of childhood, the late Philippe Ariès, this question was not put in the sixteenth century, childhood being not yet regarded as a distinct phase of life. William Gouge would later remark: 'Children are to be used as children'. That sounds promising. Were the early reformers already that enlightened? But Becon's answer is not encouraging: 'A child in Scripture is a wicked man, as he that is ignorant and not exercised in godliness'. Lewis Bayley asked in his *Practise of piety* (that religious best-seller of the early seventeenth century): 'What wast thou, being an infant, but a brute, having the shape of a man?' The intensity of Augustinian pessimism in protestant anthropology depicted the child as prone to evil, 'as the sparks fly upward'. John Robinson, pastor to the puritan group which took ship on the Mayflower, believed that the 'natural pride' of children had to be 'broken and beaten down'.[39]

Just as protestant writers censured husbands and wives for undue levity and familiarity, so they complained of parents who spoiled their children, and they objected to the father's 'cockering' and the mother's pampering. It was said that 'apes kill their young ones with hugging'. 'Why restrain ye not the horrible pride of your daughters?' asks one writer on the subject, leaving us moderns at a loss for an answer. 'Let your sons have correction and your daughters be bridled.' Parents yielded to weakness in making the schoolmaster an executioner on their behalf – 'your master shall hear of it' – when they ought to chastise their offspring in person. The conduct books discuss children largely in terms of obedience and respect, obedience having to do with such major turning-points in life as the choice of a marriage partner or a career, respect with the day-to-day behaviour of young children.

> If any man talk with them, let them stand right up, hold up their heads and look them in the face with a modest and cheerful

countenance, mixed with gravity. Let them hold their hands and feet still: let them not bite their lips, nor scratch their heads, nor rub their elbows, nor pore in their ears.

If parents were unwilling to hear what they had to say 'they ought to lay their hands upon their mouths . . . This is a token of great respect.' Steven Ozment, commenting on similar teaching in the German context, remarks that external actions, manners and even expressions were considered a profound commentary on the child's inner state and character. 'Yawning is never funny in a child.'[40]

So did the Protestant Reformation subject children to a new and intensified form of tyranny, as they descended into the bleak prison-house later associated with the fictional world of *The Way Of All Flesh* or the bitter-sweet recollections of Edmund Gosse in *Father and Son*? Historians react variously to the evidence. Some, like the New England historian John Demos who makes use of the concepts of developmental psychology, conclude that such an upbringing, especially at the infantile and traumatic stage of weaning, can only have crippled emergent personalities. Others favourably contrast the seventeenth century (or the sixteenth in the case of Ozment's sudy of Reformation Germany) with more modern epochs, such as the nineteenth century. The Puritans, unlike the Victorians, did not turn childhood into a nursery of sentimental fantasy and escape but complimented children by regarding them as responsible moral agents and provided them with an upbringing which was well adapted to the real world in which they would have to live as adults. Similarly it has been pointed out that medieval lullabies sung to children did not convey them into some unreal world of fantasy but integrated them 'immediately into the common worries of survival'.[41]

However, although Demos thinks that being a younger member of the family in seventeenth-century New England was a thoroughly unpleasant experience ('psychohistory' reminds us of the cartoon caption IT WAS HELL SAYS FORMER CHILD), the English evidence of parental attitudes, scant though it is, is at variance with the conduct books except in what they complain of: inordinate affection. William Gouge himself did not conceal the depth of his emotion upon the death of his own small daughter, telling his friend Harley: 'My sweetest child, my only daughter is gone', echoing words written in similar circumstances by Luther and sentiments later consigned to his diary by the Essex minister Ralph Josselin. The pious London furniture maker Nehemiah Wallington recorded the last words of his 'sweet child', a three-year-old daughter: 'Says she to me, father I go abroad tomorrow and buy you a plum pie'. Later Mrs Wallington had to remonstrate with her husband for grieving for little Elizabeth too long and too hard.[42]

How is this conflict between dominance and affection to be resolved? Puritan parents were concerned not merely to *correct* their children but to *convert* them. Sir Nathaniel Barnardiston used to take his children into his closet to pray over them and for them (but not with them).[43] Edmund S. Morgan's classic New England study *The Puritan Family* wonders why, when Puritans thought so little of the social virtues which led to a 'smooth, honest civil life', they nevertheless spent so much anxious effort to inculcate these very virtues in their children. Good behaviour could never save the child. But it might provide precious empirical evidence, not certain but probable, of the child's election into the Lamb's Book of Life, so serving to allay parental fears about a child's ultimate destination. Morgan believes that this ambition was so powerful as to be capable of converting the broad vision of a godly commonwealth, with which Massachusetts began, into a narrow tribalism concerned with the more limited objective of ensuring salvation within the family stock. As for affection, the Puritans loved their children too much and shrank from the overpowering strength of their own emotions. 'Puritan parents did not trust themselves with their own children, they were afraid of spoiling them with too great affection.'[44] This is a very long way from the formal frigidity which, according to Lawrence Stone in the least convincing pages of *Family, Sex and Marriage*, characterised the dealings of parents and children in this society.

It remains possible that in seeking to reconcile the corrective and affective attitudes of devout protestant parents we are considering a very narrow segment of evidence untypical of human relations more generally and characteristic of social groups which, either as an aspect of their socio-economic status or through heightened religious sensibility, lived at a more elevated emotional level than was normal. The practice of putting infants out to nurse, which in France entailed the transportation of babies for hundreds of kilometres by professional carriers, suggests a distinct lack of parental sentiment, or economic necessity so overpowering as to suppress sentiment. And, since these parents could not be ignorant that such practices greatly increased the likelihood of infant mortality, they may have amounted in extreme cases to a form of deliberate infanticide, more or less equivalent to exposure of the unwanted child. Yet the most recent study of family relations in later medieval England has found little evidence of cruelty towards children, or even of what we should regard as an unnatural absence of parental affection. In four thousand coroners' inquests into accidental deaths, many of them involving children, Dr Hanawalt found only three cases of culpable infanticide proven. 'Medieval parents did not take the casual attitude towards the loss of children that historians of the modern family have attributed to them.'[45]

VII

We have now spent some effort in trying to penetrate a resistant membrane between ourselves and the past, and to observe the inside of something called the Protestant Family, as if it really existed. Unfortunately such an assumption can no longer be made. Just as we very nearly found that the Protestant Nation is only half a subject, since many of the notions associated with Protestant nationalism were current before the sixteenth century, so there is now some risk that the Protestant Family will dissolve before our gaze.

It is a double risk. At the first barrier our advance may be halted with the advice that it is not a subject since what is meant by the Protestant Family is a collection of emotions, sentiments and values which for a period as remote and poorly documented (for this purpose) as the sixteenth and seventeenth centuries are not recoverable. And it is certainly true that in no other branch of historical study are such dubious statements so confidently made, such flatly contradictory claims staked out. One authority tells us that this was the apogee of patriarchy, another that patriarchy was 'threatened', could no longer be taken for granted'.[46] The reason is clear. The conduct books can be read either as evidence of what they complain of, the relaxation of traditional standards of behaviour, or, conversely, as an indication that the conservative lessons they taught were part of some social consensus.

We can work out what these books recommend in respect of the rearing of children. It is more difficult to discover how all but a few parents really did rear their offspring. Even the underlying sentiments are often only recorded as they were frozen in the heightened, snapshot moment at the deathbed of a child. But as to knowing what it was like to be a child, in childish perception, there is little hope. As Peter Laslett has remarked, in the pre-industrial world there were children everywhere, teeming in the streets, hanging round the farm, getting in the way, like a third world scene today. In modern Ethiopia, where crowds of small children are sometimes almost threatening, it is common practice to scatter them by picking up and hurling a handful of stones. I doubt whether this has ever been a matter of formal documentary record and I should not know it if I had not witnessed it, often, with my own eyes. Early modern children were everywhere except in the records. We do not know how their play was organised, what they played, or even whether they were encouraged to play or discouraged, what kinds of toys were given as presents, if and when children were given presents. However a little seems to be known about 'fairings'. Only two stray details come readily to mind. In the complex allegorical picture of the Edwardian Reformation which ushers in the appropriate section of Foxe's 'Book of Martyrs' a mother is seen in the act of entering a church; half her body is concealed by the wall of the building, the visible arm is clutching a small child. And in the child's grasp is a hobby horse. That vignette may in itself give a misleading impression of close parental surveillance, perhaps characteristic of the bourgeoisie. The children of the London parish of St Faith's hard by St Paul's may have been more typical in their uninhibited play. They used to urinate on the floor inside the south door of the cathedral 'to slide as upon ice', and to play 'in such manner as children use to do till dark night', to the disturbance of the service in the choir. Thomas Becon wrote in the mid-sixteenth century that 'children be naturally given to play, and are desirous of pastimes'. But Linda Pollock calls the children of the past 'indecipherable figures'.[47]

The preceding paragraph had already been written when a book appeared which suggests that its plea of ignorance with respect to the real world of past childhood may be excessive. Using the record of some four thousand coroners' inquests into accidental deaths, mostly dating from the fourteenth century, Barbara Hanawalt is able to observe the children of country people at their habitual occupations: water-carrying and fuel-gathering, catching fish in rivers and ditches and collecting shellfish on the sea-shore, gathering rushes, picking fruit and nuts, and above all herding livestock. The sometimes dangerous play of children also becomes visible as in no other source, leading Hanawalt to the conclusion that the stages of child development, for example in the mastery of motor skills, followed each other much as they do now, determined by a biological rather than cultural set of rules and conditions. To be sure these are still but flickering shadows on the wall of a cave from which we cannot escape into the sunlight of direct and unrestricted observation.[48]

And what of the real world of women? Although it is a more accessible world than that of childhood, 'women's history' is often nothing of the sort but rather the history of male attitudes and behaviour towards women. It has been said that a better object of historical investigation than women is both women and men, parents and children: that is, the entire family, in its stabilities and instabilities, as the prime and irreducible unit. But it is doubtful whether the meaning of the interaction between people so long dead and recoverable only from documents, and sometimes unsuitable documents at that, is ever accessible. It is hard enough to surmise what has happened when the marriage of a couple whom we thought we knew well falls apart, or what it is which sustains that other partnership which, somewhat to our surprise, endures.

If we push past that first barrier we encounter at the second the demoralising suggestion that in so far as we can discover anything valid and true about the English family in the sixteenth and seventeenth centuries, when reduced to generalities with merely superficial and local differences ironed out, it resembles what can be said about the family in other centuries. Family history still suffers, as political history used to suffer, from being written backwards, with the intention of discovering how we got to where we now are. This encourages the construction of progressively developmental stages, but these may prove to be quite spurious, the invention of historians. Such, it appears, are the stages of development traced by Lawrence Stone. Yet if the family has no significant developmental history, historical interest of a serious kind will not be sustained. It may be as enjoyable for recreational purposes to read about such seventeenth-century families as the Verneys or the Harleys as to visit some stately home: but just as irrelevant for any serious and contemporary purpose.

Recent revisionism with respect to this subject is like a plane, busily removing the knots and other rugosities from a plank of wood, the irregularities which make the subject interesting and a suitable case for historical treatment. First the revisionist plane comes up against the apparent singularity of what protestant and puritan writers have to say about marital and domestic matters. With one or two strokes it demonstrates that there is no great difference between what the conduct books contain and what earlier writers had already said on the same subjects, and they in turn may have restated an even older body of conventional and oral wisdom, or prejudice. A certain smoothness in the plank begins to emerge. As the plane works on it next exposes a more basic flaw. Conduct books are not at all descriptive of domestic life as it actually was but merely express the preoccupations and hang-ups of their authors or, worse still, stand in a literary tradition to which successive writers of no great originality gave a new lease of life from time to time, without contributing any new ideas. Then, as the carpenter's tool bites ever deeper into the timber, the last knots vanish and an even more depressing sameness is revealed. At this level we are beginning to encounter facts about the family established by the increasingly sophisticated methods of historical demography. And these suggest that in some essential respects, and for as far back as surviving evidence will allow us to go, the family has not changed: not in the rules governing its formation, not in its structure, not in its size, not even in social function and emotional value. At this point the over-enthusiastic Do-It-Yourself historian may find that his plank has been planed away to almost nothing and that he is left with nothing but a pile of shavings.

In the last twenty years there has been a revolution in the objective and primarily demographic history of the West European family in general and of the English family in particular.[49] These findings have a bias towards what might be called 'most people', demographic mass-observation, and away from the upper classes which, as late as 1974 and Professor Stone's block-buster, still dominated. The critical discovery has been that the restricted nuclear family was not, as Engels supposed (and he was sharing a widespread assumption), the invention of the sixteenth century but has existed, in a manner of speaking, always. Far from complex and extended families being the norm, those sharing the same living space and going to bed under the same roof (held, on debatable grounds, to be the essential criterion of family identification) had always been restricted, at least for most of the lifespan of most marriages, to two parents and their offspring. Simple families are the norm in Domesday Book. A recent study of late medieval coroners' inquests has found that the families visited by accidental death were 'almost always simple families'.[50]

Vastly important implications follow. Although parents, kin and other interested parties might intervene in various ways in the selection of marriage partners, in the social rituals accompanying betrothal and marriage contracts and in inheritance stratagems, social practice and legal doctrine (deriving from twelfth-century Canon Law) favoured the formal and often realistic principle that the parties themselves made the marriage.[51] There is good reason to believe that marriages, long before the sixteenth century, were expected to arise from mutual attraction, parents and other 'friends' contributing their 'good will' when persuaded that the young people had first given their good will to each other. The evidence of seventeenth-century popular literature is that freedom of choice and marriage for love were matters taken for granted. In anthropological parlance 'neolocal residence' was both a condition of marriage and its invariable consequence. That is to say a married couple were expected to set up a separate household without delay. In the economic crisis of the 1590s concern was expressed in one English village about young people who were wed 'before they have a convenient house to live in'. Significantly the verb *s'établir* in the French usage of the early modern period implied both the acquisition of economic self-sufficiency and marriage. Central to the making of a marriage were cultural expectations about what constituted a suitable married home. Consequently a higher proportion of the population remained unmarried than has been the case in most non-European societies and those who did marry married late: at some point between twenty-five and thirty for both sexes, which, given pre-modern life expectancy, was even later than it may seem. Nevertheless the simplicity and cheapness of much late medieval housing made neolocal residence a not unreasonable condition of marriage, equivalent to the barest of livelihoods rather than total self-sufficiency.[52]

There was not, as moderns might assume, a concomitantly high illegitimate birth rate. But when the age of marriage began to fall in the eighteenth century the illegitimacy rate, far from falling with it, actually rose from less than two per cent to five per cent. This can only mean that the force which had hitherto prevented the marriage of young people had also inhibited procreation outside marriage. It remains only to identify and locate that inhibiting force, whether in ecclesiastical discipline, community and familial expectations or low libidos. Robert Muchembled, examining the French evidence, proposes that the early modern period witnessed an unprecedented campaign of sexual repression, designed to persuade countless individuals that sexuality was a social rather than merely individual and erotic function. This was a 'major cultural revolution'. But for Martin Ingram no such 'revolution' was called for, or occurred. What happened between 1600 and 1700 was part of an 'ongoing dialogue' between varieties of official and popular culture. Taking a no less broad view, J.-P. Flandrin has proposed that the sexual repression of young people, as a cultural structure, has always been stronger in Western Europe than anywhere else, but that it intensified in the period in question to the extent that it eventually destroyed what he calls 'the ancient structures of sexual life', with observable consequences in the eighteenth century.[53] Less controversially it is clear that within marriage the birth-rate was customarily and not ineffectively controlled by prolonged breast-feeding, a biological method of contraception. The result was a mean completed family size of five to seven which, given the higher incidence of mortality, meant families no larger than those of today and a very slow rate of population accretion or, as in the disease-ridden fifteenth century, no growth at all.

Such facts, in so far as they are facts and incontrovertible, are worth more than any amount of contemporary comment or doctrine. It is better to know that fifteen per cent of the female population remained unmarried, even when nunneries disappeared from protestant societies, than to be told by Luther or the conduct books that marriage was more or less inescapable and compulsory. (Although we may note that in the harsh economic climate of the early seventeenth century William Whateley of Banbury departed far from Luther in deterring his readers from marriage, with frank warnings about the cares and troubles it involved: 'Keep as you be'.)[54]

But of course the facts are not quite incontrovertible, and the interpretation of facts remains subjective. The 'facts' which have been mentioned are statistical abstractions and they emerge from the analysis not of all conceivable statistical data but of the data which is retrievable, and precisely because it is retrievable what we have may distort the true picture. Global generalisations of the kind in which we have just indulged require the reduction of statistical irregularities which may be significant to averages and means which, while 'true', are themselves insignificant: the problem of the meaningless mean. And to establish the normal conditions of cohabitation is to say nothing about social structure and interaction, or about the distribution of resources and of economic activity outside the marital homestead, which may still have involved significant and ramified connections with kin who were not co-resident. The study of the early modern family has now moved on to a distinct and more sophisticated phase in which it is widely acknowledged that concentration on the nuclear family, as a simple unit of conjugal cohabitation, is no longer adequate. While it is certainly the case that such units of co-residence were the norm in England and neighbouring parts of north-western Europe, it was not always, or even very often, a tidy norm: death and remarriage ensured that many households were truncated, or incomplete, or included the survivors of earlier episodes of marital stability. 'Family', and its equivalents in other European languages, was not a word confined to the simple family or, in France, used in that sense at all. When a seventeenth-century legal text written in Bordeaux stated that custom dictated that 'property remain in the family', it did not mean and could not mean the simple family.[55] However 'household' (in English) *does* designate 'the living space of a group of people that is private to them in that other people may not enter it without their permission'. And as Barbara Hanawalt has observed, however many exceptions there may have been to prove the rule, medieval peasants (and doubtless their early modern successors) 'showed a strong preference for having only a conjugal family in a household'.[56]

The evidence of a marriage ceremony serves to reduce a world of constantly lived-out meaning to a single moment: the couple making a marriage contract by the exchange of promises and tokens normally did so not in isolation but in the presence of witnesses, both kindred and neighbours or future neighbours, the all-important 'friends'. This had significance beyond the simple legal consideration that the act should be witnessed. At a betrothal in Folkestone, an occasion which was well attended, the question was put (and perhaps it was a customary and almost ritual question): 'Which is she that should be our neighbour?', to which Joan Harwood replied, 'I am she'. 'And she was then called Mistress Lambard. And she said she was contented with that name and would never forsake it during her life. And she said that she trusted to be entertained there as a neighbour among them.'[57] Marriage, any marriage, necessarily subtracted from one community and added to another, altering and complicating patterns of relationship. Communities had a variety of means at their disposal to express approval or disapproval of these altering configurations. The charivari or 'riding', a cacophonous and threatening ritual, was organised to censure incongruous unions, between aged husbands or widows and young marriage partners, which threatened the interests of the demonstrators themselves, the young unmarried.[58] To reduce these complications to the barest bones of demography, married partners in a social vacuum, has artificially divorced the family from its setting and limits our outlook on society as a whole. However it is probably the case that the effect of Protestantism in England, like that of Tridentine Catholicism in France, was to reduce the scope of public secular festivities and folk customs associated with family formation, privatising marriage as a religious rite of prime interest to those celebrating it.

To move on from the data to postulate its meaning is hazardous but, like most hazardous pursuits, not without its thrills. The meaning of the raw demography as it is now understood may amount to social rather than merely biological control of reproduction as being the age-old western norm. Europe seems to acknowledge, as Asia does not, a conflict between economic wellbeing and the desire to marry and raise a family, production at odds with reproduction. And Europe seems to have resolved that conflict in favour of individual wellbeing. For Alan Macfarlane this implies the very early presence in the West of a kind of acquisitive and possessive individualism. The individual pursued his own interest and limited those who shared in it to a partner whom he chose for himself (or she for herself) and subsequently the immediate conjugal family. What early Marxists had assumed to be the consequence of early stages in the growth of capitalism was perhaps a precondition for that peculiarity of Western civilization. Western Europe seems to have resolved that conflict in favour of individual well-being, not in the sixteenth and seventeenth centuries but much earlier. Elements of the European marriage pattern are described by Tacitus. This makes not only the Reformation but also many other supposed watersheds and threshholds something less than Herbert Butterfield's 'internal displacements', in fact no displacements at all. What might be called 'bottom line' history becomes a continuum. It is not a matter of pushing back the capitalist revolution but of denying that such a revolution ever took place, or was needed, since the critical connections between distinctive marital, demographic, political and economic systems were always, in principle, present.

Thus far goes Alan Macfarlane, who has recently argued in *Marriage and Love in England 1300–1840* that the sentiments which he believes can be inferred in prudential 'Malthusian' marital and reproductive strategies were equally constant. Engels's 'individual sex-love' had been critically present in English marriage since at least the central Middle Ages, where investigation can begin. Marriage had always been companionable, with husband and wife, in all ordinarily favourable circumstances, the best of friends. When the Tudor church homily proposed as the principal reason for marriage that 'man and woman should live lawfully in a perpetual friendship', this was to express not a novel but a very traditional sentiment. Eileen Power found that the medieval world was 'full of married friends'. Barbara Hanawalt concurs: 'Partnership is the most appropriate term to describe marriage in medieval English peasant society', a partnership both economic and emotional. Husband and wife walked side by side in fifteenth-century England, even when the occasion of their walking was a quarrel.[59]

As for the children of the marriage, they were emotionally valued, enjoyed, loved, and probably always had been. A medieval lyric remarks:

> Your children you dance upon your knees
> With laughing, kissing and merry cheer.[60]

Macfarlane agrees with many other historians of the family, doubtless a majority, in doubting whether the seventeenth century witnessed any significant change in what Stone called, rather clinically, the investment in children of emotional capital. Except in the cases of the very youngest of dying infants there is no reason to suppose that high levels of child mortality blunted the edge of parental grief. The widely prevalent medieval cult of child martyrs would suggest the reverse. The seventeenth-century paramedical practitioner Richard Napier found that bereavement was the third most common cause of what we should call clinical depression among his patients, and that of a total of 134 cases of bereavement-induced depression, 58 concerned the loss of children. In all but seven of these it was the mother who was unhinged by the experience. Napier considered a woman's failure to love her children a rare phenomenon and in itself a symptom of mental disorder. It seems unlikely that these were new attitudes, resulting from economic change or new religious doctrine. If Barbara Hanawalt's fourteenth-century coroners' inquests contain rare examples of child abuse, they also suggest that society disapproved, then as now, of the neglect of children.[61]

One can but sympathise with the strength of Dr Macfarlane's negative reaction to some of the excesses involved in earlier attempts to write the history of the emotions, including unlikely theories about children and the curious notion, to which C.S. Lewis gave the widest currency, that in the Middle Ages romantic heterosexual love existed only quasi-adulterously outside marriage, never within it. This may work as an explanation for a literary genre but not otherwise. Nevertheless a book like Macfarlane's which devotes 350 pages to the theme of love without once defining that emotion invites some criticism. The puritan conduct books insist that husbands *must* love their wives, because St Paul says so. And when they go on to teach that love flows downwards, never upwards, so that whereas husbands are to love their wives, wives are required to *obey* their husbands, we are entitled to ask what this discourse has to do with the concept of romantic love as we know it, or even with sexual desire. Sixteenth- and seventeenth-century marriage begins once again to look a little remote from any experience of ours. Macfarlane seems not to notice that love in these texts is understood to be the *product* of a married relationship, not its occasion. When Ben Jonson mourned his infant son and prayed that he should not in future like so much what he loved his words suggest that he was bound of necessity to *love* his own, whether he liked to or not, but that his *liking* for the dead child was a more unpredictable emotion.[62] Similarly the fact that the word 'friend' was used in the sixteenth and seventeenth centuries primarily of parents and other close kindred, whom we might call compulsory rather than voluntary friends, suggests a society of constrained emotions, different from our own. Our plank of wood has evidently been planed a little too smooth for comfort. Macfarlane invites the criticism of other medievalists and family historians for suggesting that there were no significant differences at all between the family and the emotions then and now.

VIII

Let us return, finally, to the world of the conduct books, once thought to have expressed new values and virtues. Stone thought that they embodied 'the most far-reaching consequences of the Reformation in England'. Granted that these sources are of dubious worth as social documents, telling us little about actual behaviour, do they not nevertheless embody a new *ideal* of family relationships, and one which may have had some influence on attitudes and even on behaviour?

Kathleen Davies doubts whether the ideal was new at all. A comparison of post-Reformation and immediately pre-Reformation texts on marital questions reveals what she calls 'a monotonous similarity of highly generalised advice'. If the Puritans insisted on male sovereignty and the absolute subjection of wives, so did their precursors, writing on these matters before the Reformation. The doctrine of mutuality was taught in the 1520s and earlier. So was the principle that marriage was a contract requiring as its *sine qua non* the willing and loving consent of both partners. Even the alleged contrast between the negative appraisal of married life, said to be typical of late medieval Catholicism, and its enthusiastic endorsement by Protestants melts away when we grasp that whereas catholic works of moral theology addressed to priests naturally argued in favour of celibacy, those designed for the instruction of the laity had long adopted a more positive approach, hard to distinguish from the protestant line. Davies concludes that historians have been misled by the greatly increased volume of printed works on domestic ethics published in the century following the Reformation, which was commensurate with the expansion of publication in all other fields, a consequence of what we might call the new information technology and of advancing literacy. Market forces are certainly indicative of something. Given the sound commercial instincts of London stationers they were not likely to print books on marriage for which there was no demand. But the response to this demand is just as likely to have reinforced existing attitudes as to have changed them. Davies concludes that it may be more realistic to regard the conduct books as 'conventional texts for the market' than as 'serious attempts to tackle novel issues': 'descriptive rather than prescriptive'. Far from embodying new ideals, they described 'the best form of bourgeois marriage as they knew it'.[63]

This leaves unresolved and indeed unexplored both the extent of 'bourgeois marriage' and that question which will neither answer itself nor go away, concerning its origins. There are two revisionist possibilities. One is that the changes of attitude and value traditionally associated with the Reformation really did happen but need to be relocated, pushed back a little but not too far, into the early sixteenth-century cultural setting which the French characterise as one of 'pre-Reform': the epoch of christian humanism dominated by Erasmus and that quintessential family man, Thomas More. Kathleen Davies dismisses this suggestion, denying that her 'earlier writers' were in any sense 'proto-Puritan'. But her writers were not all that early. The books she cites were all published between 1528 and 1531, and there is no denying that they were all written by christian humanists, the most notable of whom was the monk of Sion, Richard Whitford, author of *A Work for householders*, which says many things which later puritan writers would say. Another student of the problem, Margo Todd, agrees (in effect) with Davies that the puritan conduct books were not original, but unlike Davies she thinks that if the advice they purveyed was stale by the seventeenth century it had been bright and new a hundred years earlier. 'It is to the Christian humanists . . . rather than to the Puritans that we must look for the roots of the spiritualized household.' The social morality of the generation which contained those staunchly catholic critics of current corruptions, More, Whitford and the dramatist and musician John Heywood, was in many respects 'puritanical'.[64]

Both Davies and Todd refer to the same texts but, whereas Todd thinks that they were making a new departure in about 1530, Davies, like Macfarlane, seems to think that there is nothing new under the sun. One thing which is reasonably certain is that any major cultural or ideological change which did take place did not happen all at once. So, since the Reformation itself was a long time in coming, and an even longer time departing, to go behind the Puritans who inherited the Reformation to the Christian humanists who unwittingly prepared the way for it – to discover Richard Whitford in William Gouge – may be a reasonable strategy in the attempt to establish what, if anything, was changing in the public perception of the family in this period. One recalls Christopher Hill's hunch that it was in the course of a long time-span from the fourteenth to the seventeenth centuries, and in a particular class and environment, that certain critical changes occurred. He may be right. It would be unkind to Mrs Davies to call her argument a correction of some points of detail, but in the context of Hill's suggestions it does not look very significant.

The other, more radical, possibility is that no perceptible change occurred in the doctrine and practice of the family at any time which the records make accessible to us, and certainly not in the age of the Reformation. This is the option favoured by Macfarlane and it looks rather extreme. The *reductio ad absurdum* is to trace the pedigree of the conduct books back to Tacitus, who wrote that the Germanic wife entered her husband's home 'to be the partner of his toils and perils'. More to the point, perhaps, the biblical texts on which the protestant version of marriage was erected had been a readily available resource of western civilisation for a thousand years before the sixteenth century. The principle of mutuality, which determined the organisation of the material in the conduct books and is thought by some to have constituted their major original contribution, exists in all essential respects in St Paul's Epistle to the Ephesians. Nevertheless it seems altogether too drastic and self-defeating to contend that no significant cultural change, even at the level of sentiment, occurred at any point in these many centuries. This is where our plank ceases to exist, leading to a collapse of many stout parties.

Even if it could be shown that the family had no significant developmental history this would not necessarily eliminate the Protestant Family as a topic of legitimate investigation. The occupational disease of the historian (and a Marxist might say that this in itself is a piece of bourgeois possessive individualism) is an obsession with uniqueness and with the origins of things, and not only with origins but also with a personal discovery of the origins, leading to a proprietary interest in the matter. There is, too, a romantic urge at play in this quest. To deny, like Macfarlane, that an institution has any perceptible origins is simply to turn the coin over and play the game in reverse, claiming a paradoxical triumph.

Much that we have so far discovered suggests that the Protestant Reformation was a continuum, or part of the unbroken continuum of our history, not a point of wholly new departures. As Troeltsch in Germany and Tawney in England perceived, its immediate effect was the intensification of certain very old-established preoccupations, whether about salvation or concerning the investment of money. The family can perhaps be added to this list. As for the Reformation and social revolution, there was no social revolution in the age of the Reformation and the religious contribution to revolutionary change when (Macfarlane would say if) it came was indirect and disputable. The doctrine and, so far as we can observe it in the field, the practice of early Protestantism in respect of marriage and domestic matters generally was not a total novelty, if novel at all.

But the protestant doctrine and practice of marriage can be used to provide a reference point and to stand for an ideal type of certain significant features of the Western European family, highlighting what in a comparative global context are its distinctive and even unique features. For (in England at least) it was in the form of the Protestant Family that these features became elevated to a high point of explicit consciousness and of emulation and perpetuation in successive generations. It was here that the family as we know it experienced its birth.

4 Protestant Culture and the Cultural Revolution

If 'culture' be understood, not as anthropologists understand the word (or social historians when they speak of 'popular culture'), but as meant by Goering when he is supposed to have said that whenever he heard the word he reached for his revolver,[1] then according to a certain widespread prejudice there is no need to draw a gun on English Protestantism, since it produced no culture of its own but made an iconoclastic holocaust of the culture which already existed. The efflorescence of high culture in the age of Shakespeare is conventionally packaged and labelled as the English (or Elizabethan) Renaissance, a secular achievement which involved a degree of emancipation from the dominance of religion and was consequently facilitated by the Protestant Reformation, but only in a negative sense. No one turns Shakespeare himself into a chapter of the English Reformation.

Spenser may be another matter. *The Faerie Queene* is unmistakably a Protestant epic. And later there is Milton. With these poets the total incompatibility of Protestantism and high culture becomes more doubtful. C.S. Lewis discovered a paradox, in that the flinty rocks of Calvinism were to be seen pushing through the soft turf of Sidney's *Arcadia*.[2] But if Protestantism had a cultural history, surely Puritanism (in spite of Milton) was another matter. A long-running dispute about Spenser, whether he should be classified as a Protestant or a Puritan, is sterile,[3] since it rests on a distinction which cannot in fact be made. But in this discussion there is a sense of promising paradox. If one were to demonstrate that Spenser was indeed a Puritan one would have succeeded in proving something almost unprovable: the compatibility of Puritanism and great art. Similarly Percy Scholes writing on *Puritanism and Music*, Margo Heinemann on *Puritanism and the Theatre* and Donald Davie on the lyrics of Protestant Nonconformity, all discovered mileage in subjects on which, according to conventional wisdom, there is little or nothing to be said. How was it, asked Davie of himself, that he could have been a Baptist and yet read English at Cambridge?[4] Dr Johnson claimed to have seen a book on the natural history of Iceland with a chapter on snakes consisting of the single sentence: 'There are no snakes to be met with throughout the whole island'. It has seemed, in the course of the long march away from the brief triumph of Puritanism in the mid-seventeenth century, that an equally short chapter could be written on Puritanism and Culture. And yet Puritanism was neither alien to Protestantism nor even distinct from it but was its logical extension, equivalent to its full internalisation: as R.H. Tawney suggested, the real rather than merely the official Reformation in England. So this is almost as much as to say that Protestant Culture is a nonentity.

'The Bible, the Bible only I say is the religion of Protestants.' So wrote William Chillingworth in 1638. And since for Protestants religion was not one compartment of a segmented life but all-enveloping, this must also mean that the Bible only is the *culture* of Protestants. This will do as a starting point and I think that it has to do, uncompromising and unpromising though such a statement may at first sight appear. The Bible was no narrow straitjacket but a rich and infinitely varied source of imaginative and formal inspiration. Nevertheless, just as the God of the Bible advertised himself as a jealous God, so his book in the age of the Reformation made exclusive and intolerant claims. The Bible was not rendered into the European vernaculars and promulgated on a vast scale merely to provide reading for Sundays or a religious supplement to an equally copious literature on a hundred other subjects, although the catalogue of all the books published in England in the period may give that impression. Turning to the beginning of letter A on the first page of the *Short-Title Catalogue* of books printed between 1475 and 1640 one finds that the very first titles out of more than 26 000 are, in order, *A pleasant fancie called The passionate morris dance* and *A treatise of the way to life*. These books and others like them were obliged to coexist and compete. On this first page *A briefe chronologie of the holie scriptures* sits uneasily alongside a work on rapier and sword play and a spuriously feminist satire purportedly written by one Jane Anger. Twenty of the forty-one titles on the page may be described broadly as religious, the remainder as secular, a ratio which is not different from that sustained in the remaining 608 pages of the original edition of the '*S.T.C.*'.

Non-fiction, texts on practical subjects, was, in the perspective of the godly religious mind, legitimate. Fictions were not, religious and secular literature being in deadly competition for possession of the imaginative and leisure hour. William Tyndale made polemical play of the fact that the bishops, while forbidding lay people to read the Scripture, had allowed them to stuff their heads with such fables of love and wantonness as Robin Hood and Bevis of Hampton, 'as filthy as heart can think'.[5] When Erasmus (and Tyndale following his lead) expressed the hope that wayfaring men and women would have the Scripture in their heads as they went about their business – 'that the ploughman holding the plough did sing somewhat of the mystical psalms in his own mother tongue' – they seem to have meant that *only* these lyrics should be on their lips. Miles Coverdale in the preface to his *Goostly Psalmes and Spirituall Songes* wrote: 'Would God that our minstrels had none other thing to play upon neither our carters and ploughmen other thing to whistle upon, save psalms, hymns, and such godly songs as David is occupied withal! And if women, sitting at their rocks, or spinning at the wheels, had none other songs to pass their time withal, . . . they should be better occupied than with *hey non nony, hey troly loly*, and such like fantasies.'[6] This was a vision realised nowhere in early modern Europe except in certain Huguenot villages in the Cévennes, where nineteenth-century folk song collectors found nothing to collect since the only music, even for babies in their cradles, was the Psalms.[7] The title-page of one of the earliest English metrical psalm books commended its contents for private use by 'all sorts of people . . . laying apart all ungodly songs and ballads', and in dedicating the book to Edward VI one of the authors, Thomas Sternhold, praised the boy king for delighting more 'in the holy songs of verity that in any fayned rhymes of vanity', a sentiment later echoed by Archbishop Matthew Parker:

> Depart ye songes: lascivious,
> from lute, from harpe depart:
> Geve place to Psalmes: most vertuous,
> and solace there your harte.

The tap-root of this *topos* can be traced to a letter of Erasmus's favourite christian writer and the translator of the Bible into the vernacular of his day. In a letter written in the person of one of his female companions and describing life in his monastery at Bethlehem as a 'little villa of Christ', St Jerome reported that 'apart from the singing of Psalms, there is silence. The ploughman driving the share sings an *alleluia* . . . These are the popular love-lays. This is what the shepherds whistle.'[8]

So it was in an authentically protestant tradition, but one of far greater antiquity than the Reformation, that Milton stood when in

Paradise Regained he envisaged a choice and even a conflict between 'divine' and 'humane' literature. Christ tempted in the wilderness was confronted with the rival claims of both, with Satan cast, literally, as devil's advocate for secular, pagan literature: Christ is made to say to him that the classics are unworthy to compare with Sion's songs, to all true tastes excelling. If he would delight his private hours with song, 'where so soon/As in our native Language can I find that solace?' For Milton and the three of four generations of English Protestantism which preceded and formed him 'our native Language' was a Hebrew which had learned to speak English in the pages of the English Bible, Tyndale having declared that 'the properties of the Hebrew tongue agreeth a thousand times more with the English than with the Latin'.[9] So unless we dismiss the contention of secular and sacred art as an artificial device (which in part it was) we have to face the uncomfortable fact that the pluralistic cohabitation of various literary modes and genres in sixteenth-and seventeenth-century England, the diversity of both sacred and secular, was something unintended and undesired by Protestants, the consequence of their defeat, or at best their very partial success. (Nevertheless the Herefordshire library of that impeccably godly gentleman Sir Robert Harley included, besides the entire corpus of English puritan divinity, Shakespeare's *Sonnets*, Spenser's *Shepheardes Kalendar* and Jonson's plays.)[10]

'Is there in truth no beauty?', asked George Herbert in the poem 'Jordan I', advancing a famous apologia for the 'plain style':

> I envie no mans nightingale or spring;
> Nor let them punish me with loss of rime,
> Who plainly say, *My God, My King*.

The Bible is here assumed to be plain, honest, even artless. As Nicholas Udall had written in the preceding century, divinity 'loveth no cloaking, but loveth to be simple and plain'. This was not to say that it refused eloquence, 'if the same come without injury or violation of the truth'. Truth was all and truth for Protestants was plain truth, sufficiently contained in the Bible. All non-scriptural doctrine and practice, all non-scriptural art, amounted to lies, false religion. There was no gainsaying Scripture, no substitute for it: there was scope only for some debate as to the all-sufficiency of Scripture, as to whether or not there were areas of indifference where it could be supplemented by human reason and imagination.[11] For hardline Protestants 'imaginings' was one of those words always qualified by the same adjective, in this case 'vain', often in the formula 'vain imaginings and humane policy'. It was primarily Tyndale who had put the Bible into plain speech. If the wayfaring man and the spinning woman were to fill their mouths with Scripture, the Scripture must itself speak the language of the spinning woman and the wayfaring man. It has been said that Tyndale 'hated literature. Next to a papist he hated a poet.'[12]

But Herbert's question still stands nevertheless. 'Is there in truth no beauty?' Could it be said that the Bible was not only literally and dogmatically true but also aesthetically true? Moreover this rhetorical question (for of course the answer was yes) can be extended in the direction of a more popular culture. 'Is there in truth no pastime? no mirth? no enjoyment?' The protestant play *The life and repentaunce of Marie Magdalene* sold itself as 'not only godly, learned and fruitful, but also well furnished with pleasant mirth and pastime, very delectable'. Another biblical play, the *Historie of Jacob and Esau*, was described as 'mery and wittie', an interlude on the story of King Darius as 'pithie and pleasaunt'.[13]

Looking ahead, in the first century of English Protestantism the story of truth and beauty, religion and culture falls into three stages which work almost dialectically: positive, negative, positive nevertheless. First Protestantism embraced the cultural forms which already existed and employed them for its own purposes, both instructively and as polemical weapons against its opponents. Then, in the secondary phase of the English Reformation, roughly equivalent to the first ascendancy of Puritanism and dated quite precisely to 1580 in respect of its cultural impact, many protestant publicists turned their backs on these same cultural media, which now became the enemy no less than popery itself. The consequence of this rejection, seen most starkly in the case of the drama, was an advanced state of separation of the secular from the sacred, something without precedent in English cultural history. But in the third phase protestant biblicism delivered its positive answer in ever fuller measure to Herbert's question, heard most clearly in some of the greatest of the English poets. And it was at this point that an authentically protestant literary culture emerged. If I presume to say least about this third stage of protestant culture it is not on account of any limitations in the subject but with grateful deference to Lily Campbell, Barbara Lewalski and other students of literature who are at home, as I am not trained to be, with the principles of protestant poetics. As Professor Campbell wrote in 1959: 'If I were to undertake to trace the whole movement to make the Bible the guide to Christian living, I should require more years that I can hope to live and more volumes than any printer would publish'.[14]

II

So far this book has been something of a struggle if its purpose has been to persuade the reader that the Protestant Reformation was a major watershed in our civilisation. It was not clear in the first chapter that Protestantism was the midwife of Nationalism, and in the third it was not certain that such a thing as the Protestant Family ever existed. In terms of the image used in Chapter 1, we have spoken of the Urals rather than of the Himalayas. But so far the reader may have been reminded only of the mighty Gogmagogs, which the M11 motorway has to surmount on its way from Cambridge to London. Culturally speaking, however, the Reformation was beyond all question a watershed of truly mountainous proportions. On the far, late medieval side of the range, the landscape consists of images, concrete symbols, mime, the ritualised acting out of religious stories and lessons, a certain artlessness. Religion was 'intensely visual'. Seeing was believing, more than hearing and much more than the privatised mental discipline of absorbing information from a written text.[15] On this side of the divide we confront the invisible, abstract and didactic word: primarily the word of the printed page, on which depended the spoken words of sermon and catechism. In crossing this range we are making a journey from a culture of orality and image to one of print culture: from one mental and imaginative 'set' to another.

The mimetic presentation of religion which came to an exuberant climax in the last generation or two of pre-Reformation England lacked absolutely, in protestant perception, any sense of what might be thought to constitute blasphemy and was almost totally neglectful of the Second Commandment: 'Thou shalt not make unto thee any graven image'. As anyone knows who has shared as actor or audience in the modern revival of the mystery and miracle plays, the religious drama and pageantry treated divine things with a homely familiarity which was shocking and obnoxious to Protestants who had recovered their sense of God's awe-inspiring otherness. Thus it was thought in no way indecorous for King Richard II to be welcomed into the city of London in 1392 with ceremonies which explicitly identified this mortal monarch with Christ in his entry into Jerusalem on Palm Sunday, or as making his Second Coming to inaugurate a new

Jerusalem. The Chester accountant who noted expenditure 'for gilding of little God's face' presumably felt no embarrassment.[16]

But this last reference dates not from 1392 but from 1566, at least thirty years into the official Reformation and six years after the definitively protestant Elizabethan Settlement. At York for another six years still, until it was suppressed in 1572, the annual naivety (or indecent blasphemy) of the Christmas ride of Yule and Yule's Wife continued, with Yule distributing nuts 'to put us in remembrance of that noble Nut our Saviour's blessed body'. 'For the Nut hath in it[s] body a triple union, that is to wit, *Testam*, the shell, signifying the bones; and *Corium et nucteum*, the skin and kernel, signifying the flesh and inward Soul of our Saviour.'[17] Those who scrambled for the free nuts and cracked them in their teeth were supposed to bear this symbolism in mind. Our mountain range will have to accommodate some complex and overlapping geographical features, since elements of this mimetic religious culture survived long after the Reformation is supposed to have happened: long enough for the young Shakespeare to have witnessed the Corpus Christi plays in Coventry and to have included in *Hamlet* a likely reference to them in the player who 'out-Heroded' the blustering and comically villainous character of Herod. Earlier in the sixteenth century it was said that Warwickshire preachers would end their sermons with 'if you believe not me, then for a more suerty and sufficient authority, go your way to Coventry, and there you shall see them all played in Corpus Christi play'. The formidable protestant intellectual Thomas Lever, archdeacon and preacher of Coventry, presumably claimed a better authority for his sermons. Yet for the first twenty years of Elizabeth's reign and his own tenure his preaching had to coexist with the continuing religious drama. In 1562 the Drapers Company was still paying five shillings each to 'three white souls' and 'three black souls', and in 1571 sixteen pence 'for keeping hell mouth and setting the world on fire'–surely the bargain of the century.[18]

By this time the plays were controversial. When the queen came to Coventry in 1575 'certain good-hearted men' petitioned to revive for her benefit the play called the Hock Tuesday Play, a piece which dealt with local history in the time of the Saxons and Danes, 'without ill example of manners, papistry or superstition'. They knew no reason why the play should have been abandoned 'unless it were by the zeal of certain their preachers: men very commendable for their behaviour and learning, and sweet in their sermons, but somewhat too sour in preaching away their pastimes'.[19] In 1580, the year of the earthquake and evidently as its direct consequence, the Coventry pageant was finally 'laid down', to be replaced four years later by a new and protestant play 'of the Destruction of Jerusalem' which had a brief run before, towards the end of the reign, the indigenous homegrown drama of Coventry was finally extinguished and the principal promoter jailed for his truculent behaviour towards both preachers and magistrates.[20] At York, Wakefield and Chester the plays had been put down in the mid-1570s, victims of the vigorous new broom of the Protestant régime in the north headed by Archbishop Grindal and the President of the Council, the Earl of Huntingdon. As early as 1567 the Dean of York and a future archbishop, Matthew Hutton, had ruled against any further performance of the so-called 'Creed Play', a piece now lost but apparently didactic and innocuous. Hutton advised that it disagreed with 'the sincerity of the Gospel'. 'For though it was plausible forty years ago and would now also of the ignorant sort be well liked, yet now in this happy time of the Gospel, I know the learned will mislike it, and how the state will bear with it I know not.'[21]

Subsequently the tradition of civic 'pastimes' lived on in two secondary developments: the visits of travelling theatrical companies (again as in *Hamlet*) enjoying the patronage of noblemen and courtiers like Shakespeare's Earl of Southampton; and, as at York and Chester, in fragments of the old religious drama preserved in what otherwise became purely secular midsummer shows and pageants, unconnected with any religious feast and lacking in meaningful symbolism. At Chester one of the figures in the annual summer procession was the Devil, in feathers supplied by the butchers. This can only have been a relic of the play of the Temptation of Christ in the Chester Cycle. However by the early seventeenth century the local vigilantes, and particularly mayor Henry Hardware, were cleaning up the shows, removing such unacceptable features as devils preceded by women with cups and cans, or naked boys in nets. Running races for silver cups replaced the licensed violence of the traditional Shrove Tuesday football game. In Salisbury the Whitsun festivities were reduced to 'children's dances', which disappeared altogether by 1611. This was 'civility' and itself equivalent, if culture is understood in its broader sense, to a cultural revolution. By this time some towns (but not Coventry) were closing their gates to the strolling players and even paying them to go away. This happened at Stratford-upon-Avon, seven years after the death of a local worthy called William Shakespeare. At Dorchester the leader of a travelling company was imprisoned. In Chester citizens faced fines for going out of town to witness dramatic performances elsewhere. This negative response to the travelling theatre, more or less typical of the Jacobean period, contrasts with the popularity of the players in earlier Elizabethan years, even in towns which were 'forward' in their adoption of the Protestant Reformation. Ipswich was such a town: in the 1560s it had already invested in the institution of a town preacher but in the same decade it opened its gates to many acting companies, whose patrons included the Earl of Leicester, the Duchess of Suffolk, the Earl of Bedford, the Earl of Warwick and Lord Rich, all otherwise promoters of advanced Protestantism. Ipswich also welcomed jugglers, tumblers, flute-players and bear-wards, and continued to make payments to the players well into the 1590s.[22]

III

Accounts of 'mysteries' end' (to quote the title of Harold Gardiner's standard account) often telescope this story, as if the civic religious drama was a more or less instant and inevitable casualty of the Reformation. But this was not the case. A child at the time of Henry VIII's first divorce could have seen the plays at Coventry as, by the standards of the time, an old man. The first generation of English Protestants and perhaps the second too entertained little hostility towards plays. Nor, for that matter, were they opposed to other cultural forms such as popular music and pictures, at least not *per se*. They objected only to the use of these media to convey false doctrine, what the men of Coventry called 'papistry or any superstition'. It was in no way incongruous for the Coventry martyr John Careless, later a kind of protestant folk hero, to be let out of prison in Mary's reign to play his usual part in the Corpus Christi play and then to return to confinement, where he later died.[23] At York the change to official Protestantism under Elizabeth was marked by a purging from the Play Cycle of unacceptable 'popish' elements, such as several scenes featuring the Virgin. But the plays as such survived the Elizabethan Settlement.[24] The essential point is that early Protestantism was troubled by these cultural media as potential vehicles of false religion, not as inherently false or deceptive. There was hostility to mendacious art but not to art itself.

Early Protestantism did better than merely tolerate or bowdlerise the old religious drama. It created a new religious and moral drama of its own for its own propagandist and didactic purposes. For a full generation English Protestants were what Abbot Feckenham called them in a House of Lords speech in 1559: 'the preachers and scaffold players of this new religion'. 'Preachers, printers and players trouble Winchester' was Foxe's gleeful headline over a story about Bishop Stephen Gardiner's discomfiture at the hands of the protestant dramatic satirists. Gardiner complained that he and his prelatical colleagues were lampooned 'in all manner of farces and pastimes'. It is instructive to note that in a later generation that resolute Protestant William Prynne was so hostile to the theatre in any shape or form that he sympathised with Gardiner and others of his cloth for all their reactionary Catholicism, invoking not just patristic and protestant opponents of plays but many papists and even the Prophet Mohammed to bolster his already over-burdened freight of authorities against the stage.[25]

These protestant plays and pastimes, the bulk of which have not survived, were written and perhaps directed by the reforming clerics themselves (the last clerical dramatists before this century), most of them obscure figures, but including the learned and vituperative John Bale, ex-Carmelite friar, briefly a protestant bishop in Ireland and author of self-styled 'comedies' on the Temptation of Christ and the life of John the Baptist, and most notably of the robustly anti-catholic history play *King Johan*. Bale's instinctively comedic talents – 'a man obsessed with the idea of drama' – underlay not only his ostensibly dramatic work but also his apocalyptic treatment of history in a more ambitious and scholarly undertaking, *The image of both churches*, which, suggests John King, is governed by the assumption that 'the Reformation provides an essentially comic resolution to the otherwise tragic course of history'.

Bale was also an incorrigible and irrepressible propagandist who knew that dramatic performances which appealed to instincts and prejudices below the belt and somewhat beneath the level of the highest intelligence were a more effective means of spreading the new religion than learned treatises, more telling even than sermons. As a Marian exile in Frankfurt he was encouraged by John Ponet, who in Edward's reign had succeeded as bishop of Winchester that victim of the theatre of protest, Stephen Gardiner. Ponet told him: 'Ballads, rhymes and short toys that be not dear, and will easily be born away do much good at home among the rude people. To the which studies I mind not to pluck you from other more weighty purposes but wish that you would prick other men to such easy exercises ... The ploughman's whistle is no vain instrument.'[26]

This was to teach a grandmother how to suck eggs. Bale's last days, which were spent in the semi-retirement of a canon's house in the cathedral precincts of early Elizabethan Canterbury, saw him still active in promoting satirical sketches with which to hammer home the recent and still fragile Protestant *revanche*, and which were performed by the boys of the king's grammar school. One of these late plays, *A newe comedy or enterlude concernyng thre lawes* (printed 1562) casts 'Hipocrisy' as a Franciscan friar and 'Sodomy' as a monk, and directs that they should be given suitable costumes.[27] On a Friday afternoon in May 1560 a Canterbury tailor found work to do in cutting out what he laughingly called 'an ape's coat'. This was the costume for the part of a popish friar in a play which Bale was to 'set forth' (and perhaps it was the *Thre lawes*) and which was to be given a public performance in one of the large houses of the town, with a charge made for admission. Alderman Okeden (or Ugden), a man of conservative religious views, heard these arrangements being discussed in the tailor's shop and made a fuss. Bale had given up preaching, preferring to stage plays which attacked the friars. 'Yet he himself was a friar and knew their knavery well enough.' Okeden would have nothing to do with this 'trumpery' and announced that he would take himself off to a better play at New Romney, where the famous Whitsuntide mystery plays were still serving as a magnet for conservative sentiment. So the old religious drama and the new were in competition.[28] Here is a rare, even unique, glimpse of a cultural world which we have lost: a transitional epoch of entertainments which survive only in the deceptive aridity of printed texts existing on the extreme margins of modern literary interest, where it tends to be forgotten that they were once enjoyed in provincial towns by audiences who had paid their twopences to get in.

Bale's dramatic works may be called anti-catholic rather than positively protestant. But Nicholas Udall's bible play *Jacob and Esau*, and even more Lewis Wager's *Life and repentaunce of Marie Magdalene*, are theological plays, proof that the themes of predestination and of salvation through faith alone could be convincingly treated on the stage. The audience which saw the Magdalene play was left in no doubt that the heroine's redemption was effected, not by the moral force of her own repentance, touching though the representation of this was, but by purely unmerited grace:

> There was never man borne yet that was able,
> To performe these preceptes iust, holy and stable,
> Save onely Jesus Christ.

So by faith in Christ you have Justification
Freely of his grace and beyond mans operation.

So too with the parallel dramatic tradition of the moralities. A run of
new interludes on the well-worn 'Prodigal Son' theme, with such titles
as *Nice Wanton, Lusty Juventus* and *The Disobedient Child*, reworked
the devices and conventions of late medieval morality, interlarding
heavy-footed protestant moralism with attacks on popery which cast
the vices as priestly and prelatical figures: Ignorance, Hypocrisy,
Cruelty. These little plays are all variants on the theme of hot-headed
and heedless youth, voting with its feet against the salutary disciplines
of home and school. In *Nice Wanton* Ismael tells his sister Dalila:
'Have with thee, Dalila, Farewell our school, Away with Book and
all' – and the stage directions indicate that they should literally cast
their books aside. Later Dalila dies of the pox in the stews, while
Ismael ends on the scaffold. But Juventus, who is well instructed by
the character of Good Counsel, experiences a prodigal-like if dramat-
ically not entirely convincing repentance.[29]

The strategy of the protestant dramatists, one which was as characteristic of primary protestant culture as it would have been inconceivable
a generation later, was to encase the bitter pill of these moral lessons in
the sweet coating of 'mirth', including popular songs of the time like
'Come oer the bourne Bessie' (these were musicals) and plenty of
bawdy. Both the bible plays and the moralities are, even to a modern
ear, startlingly explicit in their treatment of sex. 'Lusty Juventus' gets
into a tight clinch with Little Besse – 'such a gyrle' – and is observed by
Hypocrisie: 'What a hurly burly is here, Smicke smacke and thys
geare, You will to tyck take I feare'. Moros in *The Longer Thou
Livest* is incited by Idleness 'to kiss, to clip, and in bed to play. O with
lusty girls to singe and dance.' The stunning blonde Mary Magdalene,
whose vital statistics are dwelt upon in loving detail, is an accomplished musician. So Infidelitie urges her, most suggestively, to play
upon his recorder. 'Truely you have not sene a more goodlie pipe, it is
so bigge that your hand can it not gripe.' Evidently these clerical
playwrights would have agreed with Prynne's opponent Sir Richard
Baker in a later generation: 'To expect, therefore, that plays should
be altogether without obscene passages, were it not to expect that
Nature should make bodies altogether without privy parts?' Certainly
their taste and sense of decorum was in harmony and continuity with
the late medieval dramatic moralists in whose steps they trod, including the devoutly catholic John Heywood, whose *Play called the foure*

P ('a mery enterlude') contains equally coarse satire directed in a Chaucerian vein against the stock-in-trade of one of the 'Ps', the Pardoner, such as 'a buttock bone of Pentecost'. Invited to kiss 'All Hallows blessed jaw-bone', the Poticary (another of the Ps) exclaimed: 'I never kist a warse;/Ye were as good to kiss All Hallows arse'.[30]

Once dismissed as the insignificant tail-end of a nearly extinct dramatic tradition, as if of merely academic interest, and slight interest at that, these pieces are now understood to have been part of a living theatrical tradition which flourished in the first half of Elizabeth's reign, when many of them were first printed. The fact that they carry cast-lists and stage directions indicating how 'four may play it easily' suggests that the prodigal plays and other interludes were intended for performance not only in schools but also by the typical touring company of 'four men and a boy'. Wager's *Marie Magdalene* contains a reference to those who had paid for admission, and the later reminiscences of an aged inhabitant of Gloucester suggest that these were indeed the repertoire of the travelling players in the years of his Elizabethan childhood.[31] But from the late 1570s, as we shall see, everything began to change.

IV

If the protestant dramatists stole the opposition's costumes and scenery, protestant ballad-mongers anticipated the question put by the nineteenth-century Salvationist William Booth: 'Why should the Devil have all the best tunes?' Just as important as the sermon as a vehicle of propaganda and indoctrination, and more important than the play, because potentially more universal and pervasive, was the so-called 'scripture song'. Scripture songs included the Psalms, rendered in popular ballad metre, but were just as likely to consist of polemical attacks on the Mass or of anticlerical satires with no scriptural content at all. They bore titles like 'The Fantasie of Idolatry', a song of fifty stanzas on the folly of going on pilgrimage, preserved by Foxe 'for posterity hereafter to understand what then was used in England'. (Where should we be without Foxe and his profoundly historiographical instincts?) London merchants encouraged their apprentice boys to 'sing a song against the sacrament of the altar'. In Worcester an eleven-year-old boy composed an anticlerical ballad with the refrain: 'Come down for all your shaven crown'. We may well call these, in the language of our own century, 'protest songs'. They were sung in prison but were also provided as entertainment at wedding feasts, where they were performed by professionals, what Foxe calls 'common singers against the sacraments and ceremonies'. (The evidence of this comes from Essex.) In Mary's days Thomas Rider of Herne in Kent was accused of having conducted a mock procession in an alehouse, 'as it were in derision of the service of the Church'. Rider admitted that 'he hath divers times sung a song both there and in other places', but denied the charge of contempt.[32] Revisionist historians of the English Reformation who deny its popular character should take note of these circumstances.

This was a time when Protestantism was still a religion of protest, at ease with the culture of the streets and of other public places, including inns and alehouses and (as was said in London in 1539) 'vintners' and barbers' shops'. In the reign of Henry VIII the early protestant evangelist Robert Wisdom exhorted his Essex hearers 'to take the Scripture in their hands' when they gathered at the alehouse on Sundays and holy days and 'to talk, commune and reason of it'. When Bishop Bonner complained that this would lead to the abuse of the Bible by drunkards, Wisdom retorted that on the contrary the presence of Scripture would prevent people from getting drunk. In fact at this exciting moment of religious revolution such places were the scene of much heated religious discussion of the kind called by contemporaries 'jangling'. In Mary's reign the secret protestant congregation in London had meetings at various hostelries, where drink was liberally consumed before the sermon. And at Colchester the brethren held their christian exercises in 'the common inns of the town'. A later and more fastidious and inhibited generation of the 'godly' distanced itself from drinking houses, condemning the vices of 'good fellowship' and 'company keeping'. By 1569 it was thought inappropriate by some present that there should have been 'talk . . . of Scripture' on an alebench in Sandwich.[33]

The popular street culture of pre-industrial England consisted of inventive 'pastimes' which, while providing entertainment and a kind of orgiastic release for the participants, were also understood to perform a practical function by correcting offences against social norms or simply by allowing relatively harmless expression to tension and suppressed conflict. These were the rituals of inversion or 'misrule', celebrated at Christmas or carnival time, and also the 'rough ridings' or 'skimmingtons' with which the parish youth periodically demonstrated its disapproval of such irregularities as a cuckolded or harassed husband, or a gross discrepancy of age between marriage partners. Social historians have found the mature Protestantism of the seventeenth century intractably hostile to customs of this kind. But this was not the case in earlier days. At Christmastide in 1535 the young men of Harwich followed their usual practice of invading the church after Evensong with pipes and minstrels, preparing to choose a 'lord of misrule' to preside over the Christmas holidays. The curate plucked the pipe out of the minstrel's hand, hit him on the head with it, broke it in pieces and stamped on the fragments. Fifty years later this would have been described as typical 'puritan' behaviour. But the curate of Harwich was a religious conservative who preached against 'the new learned fellows'. And the revellers were evidently reformers, of a kind. It was said that their intention was to 'solace' the parish and to attract the youth away from dice, cards and other 'games of riot'. When the curate compared them in his next sermon to the Children of Israel dancing and piping before idols the association was indignantly repudiated. They had gathered not for idolatry but 'to eschew vice and to increase virtue'. A generation or two later these stereotyped roles would be reversed. In the mid-sixteenth century it was not orthodox Protestants who took a censoriously negative view of sports and pastimes but the radically sectarian 'free willers' who had made a schism against the Reformation itself, and whose general code of shunning anything and anybody 'wicked' led them into attitudes hard to distinguish from later Puritanism. It was the Marian Protestant martyr John Philpot who attacked 'these contentious schismatics' and 'heretics' for 'condemning of men using things indifferent as shooting, bowling, hawking, with such like', insisting that 'honest pastime was no sin'. Philpot's direct spiritual descendants were not to be noted for their spirited defence of 'honest pastime'.[34]

As with the appropriation of the drama, there was initially no rejection of the medium of balladry,[35] only of the unacceptable uses to which it had hitherto been put. An essential part of this strategy, and one which was quite deliberately populist and appealing, was to make common cause with the popular music of the time, and even with the musicians themselves. Mid-Tudor Bible-readers turning to that Old Testament book, the Song of Solomon, found it entitled 'The Ballet of Ballèts'. Secular ballads and psalms were both accompanied in the mid-sixteenth century by music which derived from the late Henrician and Edwardian court, the cultural milieu of Surrey and Wyatt. For the psalms, no less than ballads, were originally sung to an instrumental accompaniment as galliards and 'measures' (and as to what, precisely, a 'measure' was, no one seems to know). Sternhold's invitation to the boy king to exchange 'fayned rhymes of vanity' for 'holy songs of verity' did not require the monarch to alter his musical taste. And no such agonising choice confronted the public as both ballads and psalms found their way on to the streets, for both shared the same melodies.[36]

Virtually every successful Elizabethan ballad was immediately paid the compliment of a moralistic parody (and this was in itself a measure of success), employing the same tune to words which preserved the original rhythm and cadence while grossly transfiguring the sense. There were moralisations of 'Go from my window', 'The hunt is up', 'John come kisse me now', 'Maid will you marry', 'Into a myrthful May morning' and 'O sweet Oliver'. The hit song 'Row well ye mariners' with its lilting line (the tune is lost) was immediately pirated in no fewer than three distinct parodic versions: 'Roo well ye maryners moralized', 'Row well Godes maryners' and 'Row well ye Christes maryners'. In addition two more ballads, 'A warning to London by the fall of Antwerp' and 'Lamentation from Rome', were set 'to the tune of "Row wel ye Mariners" '. The famous 'Daunce and songe of deathe', beginning 'Can you dance the shaking of the sheets?', adapted the lost ballad 'Dance after my pipe'. Some of these enterprises were of heroic proportions. The miscellany of secular verse *The Court of Venus*, containing lyrics by Surrey, Wyatt and others, was answered in John Hall's *Court of Vertue*, a voluminous album, as we might now say, employing many of the same tunes. Here Wyatt's 'Blame not my lute' became:

> Blame not my lute though it do sounde
> The rebuke of your wicked sinne . . .
> And though this songe doe sinn confute
> And sharply wyckednes subdue,
> Blame not my lute.[37]

This was intended to supplant all other 'books of lecherous ballads'. (But the first and only edition was still in print thirty years later!) Again we should note that these were not Sunday ballads to complement workaday love ballads, but alternatives and rivals, intended to see secular ballads off the field. At least so they were regarded by the religious establishment. Professional ballad writers and ballad mongers like William Elderton, with his famous grog-blossom of a drinker's nose, had a different outlook and interest. They hoped that the two markets would stimulate each other (the strategy of mock-controversy called 'flyting') and were happy to supply both; they were by no means unhappy when Thomas Brice in the godly ballad *Against filthy writing and such delighting* asked his ostensibly uncompromising question: 'Tel me is Christ or Cupide Lord? doth God or Venus reigne?'

That was in 1562. Within twenty years the compromise which Brice had made by adapting the lyrical and musical language of Venus and Cupid to a moralistic purpose became, quite suddenly, no longer tolerable. Thomas Lovell's versified *Dialogue between custom and veritie concerning the use and abuse of dauncing and minstrelsie* (1581) was a landmark in this respect, although we know of it only from a single copy in the Huntington Library in California. Lovell's target was the minstrels, as aiders and abettors of whoredom. This was in harmony with contemporary anxiety about unattached popular musicians which we find reflected in sermons and in the business of the church courts. There they were cast as idle vagrants who seduced the youth of the parish out of church and into the Sunday dances, people as morally dangerous as they were sacrilegious.[38] More interesting is Lovell's onslaught on the ballad industry for seeking to be all things to all men:

Some godly songs they have: some wicked ballads and unmeet: . . .
For filthies they have filthy songs,
For baudes lascivious rimes:
For honest good for sober grave
Songs, so they watch their time.

This was to fall foul of the Epistle of St James, which teaches that out of the same mouth ought not to proceed both blessing and cursing.

With modest men they modest be
With sober they be grave
With lewd and naughtie companie
They also play the knave.

Against the plea that godly songs did more good than sermons Lovell insisted that for every one who learned honesty from the minstrels 'ten times so many learn to practise sin a-pace'. Musicians had no public office to teach. All that was required was 'the preacher with the word, the magistrate with the sword'. It is somewhat ironic that Lovell should have chosen to dedicate this work to the aged London cleric Robert Crowley, for Crowley himself, printer and poet as well as preacher and moralist, represented the kind of mid-sixteenth-century cultural mix which was unacceptable to a younger generation.

Twenty years later the Suffolk preacher Nicholas Bownd complained that ballads were everywhere supplanting psalms, which was to reverse the trend of earlier years. In every country fair and market they were being sung and sold (a scene made familiar by Autolycus in *The Winter's Tale*) and country people were sticking them on their cottage walls for want of anything better to look at. Bownd assumed that ballads and psalms could never peacefully coexist ('they can so hardly stand together') and he contemptuously dismissed the suggestion that minstrels and ballad peddlers might be engaged to popularise the psalms, as they had been in the early years of the Reformation. For the 'singing men' were so notoriously ungodly that it would be better to stop their mouths altogether than allow them to pollute such sacred songs.[39] This was the end, for the time being, of the strategy of parody or 'counterfeit', the death of the godly popular song.

To be sure two such puritan writers are not in themselves evidence of a general cultural about-face. More telling is the fact that the flood of moralistic parodies of the sixties and seventies dwindled to a trickle in the eighties and nineties. 'Greensleeves', the hit of our critical year 1580 (called in that year *'a newe northern dittye'* and in 1584 'a new Courtly Sonnet'), seems to have been a landmark. Its publication was smartly followed by 'Green Sleeves moralized to the Scripture', and other sacred lyrics seized upon its infectious tune, among them 'The godly and virtuous song and ballad' of the Coventry martyr (and player) John Careless. But both Thomas Nashe and Shakespeare wrote disparagingly of this 'device', and with specific reference to 'Greensleeves' Mistress Ford in *The Merry Wives of Windsor* complained that Falstaff's words 'do no more adhere and keep place together then the hundred Psalms to the tune of Green Sleeves'. In 1597 a Kentish vicar sued his parishioners for slander when they accused him of leading the congregation in a rendering of the 25th Psalm ('Unto thee, O Lord, do I lift up my soul') to the tune of 'Greensleeves'.[40]

Subsequently there was a substantial (if never total) divorce of secular and sacred music. 'Psalms' came to mean the Psalms of David and little besides, slow and measured *hymns* mainly designed for congregational singing and no longer enjoying any affinity with that 'small music' of country inns and weddings which George Puttenham sneered at in *The arte of English poesie*. Whereas songs and dances would be published in crotchets and quavers by seventeenth-century musical promoters such as John Playford, psalms were printed in minims and semibreves and sung after the parish clerk, note by note and dwelling as much as two seconds on each. George Wither insisted that to sing the Psalms of David to 'roguish tunes' and 'profane jigs', or to set psalm tunes to profane words, were two equally inadmissible procedures. The implications of this alteration in sensibility can hardly be underestimated. Professor H.G. Koenigsberger has remarked that 'it is difficult to escape the impression that Calvin was profoundly uneasy about music', precisely because he knew that it had 'great power to move the hearts of men', a power which was sensual. If anything this was more true of his heirs, the Calvinists and Puritans. If Koenigsberger is also correct in his hunch that the European musical tradition, as it was to develop in the succeeding centuries, represents one form of secularisation of the religious impulse, the filling of 'a kind of emotional void' which the retreat of religion had left, then at this point of our investigation we are indeed pausing at a significant crossroads, equivalent to what T.S. Eliot called the dissociation of sensibility.[41]

V

The year 1580, or thereabouts, was a date equally critical to the history of Protestantism in its relation to the drama, but here it marked an even more absolute and irretrievable divorce. It is well known that the movement conventionally described as the puritan onslaught on the theatre was a storm which blew up with surprising suddenness in about 1577, its timing apparently linked to the full institutionalisation of the drama with the opening of the first permanent public theatres in London. This was the epoch marked by incessant attacks from the pulpit at Paul's Cross and by the sustained polemics of Gosson, Northbrooke and Stubbes, as well as by Sidney's riposte in the *Defence of Poesy*. Among the reasons propounded for this profound anti-theatrical reaction some may be described as rational and pragmatic: concern with the unfair competition offered to the pulpit, or fear among the city fathers of the threat to public order and decency posed by the playhouses and their inducements to idleness and casual vice. More interesting for our purposes were motives which might be called instinctive, even subliminal: the rejection of dramatic fictions as lies, with a particular objection to the transvestite lie implicit in the acting of female parts by boys; the revulsion against 'filthiness', that is theatrical eroticism; and the urge to close up what has been called 'the idolatrous eye'. Anthony Munday wrote that 'there cometh much evil in the ears, but more at the eyes'. But all in all the reaction seems to any dispassionate and modern eye one of quite unreasonable and unwarranted severity. As Thomas Nashe insisted in *Pierce Pennilesse*, 'Our players are not as the players beyond sea, a sort of squirting bawdy comedians that have whores and common courtesans to play womens' parts and forbear no immodest speech or unchaste action that may procure laughter'.[42]

For the study of protestant culture the most significant and problematical aspect of the anti-theatrical reaction was the particular attack mounted by both Gosson and Stubbes on the religious drama, moving in Gosson's case from an initial endorsement of some plays as 'good' and 'sweet' to condemnation of 'divine' plays as the worst of all, an argument which is elaborated in Stubbes's *Anatomie of Abuses* (1581). Stubbes found it intolerable that the glorious majesty of God should be handled in these 'sacrilegious' performances 'scoffingly, flauntingly and jibingly'. The merits of Christ's Passion were not available to be 'derided and jested at, as they be in these filthy plays and interludes', which was as much as to 'mix scurrility with divinity', or, wrote John Northbrooke, 'to eat meat with unwashed hands', a commonplace probably derived from Erasmus's essay based on the classical adage *illotis manibus*.

Stubbes was the victim of what Nashe called a 'melancholic imagination', but in this case he had caught the crest of a wave. Bible plays would continue to be written and performed for a few more years. As many as fourteen can be traced in Henslowe's Diary and other sources of the 1590s. But even Thomas Lodge, who had clashed with Gosson and whose own own Jonah play was staged as late as 1594, wrote in 1596 that stage plays based on Scripture were 'odious'. After the Blasphemy Act of 1605 they became illegal, and when William Prynne wrote in *Histrio-mastix* in 1637 that the more sublime the matter of the play the more pernicious its fruits he was expressing a commonplace which commanded widespread assent. The reasoning behind the commonplace can be found in Stubbes and represents a drastic repudiation of centuries of religious culture. This, however, happened not in the 1530s but in the 1580s. To *represent* the Word of God mimetically rather than to expound it faithfully was to turn it into an object of mockery. For, as we read in the opening words of St John's Gospel, 'the word is God, and God is the word'. For Stubbes that was an open and shut case.[43]

The consequence was a divorce of the sacred and secular even more complete than that which we have already observed in the field of popular music and verse. The ambition of the reformers and complainers was to close the theatres, Prynne being willing only to allow the *reading* of a select list of play texts. This ambition was not fulfilled until 1642. While Charles I sat secure on his throne Prynne's vast polemical exercise *Histrio-mastix*, a work of hundreds of pages and thousands of learned citations, was a gesture of impotence. The drama was not suppressed but now advanced to its greatest artistic achievement. But having been left to its own devices it became, in the perception of the hyper-religious public, 'filthier', more abandoned than ever. From a more sympathetic and less pejorative viewpoint it must appear that dramatists were now better able to explore the moral and social complexities of the human condition on their own terms and in their own language. After all it would require a singular perversity to prefer *The life and repentaunce of Marie Magdalene* to *Hamlet* or *Measure for Measure* (where, however, theology is still resonant), or even to the more modest and domestic dimensions of, say, *A Woman Killed with Kindness*. So, unwittingly, the about-face in protestant cultural attitudes emancipated the English theatre by completing its secularisation. Now religion would only be seen on stage when stage Puritans, like Jonson's Zeal-of-the-Land Busy, were pilloried, as the popish bishops had once been pilloried, to the infinite vexation of Paul's Cross. And now preaching itself became less histrionic. Prynne deplored 'playerly gestures' as unseemly. 'He is the best Minister who is most unlike a Player, both in his gesture, habit, speech and elocution.'[44]

The cultural evolution and revolution which we have now traced may be reduced to the précis of an alliterative sixteenth-century conceit of the four, or three, Ps. In the 1530s the court musician and dramatist John Heywood, no Protestant and an enemy of Archbishop Cranmer, produced his *Play called the foure P*, a Chaucerian satire of the estates with four principal characters, a Pardoner, a Palmer, a Poticary and a Pedlar. Foxe later suggested that Stephen Gardiner was the victim of three Ps: 'Printers, Players and Preachers'. At this point stage-players were still allies of the Gospel. But Gosson's *Schoole of Abuse* launched a vicious attack on three different Ps: 'Poets, Pipers and Players'; and in 1610 a Paul's Cross sermon defined the enemies of religion as 'the Devil, Papists and Players'. Meanwhile John Awdley had written in *The wonders of England* (1559) that in 1553 (at the death of Edward VI) God had announced judgement on England: 'I shall plague Prince, Prophet and People all'.[45]

VI

It is possible to identify a similar watershed, and at about the same time, in the pictorial arts, and for this we have been prepared by what Stubbes asserted about the wordiness of God as Word. Dr R.W. Scribner has demonstrated in his book *For the Sake of Simple Folk* the extensive and resourceful use of visual propaganda in the early Lutheran Reformation in Germany. The woodcut, reproduced and sold in the form of cheap broadsheets, was a means of communication well adapted to the illiterate and semi-literate, and already available when the Reformation began. It was a medium readily exploited for the mass reproduction of satirical anti-papal cartoons, but also for the clever adaptation of established iconographical types and figures, some of which were used to turn Luther himself into a conventional saint, complete with nimbus and dove. Such propaganda was 'highly successful in exploiting the heritage of the past' and like the English protestant drama was janus-like, looking backward to its models and forward to its objectives. Study of these materials suggests to Scribner that we must modify our impression that the Reformation was propagated chiefly by the written and spoken word. Rather it operated through the hybridisation of media in which visual propaganda played an important part.[46]

The Reformed, or Calvinist, wing of the Reformation was more inhibited in its use of imagery as propaganda, although the technical capacity of the Zürich engravers who illustrated Conrad Gesner's *Historia Animalium* and of the French engravers matched the best that Lutheran Germany had to offer. In 1567 Queen Elizabeth was sent from Geneva a presentation copy of a brilliant satire in the form of a map of the world, the *Mappe-monde novelle papistique*,[47] purporting to be the work of one 'Frangidelphe Escorche-Messes'. This prodigious work of art, evidently originating in Lyon, shows the Catholic world, its cities and inhabitants surrounded by a huge and beautifully depicted octopus, every tentacle and sucker engraved with attentive realism, representing the non-Catholic peoples on the periphery of Europe, including the faithful inhabitants of these islands, 'Anglois, Ecossois, Irlandois'. This is a striking demonstration of what Calvinist artistic satire was capable of achieving, if only it could let its hair down. But, as it was, a reformed *Calendrier historial* (or almanac, the popular literature of the time) which was published in great quantity at Geneva, Lyon and other Calvinist centres in the 1560s, eliminated most of the pictures which had always accompanied such publications, replacing them with verbal information and historical data, both biblical and post-biblical.[48]

In England protestant publicists and evangelists addressed themselves to the same mixture of literacy and illiteracy, which demanded the use of images if a general appeal was to succeed. And initially England differed from Lutheran Germany only in the relatively underdeveloped capacity of its commercial artists and printers to mass-produce suitable pictures. Or so it seems. Such material was so ephemeral that we shall never know how much, or how little, of it there may once have been. But it seems unlikely that the artistic and industrial capacity existed in London for a response to the Reformation challenge on anything like the German scale. Significantly, early Elizabethan broadsheets and ballads were sometimes adorned with pictures printed from old and pre-Reformation stock. For example, *A newe ballade of a lover* 'to the tune of Damon and Pithias' (1568) is incongruously illustrated with old cuts of the saints. But at this very time, in the late sixties, Gyles Godet, a member of the London Huguenot congregation, used the Blackfriars as a forward base for publishing and marketing in England albums of ambitious and highly sophisticated biblical prints in the Parisian manner. These depicted in richly circumstantial detail the story of the Prodigal Son, the History of Joseph, the Life of St Paul and the Creation. Individually these cuts, which were coloured in by children employed for the purpose before they were sold, were as suitable for sticking on the walls of modest middle class homes as the ballads which Bownd complained he had seen in Suffolk cottages. They seem to have cost a penny each. But Godet, who had arrived in England in the 1540s, died in 1571, a little before Bible pictures ceased to be acceptable to English protestant taste.[49]

Mid-sixteenth-century English bibles were copiously illustrated, as well as being equipped with maps and other visual aids. And, very famously, Foxe's 'Book of Martyrs' incorporated a stunning range of varied graphical material. This included the dumb show of an array or 'pageant' of popes and a visual display of the ten great persecutions of the Church. There were historical narrative pictures of the Emperor Henry IV at Canossa and of the poisoning of King John, plenty of stylised martyrs in the flames, which were repeated whenever the text called for them, and a sharply observed caricature of Bishop Bonner caning the bare backsides of protestant prisoners in his orchard at Fulham. This last picture was perhaps Foxe's own work (we know that he drew, from the marginalia of his correspondence), for when Bonner was shown it in prison he is said to have roared with laughter, exclaiming: 'A vengeance on the fool! How could he get my picture drawn so right?'[50] Dr Tessa Watt believes that some of these pictures, especially a number of ambitious folded pull-outs, were also detached from the book and stuck on walls. One set, surviving in Cambridge, has been coloured in, evidently for this purpose.

So up to about 1580 a very positive answer could have been given, and in the protestant tradition of plain sincerity and biblical and historical truth, to the question later put by Francis Quarles. Christ is presented in the Scripture as Sower, Fisher and Physician: 'And why not presented so, as well to the eye as to the ear?' Quarles asked.[51] But from the 1580s Protestants began to direct the eye, that potentially idolatrous eye, inward, rejecting realistic religious pictures as unreservedly as bible plays and godly ballads. Bibles for the most part ceased to be illustrated. Other newly published works which seem to cry out for illustration, like Thomas Beard's collection of instructive providences, *The theatre of Gods judgments* (1597, 1612, 1631), are totally devoid of pictures. Book illustration in England seems to regress, just when we might expect it to advance. The later editions of Foxe (1596, 1620, 1632) continued to carry the same brilliant illustrative apparatus. But the same old woodcuts were used over and over again (to be replaced in 1641 with copper engravings of the same subjects) and I do not think that these pictures would have been newly commissioned at any time between 1580 and 1630.

'These are certain pictures', wrote the Somerset minister Richard Bernard in 1610, introducing his book *Contemplative pictures with wholesome precepts*. But there *are* no pictures in the ordinary and literal sense, only what might be called word pictures, of God, Goodness, Heaven; the Devil, Badness, Hell. Bernard explains that his pictures are not 'popish and sensible for superstition, but mental, for divine contemplation'. By this time Protestant England had moved from a cultural phase which may be described as iconoclastic, characterised by the attack on unacceptable images but consistent with the enjoyment of good images, to an episode lasting some few decades around 1600 which Karl-Josef Höltgen has called iconophobic, rejecting all material images and implying an advanced and radical application of the Second Commandment of the Decalogue.[52]

The continued use of religious pictures by Catholics as objects of devotion at a time of exceptionally intense confessional tension encouraged a protestant attitude of total rejection of all art work of this kind as necessarily popish and illicit. Writing from the Tower of London to the Earl of Leicester about one of the Duke of Norfolk's principal agents, implicated in the Ridolfi Conspiracy of 1571, Sir Owen Hopton wrote: 'I have sent you a picture of Christ which was in [his] comb-case, whereby is partly seen the lewdness of his religion'. Witness, too, these items in inventories drawn up in 1584 of the contents of various Catholic houses which had been raided in the search for incriminating evidence or suspected persons: 'twelve printed superstitious pictures', 'certain pictures . . . and one crucifix', 'a picture of (as it is termed) the Judgment Day', 'a picture of Christ'. It was images of this kind ('eight or ten pictures of the Passion of Christ') which the doomed Mary Queen of Scots stuck above the chimney piece of her chamber at Fotheringhay Castle, after her keeper, Sir Amyas Paulet, had removed from the same position her cloth of estate: an ironic reversal of the procedure which in ten thousand English parish churches had replaced the rood imagery of the Passion with the Royal Arms. In 1500 for a lay person of humble status to be found in possession of a book (almost any book) was to be suspected of heresy. It seems that by 1600 to be found in possession of a picture (almost any picture) was to be a suspected papist.[53]

It is a good question how many pictures, and of what kinds, were regularly seen by late Elizabethan men and women. Research based on 613 fifteenth- and sixteenth-century household inventories, mostly detailing the contents of comfortable and well-furnished homes, reveals that only 63 list pictures or other works of art of any kind, suggesting that 'the majority of even the most prosperous classes in Tudor England did not own any paintings or sculpture at all'.[54] Wall paintings had been wiped out in many, probably most, parish churches in response to the Elizabethan injunction against 'feigned images of idolatry', even the official church homilies declaring that the seeking out of images was 'the beginning of whoredom'. Much stained and painted glass had equally fallen foul of the Injunctions and of private acts of iconoclasm. It is often suggested that the vacuum left by this devastation was filled by the alternative cultic image of Queen Elizabeth, literally taking the place of the previously popular Virgin Mary as Queen of Heaven. The argument would have more force if pictures of the queen had in fact been placed in parish churches. But the replacement of the rood imagery by the wholly abstract symbolism of the royal coat of arms meant that churchgoers were not required to look at different pictures but at no pictures at all. In one Essex church scriptural texts were inscribed in the walls warning against the unlawfulness of pictures of God the Father and of Purgatory which had survived and were perhaps hard to eradicate.[55]

Professor Höltgen suggests that the only picture to penetrate the iconophobia of the Elizabethan schoolroom was the cut at the back of every edition of Lyly's Grammar, showing three boys raiding a pear tree. The young Henry Peacham was beaten after being caught copying this picture. There were no picture books for children.[56] We are left with woodcuts which, printed on broadsheets and the like, were perhaps more widely available than we now have any means of knowing. Since no Englishman of this generation thought to preserve in any systematic fashion the ephemeral woodcuts of the age, very few survive: as few as 300 examples out of perhaps 3000 titles, representing as many as 3 million copies, a survival rate of one in ten thousand.[57] Less still survives of the most prevalent art work of the period, painted wall hangings. Keyboard instruments, which were to be found in most 'comfortable' homes, were richly decorated in thoroughly representational modes.

Nevertheless Höltgen envisages a society suffering from severe visual anorexia, and gives a sympathetic account of three turn-of-the-century writers whose efforts to make bricks without straw in recovering some native appreciation of art and the makings of a theory of art heralded the Jacobean and Caroline artistic revival to come. These were Robert Dallington, Henry Peacham and Richard Haydocke. Haydocke, in particular, was in a peculiar position, even if one leaves out of account his odd accomplishment of preaching in his sleep, which James I took pains to expose as fraudulent. An Oxford scholar and provincial medical practitioner of ostensibly conventional protestant views, Haydocke undertook the translation of Lomazzo's *Trattato dell'Arte*. This was the bible of late Mannerism, in which religious pictures were considered 'essential elements of faith and devotion'. Haydocke betrays his discomfort in a note appended to Lomazzo's ruling that God the Father ought to be painted only with perfect colours: 'And I think he should not be painted at all'. He mistranslated the term *culto divino*, proposed by Lomazzo as the highest function of art, as 'civil discipline'. That was a desperate attempt to naturalise the high priest of advanced Counter-Reformation art in a wholly alien environment where pictures, if allowed at all, were objects to be read for the civil lessons they contained rather than used as stimuli for the sense and spirit.[58]

Nevertheless Professor Höltgen's odd trio point the way forward to the more extreme revision of religious aesthetics which we connect with the anti-Calvinist reaction of Arminianism and, presently, with Archbishop Laud's associated programme of liturgical enrichment, the 'beauty of holiness'. After all the age of extreme iconophobia was quite short, equivalent to little more than a single generation. As early as 1626 even a conventional provincial preacher, albeit occupying the pulpit in Canterbury Cathedral, 'a wonderful piece of work to the beholder', could articulate a revived apology for images as the books of the ignorant and illiterate. Describing an elaborate stone conduit erected in Canterbury at the expense of Archbishop Abbot and decorated not only with heraldry and inscriptions but also with 'lively images' in the shape of sculpted representations of the Seven Virtues, James Cleland spoke of 'the speaking power of *Pictures*': 'For herein the gross conceit is led on with pleasure, and informed while it feels nothing but delight. And if *Pictures* have been accounted the Books of *Idiots*, behold here the benefit of an Image without Offence'. The sentiment matches George Herbert's near-contemporary lines in 'The Church-porch':

> A verse may finde him, who a sermon flies,
> And turn delight into a sacrifice.

These were modest enough beginnings. But within ten years, and under the mastership of William Beale, the chapel of St John's College Cambridge, a place not noted for ignorance and illiteracy, was 'dressed up after a new fashion'. It had an altar frontal depicting the deposition from the Cross and large gilt-framed pictures around the walls portraying the life of Christ 'from his conception to his ascension', with a large crucifix behind the altar which was surmounted with a canopy painted with angels and a 'sun with great light beams and a dove in the midst'. By this time the vicar of Sturry, near Canterbury, a man 'famously noted for a forward agent in superstitious and popish innovations', had a large painted crucifix framed and hanging in his parlour. Such were the aesthetics of English Arminianism.[59]

Meanwhile, pending the restoration to 'gross conceits' of images, it is a good question what the mind's eye sees if it has not been fed with pictures, has never been taught to see in that way. Exponents of Renaissance rhetoric and logic and its affinity with the printed book tell us that the educated minds of this generation had their image-forming capacity replaced with the lines and brackets of severely practical Ramist logic, these forming abstract mnemonic patterns which almost literally imprinted the scheme of salvation and other syllogistic arguments on the memory in diagrammatic form. The third Earl of Huntingdon, Queen Elizabeth's lieutenant in the North of England and a top administrator rather than a scholar, had nothing to decorate the walls of his headquarters in York (the enlarged and enriched former mansion of the abbots of St Mary's Abbey) save some maps, a 'table' of the Ten Commandments, and another 'table in a frame, containing the cause of salvation and damnation'. Such tables resembled the 'Hustavla' which, with its Bible verses, hung on walls throughout protestant Sweden, inculcating religious doctrine associated with church, state and household.[60]

Ramist diagrammatic logic was, in the perception of Walter Ong and Frances Yates, only one particularly arresting demonstration of the significance of print (Ramus being in Father Ong's view a mere 'epiphenomenon' of the age of print), for print was far more than a mode of information diffusion. It was a mechanism for sequestering words from their natural habitat – sound, a humane habitat of unforced, instinctive interaction and participation – by imprisoning words on the page as simply 'marks', whose spatial relations became important, rather than the sequence of things said. Now the lecturer or preacher could say: 'Look at page seven, line three, the fourth word'. Here, for the student of Protestantism and of mentalities, is the significance of those seated figures depicted (just before pictures disappeared from their world and they ceased to be visible) with their Bibles open on their laps as the preacher expounds. Of the 'She Puritan' John Earle remarks that her piety is much in the turning up of her eye and the turning down of the corner of the leaf when she hears named chapter and verse. Sensing the deep and structural consistency of print culture with Calvinism, Frances Yates spoke of the 'inner iconoclasm' enforced by Ramus.[61]

VII

However no man can live by diagrams alone. Nor is it clear that the mind which is fed on print alone sees only print. This is to say that Calvinism did not succeed in killing the imagination, even if that was its purpose, which is a dubious proposition. Richard Bernard's *Contemplative pictures* were, he tells us, *mental pictures*, and they exceed in visual power what any country artist could have hoped to achieve in rural Nottinghamshire or Somerset, the counties where Bernard ministered. And yet they are of no special distinction, consisting of language well within the reach of any competent Jacobean preacher: 'The azured sky his comely curtain, his privy chamber, the place of unspeakable pleasure. His face is a flame of fire, his voice thunder, his wrath dread and terrible horror'. This is Bernard's mental picture of God and it recalls Sir Philip Sidney's *Defence of Poesy*, in which the Psalms are called 'a divine Poem', the psalmist 'a passionate lover of that unspeakable and everlasting beauty to be seen by the eyes of the mind'. For David 'maketh you, as it were, see God coming in his Majesty'. Horace expressed the thought in his double-edged epigram, *Ut pictura poesis*. But we should note that it is *poesis* which is Sidney's subject, not *pictura*. Considering the case of a man who has never seen an elephant or a rhinoceros, he suggests that all the description in the world will be no substitute for pictures of those beasts 'well painted', which would at once give him 'a judicial comprehending of them'. But this is merely intended to strengthen the main argument, which is that poetry, a *speaking picture*, performs an analogous and enlightening function. Sidney was a man of letters, not an artist (in our modern sense), still less an art theorist, and he was far from proposing a general scheme of aesthetics. He did not suggest that sometimes a picture may serve as a painted poem.[62]

Behind Sidney there stands Erasmus, who we have no reason to believe ever looked at a picture with any aesthetic appreciation, or lifted those elusive eyes long enough from the printed or manuscript page to do so, but who wrote that the text of the New Testament conveys 'the living image of His holy mind, and the speaking, healing, dying, risen Christ himself'; rendering him 'so fully present that you would see less if you gazed upon him with your very eyes'.[63] But what, we must ask again, was it, is it, to 'see'? Did a Protestant like Richard Bernard expect or even permit his hearers and readers to respond to his contemplative and verbal pictures by forming mental images in the manner of the Ignatian spirituality expressed by John Donne when he wrote: 'Mark in my heart, O soul, where thou dost dwell,/ The picture of Christ crucified'?

That is where an account of protestant culture ought to begin, not end. In one direction it would lead us to those pictures to be read, the protestant emblems. Emblems locked an almost gnomic message into the enigmatic combinations of allegorical image, some lines of verse and a terse motto. Like the parables of the New Testament (and the emblemist Francis Quarles called them 'silent parables') they concealed the truth as much as they revealed it, so that, as Christ says in Matthew 13:13–15, seeing they should not see, and hearing not hear, lest at any time they should understand in their hearts and should be converted. The Geneva Bible comments on this text: 'All men cannot understand these mysteries'. This resembles Sidney's poetic theory, that fictions which represent divine truth metaphorically, 'feigned poems', may be more instructive than plain factual statements. It is a sixteenth-century version of the principle, dear to the Tractarians of the nineteenth century, of 'reserve in the communication of religious knowledge': what a more vulgar age (our own) calls 'economy with the truth'.

It was also true to Renaissance hermeticism, the taste for the cryptic and mysterious. But if there was a literary Renaissance there was also a literary Reformation, which affirmed truth in the plain beauty of Scripture, eliciting from the disciples that cry of relief: Now thou speakest no parables. It was to this tradition that Milton was heir when he declared that the rich variety of biblical forms exceeded the pagan classics 'not in their divine argument alone, but in the very critical art of composition', in which 'over all the kinds of lyrical poesy', Scripture was 'incomparable'. As Barbara Lewalski has observed, the dependence of the English poets on the cadences of only one body of biblical material, the Psalms, is material in itself for a major study: but not one which this modest essay will attempt.[64]

However one observation may be allowed to a mere historian, and one who in the manner of modern social historians lives some distance down-market from the great seventeenth-century poets and spends his time trying to penetrate commonplace mentalities rather than to converse with the majestic mind of John Milton. When George Herbert heard the Bible, or read it, he made sense of it as any other Protestant did, in terms of its supposed inner coherence and integrity, scripture employed to unlock scripture. Or so he indicates in the poem *The Holy Scripture*: 'This verse marks that, and both do make a motion/Unto a third, that ten leaves off doth lie'. A Ramist diagram forming a preface to my own copy of the Geneva Bible, an edition of 1603, tells the reader, as it were the ordinary reader: 'Mark and consider the coherence of the text, how it hangeth together'. Even the formally illiterate were capable of this kind of scriptural understanding. Robert Passfield, a servant of the exemplary Chester Puritan John Bruen, was said to be 'utterly unlearned, being unable to read a sentence or write a syllable'. Yet he was 'so well acquainted with the history of the Bible' that if asked where such a saying or sentence occurred 'he would with very little ado tell them in what book and chapter they might find it'.[65]

The coherence was as much typological as it was logical and textual, the plain truth not excluding the symbolic mode. Among the endlessly rich catalogue of biblical types and tropes Professor Lewalski draws our attention, in order, to sin as a state of sickness, Christ as healing ('is there no balm in Gilead?'), death and life, sin as darkness, Christ as light, sin as bondage, salvation as the release of captives, the Christian life as pilgrimage ('strangers and pilgrims'), as childhood ('except ye be converted and become as little children'), as chastisement, purgation, trial through affliction (the metaphor of Job), the Christian as sheep with Christ the shepherd, as 'God's husbandry', a seed, a plant, a vine, the Church as vineyard, or as a lodge in a cucumber garden, a barren fig tree, or, most compelling of all, a building composed of lively stones. The single word 'sacrifice' was the central jewel of a cluster of precious associations or, to vary the image, a mansion the many rooms of which the protestant mind never finished exploring.[66]

What should be grasped by the social and cultural historian who may have been too much swayed by recent talk of the growing division of élite and popular cultures in early modern Europe is that all this fertile imagery was as accessible to the obscure and ordinary bible scholar and sermon-goer as it was to the erudite. Indeed this was shared ground. The Geneva Bible advises the reader to 'diligently keep such order of reading the scriptures' as his calling will allow: 'At the least twice every day this exercise to be kept . . . The time once appointed hereunto after a good entry be no otherwise employed.' This was how the imaginative world of the Bible became the mentality of the literate or scarcely literate lay person, whose mental powers are consistently underestimated by those historians who assume that Protestantism was a message which must have passed clean over his head. The proof is in the many tedious but still deeply impressive letters printed in Foxe's book, written by or to the artisan martyrs of the Marian persecution, which suggest minds so steeped in the cross-references and resonant concordances of Scripture as to be incapable of exercising themselves in any other way. As the martyr John Bradford wrote to a certain Joyce, 'a faithful woman in her heaviness': 'You are one of his lively stones – be content therefore to be hewn and snagged at . . . You are of God's corn, fear not therefore the flail . . . You are one of Christ's lambs, look therefore to be fleeced, haled at, or even slain.'[67] This was protestant culture, and while it was the culture of Herbert and Milton, it was also a kind of popular culture.

POSTSCRIPT

This chapter was written before I had the opportunity to read Ernest B. Gilman's monograph *Iconoclasm and Poetry in the English Reformation: Down Went Dagon* (Chicago, 1986), a book which investigates in the poetic record of the age 'the continuous interplay, and the occasional major collision, between strongly iconic and strongly iconoclastic impulses', embodying 'the modifications forced on Italian assumptions by the Reformation'. Gilmore begins with 'the most unassimilable, and yet . . . one of the most attractive doctrines of the Italian humanists – the set of assumptions about the indissoluble bond between language and the visual image that were compressed into the old Horatian phrase, ut pictura poesis'. These assumptions in their English protestant transmogrification conveyed 'a kind of linguistic imperialism', paintings themselves comprehended as a form of language. Yet the word itself was invested with strongly iconic properties.

The protestant English emblem had a strange birth in the midst of iconoclasm and logocentrism. The Calvinist divine Andrew Willet's *Sacrorum emblematum* was a 'blind' emblem book, without pictures. So was Ben Jonson's *Epigrammes*. Its author, deeply uneasy about his unequal association with Inigo Jones, held that 'of the two, the Pen is more noble than the Pencill'. Francis Quarles, the greatest English emblemist, was heir to this tradition but as a Laudian was also partially emancipated from it, the plagiariser but also the protestant bowdleriser of Jesuit images. This represented 'a difficult attempt to insert a pictorial element into . . . a potentially hostile literary culture'. John Donne navigated in these same treacherous waters between the adoring and scorning of images. He filled the Deanery at St Paul's with pictures; but as a preacher insisted that St Paul's rapture was not 'in a *Vidit*, but an *Audivit*. It is not that he *saw*, but that he *heard unspeakable things*.' 'The eare is the Holy Ghosts first doore'. According to Dryden, John Milton 'saw Nature . . . *through the spectacles of books*.' Yet blind Milton too was 'schizoid' rather than simply iconophobic. But in his thwarted vision the iconoclastic impulse of the Reformation was amplified and transmuted into a revolutionary aesthetic. Spenser, Quarles, Donne and Milton all had to manage the 'confrontation none of them could avoid between the image and the Word'.

5 Wars of Religion

I

'Curse ye Meroz, said the angel of the Lord: curse ye bitterly the inhabitants thereof; because they came not to the help of the Lord, to the help of the Lord against the mighty.' These words sounded a discordant note in the otherwise ecstatic song of that Joan of Arc-like figure, the prophetess Deborah, to whom Queen Elizabeth was compared, victorious leader of Israel against the foreign oppressor Sisera. If Meroz was cursed for its neutrality, Zebulon and Naphtali were praised as tribes which had hazarded their lives unto the death in the war now won. 'And the stars in their courses fought against Sisera . . . So let all thine enemies perish, O Lord.'

Not many sermons are now preached on Judges chapter five. Whole tracts of the Old Testament, which have to do with war and slaughter, are found to have little to say to our condition and are left to return, as it were, to a state of nature. It was otherwise in the mid-seventeenth century when Stephen Marshall, minister of the Essex village of Finchingfield, preached on no fewer than sixty occasions on Judges 5:23, the cursing of Meroz. The sermon originated as a parliamentary 'fast sermon', delivered to the House of Commons in February 1642 on the eve of the Civil War. Later, in one of the minor military engagements of the war itself, a group of parliamentary soldiers who fell into enemy hands cited this sermon as the reason why they had taken up arms. Perhaps they had printed copies of it in their knapsacks.[1]

'Wars of Religion' is a phrase capable of more than one construction. The Christian religion itself is often compared to warfare, following St Paul's imagery of 'the whole armour of God' in his letter to the Ephesians, and some of its institutional expressions, from the Templars to the Jesuits and on to the Salvation Army, have assumed military or quasi-military forms. To this very day church-goers still sing some of the old military hymns: 'Onward Christian Soldiers', 'Soldiers of Christ Arise'. In the sixteenth century even the near-pacifist Erasmus could publish a book of spiritual edification under the title *Enchiridion Militis Christiani*: literally 'the stabbing sword of the Christian soldier'. Later, in the post-Reformation English Church, the metaphor remained accessible and attractive. One notes in the early seventeenth century titles like *The christian conflict, The warfare of christians* and, somewhat later, Bunyan's *Holy War*. In Mary's reign Bishop Ridley wrote to his fellow-martyr John Bradford of 'this chivalry and warfare, wherein I doubt not but we be set to fight under Christ's banner and his cross against our ghostly enemy the devil'.[2]

Read in isolation it is not obvious from Stephen Marshall's sermon on Meroz Cursed that he was talking about a material rather than a ghostly enemy, or about warfare in a literal sense. He was not the first English preacher to handle this scripture. Preaching in Canterbury Cathedral in 1622, with no thought of literal warfare in mind, a canon of that great church spoke of the bitter curse laid on the inhabitants of Meroz: 'And no less curse doth lie on the Inhabitants of any Place and Country, when the Lord is in arms, that do not by their prayers help the poor weak Church'.[3] England was about to go, half-heartedly, to war. But this was not a recruiting sermon. Only towards the peroration of his 1642 sermon does Marshall say explicitly: 'It may be some of you may be called, as soldiers, to spend your blood in the Church's cause'. And whether 'the Church's cause' was to be defended in Ireland or in England itself, Marshall did not say.

The military paradigm is so apt and so vivid that sometimes Christian publicists have started at a spiritual and metaphorical level with the analogy of holy violence and have ended up in the midst of actual violence. Thus Thomas Müntzer, the arch-radical and Guy Fawkes of the continental Reformation, became intoxicated with his own violent rhetoric and while announcing in eschatological and millenarian terms the triumph of God's elect found himself at the head of an insurgent army in the Peasants' War. How far this was intended remains uncertain. Eastern Europe under Socialism has identified Müntzer as leader of a people's revolution. But it appears that his sword was the sword of the Lord and of Gideon, not an instrument of social insurrection or a violent midwife, as it were, to the modern world. He was neither a socialist nor a naturally violent man. While his peasants went to their slaughter in the rout of Frankenhausen their leader took refuge in bed, feigning illness, to be ignominiously dragged to torture and execution. Perhaps it had all been a terrible mistake.[4]

Professor Olive Anderson has shown how the Victorian age transformed the British soldier from a near-criminal object of fear and contempt to a specimen of exemplary Christian perfection. One or two well-publicised examples helped. The man of letters Edmund

Gosse later remembered how his mother had returned home with a giant guardsman, whom she seems to have picked up on a bus, and whom she proceeded to convert to her own evangelical faith. Subsequently the man died an edifying death in the Crimea and Mrs Gosse told the story of 'The Guardsman of the Alma' in a tract which sold more than half a million copies.[5] Soon it was a common expectation that military men would not only keep their powder dry but trust in God. In the 1914–18 War the Church organised a 'National Mission of Repentance and Hope', principally because the evidence of venereal disease among our magnificent fighting men jarred with these notions about the consistency of martial valour and moral, indeed Christian, rectitude.[6] The sermons preached in wartime by Bishop Winnington Ingram of London differed hardly at all from those he had delivered before the war. Then 'Into the Fighting Line' had been an address on missionary work. Now the subject was killing, literally, but in the same righteous cause. When Sir Henry Newbolt wrote 'The Vigil', long before 1914, did he envisage anything like the Somme, was it war in the ordinary sense that he had in mind?

> Think that when to-morrow comes
> War shall claim command of all,
> Thou must hear the roll of drums,
> Thou must hear the trumpet's call.[7]

This was what was said to young men at Clifton (or, in Winnington Ingram's case, Marlborough) in the Edwardian age, whatever, if anything, was meant by it. Later Newbolt was embarrassed by 'Lampada Vitae', as was Sir Edward Elgar by 'Land of Hope and Glory'.

A good subject for a PhD thesis exists in the convergence of religious rhetoric and martial enthusiasm in post-Reformation England, another age of militant Christianity and of Christian militancy. We have heard already from Bishop Aylmer ('God is English' Aylmer) who berated 'milksops' and boasted: 'It hath been always said of the English and yet is . . . that either they will win or they will die'.[8] Those words belonged to an era of dynastic wars which was coming to an end in the very year that they were uttered, 1559. But in the epoch of religious conflicts which followed, protestant preachers were welcome and at home in the armed camps and behind the siege works: on the ramparts at Berwick, or at Le Havre in 1562, or in the English expeditionary force to the Low Countries in 1585 when the commander, Leicester, put at the head of his orders for the day the maxim that 'no good event of any action can be expected wherein God is not first and principally honoured and served'. Preaching and psalm-singing were established in the army before they became generally available amenities of civilian life.[9] In 1589 there appeared from the press *A forme of prayer thought fitte to be dayly used in the English armie in France*. Of a professional English soldier, the veteran of no fewer than seven campaigns, it was said after his death in 1632 at the Siege of Maastricht: 'He carried into the army not only sword and spear, weapons for a soldier: but for his Christian warfare he had his Bible, his Prayer Book, and other authors of holy devotion'.[10]

One respect in which English Protestants remained backward-looking and unprogressive was in their attachment to antique military values. This was an aspect of the quaint and insular archaism of English values, architecturally recorded in the early years of the seventeenth century in the conceit of the mock medievalism of Bolsover Castle, built by the Cavendishes on the perch of a Derbyshire hilltop, Spenser's *Faerie Queene* in stone. For English Protestants sin was not only wicked. It was also degenerate and effeminate. Almost the only pastimes of which Puritans approved, the only truly lawful games, were archery and other martial arts. When the Chester magistrates cleaned up the midsummer shows they replaced those naked boys in nets with a knight on horseback in full body armour.[11] 'This of old', ran the caption on one side of an illustrated title-page designed by an Ipswich preacher, and the pictures show a booted and spurred foot, an open Bible and a mailed fist grasping a lance: images which were matched with a contrasted collage of modern values, a stockinged leg and fancy shoe, cards, dice and a delicately gloved hand holding a drinking glass. The Parliamentarian of the 1620s, Sir John Eliot, expressed a desire to stand erect in church to repeat the Creed, drawn sword in hand.[12] A book by the Somerset preacher Richard Bernard, *Bible battels*, was not a book about spiritual combat but a treatise which proposed that modern armies could do worse than study the strategy of Joshua.[13]

The attractiveness of Prince Henry, James I's eldest son who died young in 1612, lay in part in his personification of such values. He was an ardent figure whose very name (as an echo of Henry VIII), together with a reputation for soundness in religion, promised to bring about that convergence of military glory, macho monarchy and protestant zeal which was the natural potential of the English Reformation (as too of the Swedish) but which because of the vagaries of dynasticism had not been realised in the reigns of a child, a woman and James I, *rex pacificus*. Nor was this ideal to be realised subsequently, except belatedly in the divisive and unacceptable shape of Oliver Cromwell. 'Give me leave', wrote the translator of a French work on the *Mysterie of iniquitie* (that is, the papacy) in dedicating the book to Prince Henry, 'that I may live to march over the Alps, and to trail a pike before the walls of Rome, under your Highness standard.' A bishop hoped that the prince would prove 'a terror to that self-exalting Kingdom and Monarchy of the great Capitolian Priest'. After his death one of his chaplains declared that 'all the world were sat to see and hearken how his Highness's hopeful, youthful age should be employed'.[14]

For the historian these sound like echoes of an event still to come: the Civil War of the 1640s, a war fought on the parliamentary side by Christian soldiers in a special and double sense. In the first year of that war an enterprising publisher offered for sale *The souldiers pocket Bible*, a cheap little pamphlet of sixteen pages furnishing 'a fit soldier to fight the Lord's Battles' with a collection of essential scriptural texts 'to supply the want of the whole Bible, which a soldier cannot conveniently carry about him'. The 116 verses from the Old Testament and just three from the New Testament were grouped under such headings as 'A Soldier must be valiant for God's Cause', 'A soldier must put his confidence in God's wisdom and strength' and 'A Soldier must pray before he goes to fight'. Two Old Testament narratives were included in their entirety, neither of which were much emphasised even during the wars of the twentieth century, let alone by today's more pacific Christians. The first was a story from the Book of Judges of the war between the Children of Benjamin and the Men of Israel, when Benjamin put into the field twenty-six thousand men 'that drew sword' and succeeded in slaughtering in two successive days of battle a grand total of forty thousand Israelites, only to suffer ninety-six per cent casualties themselves on the third day. 'And the Israelites gleaned of them by the way five thousand men, and pursued after them unto Gidon and slew two thousand men of them. So that all that were slain that day of Benjamin were five and twenty thousand men, that drew sword.' The second story was no less bloody but, for the comfort of the godly military mind, less ambivalent. In the Second Book of Chronicles Abijah with an army of four hundred thousand confronted Jeroboam with eight hundred thousand. But though outnumbered two to one Abijah had the Lord on his side: 'We belong to the Lord our God and have not forsaken him.

And behold this God is with us as a Captain. O ye Children of Israel, fight not against the Lord God of your fathers, for ye shall not prosper.' Nor did they. In the ensuing engagement Jeroboam's cunning ruse of an ambush failed and he lost 'five hundred thousand chosen men'.[15]

A study of this subject which stops short of the Civil War invites some sense of irony, for a great deal of the martial ardour of the age existed only in the mind, in this Rambo-like world of God's Old Testament killing machine. Before 1642 England was not in fact a highly or even effectively militarised society. Since the days of Henry VIII the country had engaged only sporadically and with marked lack of success in ground operations on the European mainland. Expeditionary forces were rare events. Both the political will and the administrative capacity to tap the manpower and wealth of the commonwealth for military purposes were conspicuously absent, and England played little part in the generalised European conflict of the Thirty Years' War. Such part as was played is vividly enshrined in Canterbury Cathedral, where a number of garishly baroque and military monuments remind us that the 1620s were the only decade of significant hostilities between the 1590s and the 1640s. The outcome of these adventures was as futile as their motivation was confused. Clarendon observed in the opening pages of his *History of the Rebellion and Civil Wars in England* (making the moralistic point that nations do not know when they are well off) that the English people at that time were eager to engage in the European struggle but reluctant to will the means.[16]

II

Nevertheless a good case can be made for regarding the Civil War which followed in the 1640s as the Thirty Years' War which England had lost out on, 'England turned Germany'. A group of Puritans preparing to leave Herefordshire for New England in the 1630s expressed regret at having to abandon 'the stage of Europe, where we are all to act our parts in the destruction of the Great Whore'.[17] If these men had stayed at home they would have seen the action they thirsted for, if not quite in the form and scenario which they had expected. The village from which they wrote was soon the scene of siege warfare as the local Royalists moved in on Brampton Bryan Castle, defended in her husband's absence by the redoubtable Lady

Brilliana Harley. The Puritanism of Robert and Brilliana Harley was the only indigenous factor in Herefordshire favouring the outbreak of a civil war, for religion was the only point of difference between this family and its dependents and the other gentry families of the county with whom they would otherwise have been on the best of terms. For the Harleys the Civil War was quite simply a war to defend true religion.[18] Certainly Charles I was not 'the Great Whore' in his own right and person, and it was not until after the first Civil War that the appellation 'Man of Blood' came to be attached to him. But he had persuaded his opponents that he was incapable of withstanding the forces of the Romish Antichrist and so had betrayed his sacred trust in the most critical area of its application, rendering himself unfit to govern. That was why the divine Richard Baxter took the parliamentary side, not because he wanted to alter the political constitution of England but because Protestantism was not safe under this man's government.[19]

Consequently Anthony Fletcher, concluding a book of four hundred pages on the outbreak of the Civil War, writes that 'there is a real sense in which the English Civil War was a war of religion'. And John Morrill, in a foretaste of a major study yet to come, suggests that comparison between what some historians call 'the English Revolution' and events elsewhere in 1789 and 1917 have missed the point: 'The English civil war was not the first European revolution: it was the last of the Wars of Religion'.[20] There were, Morrill suggests, three distinct and separable perceptions of misgovernment or modes of opposition in the Long Parliament which, contrary to all expectation when that body first assembled in November 1640, found itself at war with its king two years later. These were *localist* (resentment of intrusive misgovernment, associated with ideal sentiment and material interest at the county level), *legal-constitutionalist* (resentment of the invasion of rights and liberties by arbitrary government, expressed in legal and philosophical terms of a secular order) and *religious* (resentment of the betrayal of orthodox religion, not only by 'popery' but by covert popery, thinly disguised as 'Arminianism'). Of these oppositional modes Morrill considers that only the third was capable of launching and sustaining a civil war, since localist and legal-constitutionalist perceptions of misrule lacked the necessary momentum and passion. 'It was the force of religion [and, Morrill seems to be saying, *only* the force of religion] that drove minorities to fight, and forced majorities to make reluctant choices.' Religious opposition differed from other forms of opposition in its passionate intensity and in the extremity of its rhetoric (Meroz Cursed) which, in its divisiveness, was mainly responsible for conjuring up the opposite, reactive, side. Without the Royalists a civil war could not have been staged, and Royalism was initially a religious cause as much as, if not more than, it was a political one. So far Morrill has not discussed the affinity, as mental and rhetorical structures, of religion as conflict and the actual violence of real warfare, which would strengthen the argument.

Meanwhile there are signs that Dr Morrill's attempt to reclassify the Civil War as a war of religion will meet with resistance from other seventeenth-century historians and may be seen as a regression towards what had been considered the thoroughly outmoded notion of a 'puritan revolution'. Christopher Hill utters his warning against isolating 'religion' as a self-sufficient explanatory factor. And what, it will be asked *is* a 'war of religion'? Some historians have contrived to discuss the so-called French Wars of Religion (which is where the phrase comes from) without much reference to religion at all. While this is perverse it is certain that these were not only or simply religious wars. That may actually assist Morrill's case, if restated in the form that the English Civil War was *no less* a war of religion than events in France in the later sixteenth century and was perhaps more simply, even naively, religious than the Thirty Years' War. Other critics are going to be sceptical about Dr Morrill's three watertight 'modes of opposition' and will wonder why he insists that only one of them acted as the precipitant of civil war. Would it not be more plausible to explain the conflict in terms of the interaction of all three 'modes'? Or they may suggest that men are prone to put an idealistic construction on their dubious motives, in order to persuade others and perhaps themselves of the rectitude of what without the sanction of religion would be inexcusable conduct. This we may call the Mandy Rice-Davies argument: 'He would, wouldn't he?' said Miss Rice-Davies in a once famous trial.

These critics would be right, but then Dr Morrill is not necessarily wrong. The role of religion in the wars and insurrections of the age of Reformation (and not only of that age) seems to have been threefold. It served to precipitate action which without it would have been prevented by natural inhibitions in codes of conduct and political convention. It was a means of bonding into a united whole elements which would have been disparate and fragmented but for shared religious values. (This principle worked negatively too: religion made enemies look more homogeneously awful than they really were.) And thirdly it provided legitimation for otherwise illegal and violent acts. Each of these functions of the 'religious factor' was in a sense indispensable, but there is no reason why this should lead to the conclusion that events like the German Peasants' War or the Pilgrimage of Grace were entirely or even mostly 'about' religion, religious in 'content'. That is to conduct the argument on the wrong terms, not so much mistaking the function of religion as failing to begin to ask what that function may have been.

Finally it has to be admitted that, with respect to violence, there was in the Christian tradition, or at least in one strand of Christian tradition, something which actually inhibited the taking up of arms in the cause of religion. Francis Bacon gave expression to this in his essay 'Of Unity in Religion' in which, having stated the commonplace of the two swords, spiritual and temporal, he disowned a third, 'Mahomet's sword'. We may not propagate religion by war, still less nourish sedition and authorise rebellion in the name of religion. However Bacon allowed the use of the sword 'in cases of overt scandal, blasphemy, or intermixture of practices against the state'. This suggests that some conscientious Christians would hesitate more over a 'war of religion' than over engagement in a just temporal quarrel, and perhaps there were some such hesitations in 1642.[21]

As an account of the meaning of the Civil War, Dr Morrill's analysis has to be squared with a more traditional view which often rests itself on Cromwell's well-known remark that while the war was not initially fought on the religious issue, it 'came to that at the last'. Cromwell seems to have had in mind the particular matter of religious liberty. However historians now invoke the remark in a rather different sense to illustrate what is sometimes called the process of 'functional radicalisation': that is, the tendency of any set of revolutionary circumstances to bring to the fore men of extraordinary and radical motivation. In these particular circumstances such men were defined in religious terms, so that what we might call the left wing or militant tendency came to be known (significantly) as 'the godly party'. In invoking religion to explain how the Civil War *began* Morrill is reacting against an interpretation to which he himself has contributed, that the war happened in spite of the disposition to neutrality of probably the greater part of the politically active nation and against all their natural instincts. According to an unkind critic this was as much as to explain 'why no Civil War broke out in England in 1642'. Equally Ronald Hutton, in a study of royalist armies, found that the war could not be explained by reference to the natural political forces and antagonisms building up in the counties where the armies were raised and the battles fought. Rather it amounted to 'an artificial insemination of violence into the local community'.[22]

The more one thinks of it, the less satisfactory 'artificial insemination of violence' seems as a concept, especially when taken with Hutton's somewhat lame plea that while some of those who took up arms for the king were presumably strongly motivated, it would be difficult to discover who they were or what their motivation was. Carried to logical conclusions this analysis of the Civil War as an undesired, unintended event, avoidable but for a failure of trust and competence at the political centre, implies that the profound political tensions and divisions which defined themselves after the Restoration of 1660 were a legacy of Civil War and cannot be traced back behind the war, still less invoked to explain how the Civil War happened in the first place.

III

The intention here is not to enter any deeper into the ongoing debate about the causes, or origins, of the Civil War, which would be like walking unprotected into the proverbial minefield. My ambitions are limited to the suggestion that not all the violence, or potential for violence, in what Christopher Hill has called 'pre-revolutionary England' was artificially induced or inseminated. We shall be investigating some of the inbuilt religious and moral tensions of the early seventeenth century. This will take us beyond the point reached in the first chapter, in which it was suggested that the identification of England with Israel, originally a principle of national unification, threatened to become divisive as English Protestants internalised the harsh intricacies of prophecy.

After the Civil War the great divine Richard Baxter was to recall that 'the war was begun in our streets [the streets of Kidderminster] before the King and the Parliament had any armies'. The French Wars of Religion were accompanied and in some places anticipated by spontaneous killing on the streets, as when a party of Protestants returning from a sermon were cut down and massacred in Rouen. Baxter was not referring to anything as grim as that and his telling phrase 'the war in our streets' brings us back to the metaphorical rather than literal language of war, since it refers to a moral and

cultural confrontation. 'The malignant hatred of seriousness in religion did work so violently in the rabble where I lived, that I could not
stay at home with any probable safety of my life.' Another good
example of what Baxter had in mind might be the condition of Exeter
in the 1620s, when among other severe and local crises including a
devastating outbreak of plague, the mayor, Ignatius Jordan, was one
of those moving heaven and earth to achieve the strict observation of
the Sabbath, suppressing both Sunday trading and Sunday sports. His
efforts met with eventual success but, we are told by Jordan's
biographer, 'not without much reluctancy, opposition and some
danger at the first, for there were commotions and tumults, and great
resistance made against him'.[23]

To the north and east of Exeter, in Somerset, Dorset and Wiltshire,
Professor David Underdown has recently detailed the history of early
seventeenth-century 'commotions and tumults' in a number of places,
so many particular eruptions in a thermal zone of cultural conflict
which covered the whole three-county region. Particular 'moral pan-
ics' (Underdown's term) occurred in Dorchester (1606), Lyme Regis
(1606–10), Wells (1607), Wimborne Minster (1608) and Weymouth
(1618), not to speak of similar outbreaks in numerous rural
parishes.[24]

Space will allow of only one example in detail and depth. Since we
have now heard so often in this book from its 'roaring boy', William
Whateley, we shall take it from the Oxfordshire market town of
Banbury,[25] where 'the war in our streets' can first be glimpsed in the
historical record of 1589. In that year, as the month of May
approached, the season for merry-making or 'Maikin' as it was called,
Whateley's uncle, a local shopkeeper and high constable of the
hundred, ordered the constables under his authority to 'presently
take down' all maypoles and to suppress all Whitsun ales, maygames
and morris dances, together with any fairs kept on the Sabbath. His
order was endorsed by the deputy lieutenant of Oxfordshire, Sir
Anthony Cope, and perhaps by the lord lieutenant himself, Lord
Norris. But to the grave embarrassment of all parties, including the
Privy Council, the high sheriff, Sir John Danvers, issued a flatly
contradictory order, instructing the constables not to disturb a single
maypole. The Privy Council took refuge from a scandalous dilemma
by advising Lord Norris that there was no reason why the people
should be forbidden their legitimate sports and pastimes, provided
these did not get in the way of their religious obligations and involved
no disturbance of the peace. This was to be the policy of the royal

Book of Sports, issued in 1618 by James I and reinforced by his son in 1633.

Behind these local Clochemerles contemporaries suspected, and perhaps we should too, the presence of a papist. Danvers, the sheriff who had intervened to protect the maypoles, was virtually a popish recusant and certainly what was known as a church papist, a reluctant conformist. According to his enemies (and such circumstantial dirt is engrained in these affairs), having first married impetuously for love he had then fallen out with his wife so drastically that they slept at opposite ends of the house, where each sought more congenial company. There were rumours of incest and the daughter implicated in the charge lured the vicar of Banbury, one Thomas Brasbridge, into the house, where she and her sister and their servants assaulted the poor man with fists and a knife, 'putting the said minister in fear of his life'. So much, at least, was alleged by Danvers's enemies. On the other hand the deputy lieutenant, Sir Anthony Cope, who described Danvers as 'mine adversary', was the radically puritan Member of Parliament who in 1586 had tried to revolutionise the constitution of the Church of England by legislation; it was also he who promoted the cultivation of the labour-intensive crop of woad with the religious and charitable intention of keeping the women and children of the poor in work. 'I hear of one Cope greatly commended', wrote the Earl of Leicester, and he was put in charge of the catholic prisoners in Banbury Castle.[26]

Ten years after the affair of the maypoles the two Whateleys, Richard and his brother Thomas, father of the preacher and twice mayor of the town, had tightened their grip. According to their opponents they and their allies were seeking to establish a corrupt monopoly of local office and had boosted their dignity by spending large sums of public money on a new silver mace. Whatever the truth of these allegations the Whateley regime was strongly ideological (it was called 'a precise course of government') and characterised by frequent arrests of countrymen coming into town to 'make merry', and by raids on tippling houses which sometimes led to the imprisonment of prominent townsmen for playing shovelboard or other unlawful games. When one of those threatened with arrest protested that he hoped that the queen's laws would allow him to invite a friend to supper, Richard Whateley, then bailiff, was said to have replied 'that if the queen do allow it, yet I will not allow it'. In a particularly violent episode Henry Wright, landlord of the Crown, was called out of church to attend to the needs of an arriving guest. He was promptly arrested at the church door, whereupon the entire congregation poured into the churchyard, leaving the unfortunate preacher to utter the final prayer to bare walls. Elizabeth Daunt, a 52-year-old matron, was carried along in the throng, 'having no purpose to meddle with any person there'. But Wright's wife, aged 40 and pregnant, had every purpose to meddle, When her children ran in to tell her that some men were fighting with their father in the churchyard she rushed to the rescue with a large stone in each hand.

This was the stuff of England's street wars of religion, and in Banbury they came to a climax with the demolition of Banbury Cross, or rather of the two famous market crosses which were the chief ornament of the town as well as a useful amenity for retailers and shoppers. Two versions were told in Star Chamber of this episode. According to one the two fair crosses were outrageously overthrown in riotous and unlawful manner by lawless iconoclasts who, when the spire of the High Cross fell to the ground, cried 'God be thanked! Dagon the deluder of the people is fallen down!'; they proceeded to hack at carvings of Christ on the Cross, the Virgin and Child and some nameless saint. This act of senseless violence had robbed the town of shelter for as many as two hundred butchers and market women. According to the other side the two crosses were taken down legally, by due order of the magistrates, any disorder being occasioned by the violent resistance offered to the workmen who arrived with appropriate tools to carry out the work of demolition (but at five o'clock in the morning!). As for the market amenities, these were well provided for by the erection of a new and more rationally designed market house, 'far more spacious and convenient' – but apparently charging higher rents. After these events the ascendancy of civic Puritanism in Banbury was no longer challenged. The town became a byword for smalltown godliness, the Jacobeans enjoying their Banbury jests no less than the English their Irish jokes. It was a Banbury cat which was hanged on Monday for killing a mouse on Sunday, and a Banbury man who in Jonson's *Bartholomew Fair* gave up his trade of baking because his Banbury cakes were enjoyed at 'brideales, maypoles, morrises and such profane feasts and meetings'.

IV

Lawrence Stone has described the seventeenth-century English village as 'filled with malice and hatred',[27] which has raised a few eyebrows. Banbury was like many other towns which were locked in the politics of faction. How subject to feuding and fighting was English society at this time? Were street wars a more or less normal state of affairs? Leaving grievous bodily harm aside, the evidence of verbal abuse, relating to legal actions for redress of character assassination, is voluminous but its interpretation is problematical. Should we conclude that neighbours were forever at war? Or, conversely, that such quarrels were scandalous and regrettable, and that litigation was undertaken with the motive of restoring peace and harmony, which was as much as to say normality?[28] Utterly typical is the record in the diocese of Canterbury of a woman of Ash whose behaviour (in 1593) was 'greatly offensive to well disposed persons dwelling near unto her', and of another woman who was 'grown to be offensive to her honest and near-dwelling neighbours'.[29] How well-disposed were well-disposed persons, how easily offended, how readily mollified? On top of these 'routine' and secular levels of antagonism, friction and reconciliation, we have to superimpose the dislikes and even the hatred to which religious differences actively contributed: differences which might arise from the presence, or suspected presence, of Catholics in the community, and from the tension arising between ordinary and extraordinary patterns of religious and moral behaviour, that is between a puritan minority and the generality of its neighbours.

How deep-seated were these religious and moral divisions? It is difficult to attempt an answer when we remain uncertain as to whether seventeenth-century communities, which are assumed to have been 'face to face' communities, were able to tolerate for any length of time a situation in which some people were not speaking to others, or regularly avoiding contact with them; or whether (and in what size and kinds of settlement) it was feasible, or considered desirable, to maintain a situation of general social neutrality.

In my book *The Religion of Protestants* I argued that the conditions which had divided the Elizabethan Church into puritan and anti-puritan, nonconformist and conformist parties, had to a great extent altered by the second decade of the seventeenth century, and that among the clerical and well-informed the advanced, evangelical, Calvinist Protestantism which was then in the ascendant was almost consensual. It therefore took the unexpected provocation of Arminianism and Laudianism, the imposition of an alien and innovative religious policy, to re-politicise the religious scene, redefining Puritanism as a reactive and broadly-based platform of opposition to Laudianism which, in a sense, carried the revolution of 1640–1 and swept on into the war of 1642. I would still defend this account of the sequence and rationale of what happened in English religion in the first half of the seventeenth century, including the emphasis on Archbishop Laud as the principal *agent provocateur* of religious revolution. At the level of politics, including ecclesiastical politics, the argument is, I think, impeccable, although it is not universally accepted. But it runs the risk of undervaluing both the scale and the intensity of localised conflicts of the Banbury variety, and also the relevance of these issues to an understanding of what was fought for in the Civil War.[30]

There has never been any mystery about what these locally contentious matters were. Reduced to the shortest possible list they included, as incidents of daily routine and habit, swearing, drinking and the associated sociability of the alebench; the weekly challenge of Sunday, affecting especially dancing, football and other regular sports and pastimes, which in London embraced theatres, bearpits and other sophisticated, commercialised entertainments; and the seasonal episodes of the festive year, especially maypoles in early summer and, later in the year, the church festivals known as revels, with other occasional church 'ales' held for fund-raising purposes. Particular controversies surrounding these contentious activities are familiar landmarks in seventeenth-century history: the storm in 1618 over the royal Book of Sports in Lancashire, which broke out afresh on a national scale when in 1634 it was read by royal order from the pulpits; the *cause célèbre* of church ales in Somerset in 1633. What has been lacking until recently has been an adequate sense of the magnitude of such things in the contemporary scale of values: both the positive value placed on them by their proponents and the enormity of the wickedness they represented in the perception of their puritan opponents. That a royal edict allowing dancing or football after Evening Prayer should be interpreted as an unprecedented endorsement of wickedness by law and should have made up the minds of hundreds to migrate to the American wilderness seems disproportionate, as does the proposition that a civil war should have been fought over the erection or non-erection of maypoles. After all such matters have been mentioned, if at all, only in the subsidiary chapters of textbooks or in soft-centred books on social history, once defined as history with the politics left out. And yet England's wars of religion began, in a sense, with a maypole. For as early as 1572 a young Sussex carpenter called, appropriately, Noah walked the six miles from his village of Hailsham to Warbleton to assist others in the removal of a maypole from the village green, only to be shot in the neck and killed.[31]

It has taken a certain injection of anthropological understanding and some assistance from the folklorists to help historians see that the weekly and seasonal rhythms of 'pastime' in early modern English society amounted to a carefully contrived structure, a way of life to which has been accorded the title 'the festive community', designed not merely to entertain but, in Keith Wrightson's words, to excite sentiments necessary for the continuing life of the community and to give life to the social structure. It was a means of maintaining order and social stability according to a set of values strongly implied in such phrases as 'good fellowship' and 'company keeping', but also a safety-valve for the expression, containment and even resolution of sectional interests and conflicts.[32] In justifying the contentious Somerset church ales the bishop of the diocese said in 1632 that they were valued 'for the civilizing of people, for their lawful recreations, for composing differences by making of friends, for increase of love and amity, as being feasts of charity, for relief of the poor, the richer sort keeping then open house, and for many other reasons'.[33]

But what was it to 'civilise' people? The ambition was general, consensual. But with their rival motto 'godly discipline' the religious virtuosi, as the heart and sinews of the contrasted, godly community, promoted nothing less than an antithetical doctrine of what it was to be a human being, and certainly of what was involved in taking one's place in a Christian society. The instruction given by John Angier in about 1638 to his flock at Denton near Manchester will amply justify this proposition, concerning as it does merely behaviour in church, from which much besides can be inferred. Church-goers should not arrive late or leave early. They should not walk or talk in the churchyard or lie on the grass. They should not kneel in ostentatious private prayer. 'This private praying is a sin, for it is a despising of the worship of God in hand.' Church-goers were not to whisper to one another, still less to indulge in smiling or laughter. Above all they must not stand up in order to gaze about, 'to see who of our friends we can espy, or who comes in, or what apparel others wear'. Do we not remember, Angier went on, that 'before God brought us home to him' we ourselves made a sport of sin and Sabbath-breaking?[34] Set this decorous model against the reality of what happened in the Yorkshire village of Alborough on the Feast of the Epiphany 1597, when the villagers, having been up all night drinking, burst into church in the midst of Morning Prayer with their 'mammet' (presumably an effigy of the Christ child) in a wheel barrow, 'with such a noise of piping, blowing of a horn, ringing or striking of basins and shouting of people that the minister was constrained to leave off the reading of prayer'.[35] At Harwich in 1535[36] protestant Christians had approved of such goings on as harmless high spirits, serving a useful social purpose. Not so their grandchildren.

V

Other historians (with ecclesiastical interests) have been slow to appreciate that it was in the context of the confrontation of these startlingly different moral economies that the stigma of 'Puritan' acquired meaning, substance and historical importance. There is little point in constructing elaborate statements defining what, in ontological terms, Puritanism was and what it was not, when it was not a thing definable in itself but only one half of a stressful relationship. For such terms of abuse often tell us as much or more about those deploying them than about those to whom they were attached. And most of all they draw our attention to the totality of the situation in which the stigmatisation occurred. We do not need to know whether those who were nick-named Puritans behaved in all respects as they were alleged to behave, or whether Anti-Puritans were fairly dismissed by Puritans as 'carnal', 'worldly' or even 'wicked'. In all probability they included some very nice people, people who nowadays would seem downright devout, or at least conspicuously regular in their attention to their religious duties. But the important thing is that a relationship of dynamic and mutual antagonism existed in principle between two well-defined and sharply differentiated kinds of people, the most telling index of which was the abusive language of identification which they employed against each other.[37]

The extremity of the radically disharmonious situation which this implies existed on paper and in the mind, and perhaps only in those places. How far extreme situations existed in the real world may be another matter. Puritans were constrained by their own principles to relate to the community at large in a manner which, in principle, maximised social stress. In their perception the established Church was both defective and deficient: defective in many aspects of worship and ceremonial detail, deficient in its lack of scriptural discipline and order. Yet these faults were not so disabling as to necessitate withdrawal from the church as if it were no true church at all but part and parcel of the 'Antichristian' Church of Rome. The author of an early puritan manifesto wrote that 'we in England are so far off from having a church rightly reformed that as yet we are *not* come to the outward face of the same', but he then evidently thought better of such an utterly dismissive statement and altered 'not' to 'scarce': we are scarce come to the outward face of the same.[38] As adherents of the national Church Puritans lived in the space created by that word 'scarce'. They did not presume to know who were the members of Christ's true, invisible Church, which was a mystery known only to God, and it is a mistake to suppose that they identified themselves with the elect and thought it possible on the basis of this identification to make the true Church visible by gathering in separatist conventicles. Even those who did separate and desert the parish churches were not so presumptuous, but constructed their gathered congregations out of the visibly worthy, in 'judgment of charity'.

Non-separated Puritans (the vast majority of those to whom the term Puritan can be usefully applied) agreed that the membership of the visible Church, the Church in society, should be so regulated by discipline as to exclude from sacramental communion the visibly *un*worthy. But the difference in their position was that, far from removing themselves, the unseparated considered that it was the unworthy who ought to be ejected, or at least denied the sacraments, like Abraham's rejected wife Hagar and her son Ishmael, who were sent out from the tent into the wilderness. But, given the constitution of the Church of England and its defective discipline, it was only to a very limited extent (in most parishes) that puritan ministers, let alone the lay rank and file, could exercise this power. Consequently they were obliged by conscience and simple necessity to continue an uneasy coexistence, even at the sacramental board, with fellow parishioners whom they considered carnal and wicked.[39]

This anomalous situation was pragmatically advantageous in that for two or three generations Puritans were able to evade the logical consequences of their own arduous and exclusive criteria of church membership. It was assumed that the godly or visibly worthy were almost everywhere in a minority. We have heard William Perkins complaining that the good corn was thinly scattered.[40] Arthur Dent agreed. If 'the prophane multitude' were to be 'separated out', leaving only 'sound, sincere and zealous worshippers', 'I suppose we should not need the art of Arithmetic to number them ... I doubt they would walk very thinly in the streets, so as a man might easily tell them as they go.' One writer thought the ratio of 'good' to 'naught' might prove to be one to nineteen; Thomas Shepard thought one in a thousand.[41] The clear implication that in all probability God had intended and provided for the ultimate destruction and dereliction of ninety-five per cent of his creation is very stark, but not to be ducked if we are to enter imaginatively within that austere edifice which Perry Miller called the Puritan Mind.

But in what sense would the Church continue to be parochial and nationally established if only five per cent of the tithe-paying inhabitants were fit to be admitted to the congregation? As it was those who had the power to separate out the remaining ninety-five per cent, the legal ecclesiastical authorities, chose not to exercise it, while those who professed to want to do it lacked the power. So the Puritans were not, in practice, forced to choose between two radically different and incompatible ecclesiologies but contrived to live with both, eating their cake and having it. It was said to be an uncomfortable experience, distressing to a sound and sensitive conscience. But even more painful decisions were indefinitely postponed, for a whole lifetime in the case of those dying before the more generally disruptive 1640s.

The puritan position was consequently the exact reverse of that taken up by the Separatists, and on the face of it more threatening to the general tranquillity and wellbeing of society. The Separatists, having stepped outside the parochial economy altogether and having emigrated, as likely as not, to Holland, could insist that in church matters the saints (themselves) were to have no communion with the wicked (all the rest). But outside religion and in all secular affairs it was permitted to them to live and deal normally with those living around them. In Amsterdam this casuistry involved the minimum of discomfort and stress. But back in England the non-separated Puritans were taught that they had no choice but to gather with the wicked and promiscuous multitude in the public exercises of religion. The law required it and the remedy was not in their hands. However in all other non-public respects, 'familiar accompanying in private conversation', they must separate severely, or 'as lawfully and conveniently as we may'. Thomas Hooker of Chelmsford taught that he had no authority to fling a man out of the open congregation, which was like a common field for every man's cattle. But he could certainly keep him out of his own house.

The question put by one writer was whether this drastic doctrine of shunning applied to such occasions in life as marriage, parenthood, civil obedience and commercial bargains. In other words, could the godly man divorce his wife, repudiate a bargain or break the law, all on the grounds of spiritual incompatibility? The answer was no. We must not be unnatural. But such necessary duties, when performed towards the carnal and wicked, must be undertaken with a 'kind of mourning or affliction for their sakes'. This meant that a wife must not refuse her ungodly husband his conjugal rights. But she must on no account appear to enjoy it. And all other unnecessary occasions, such as 'needless' company keeping, were to be avoided. Thomas Wilson of Canterbury, advising the congregation at a funeral on 'the practice of the saints', suggested that conscience should dictate 'eschewing all needless familiarity with all such whose hearts are seen not to be right by the crooked steps of their life'; but to be 'inward' with 'some godly Christians which walk wisely in a perfect way'.[42]

This was as much as to say that involvement in the common life of the community should be reduced to a minimum. Such a strategy would lack provocation only in circumstances in which the community had little common life, in effect no real existence. This may often have been a possibility since 'community', with all the resonances with which we invest it, is a piece of post-industrial nostalgia about a partly fictitious pre-industrial past. How many 'communities' in early modern England were in fact no true communities at all is something which social historians would dearly like to know.[43]

The black and white sense of absolute and unreserved difference and antipathy between godly and ungodly, which is fundamental to these texts and the strategies they embody, was at the root of 'the wars in our streets', and it provides what Anthony Fletcher and John Morrill have identified as a necessary mental condition for the outbreak of the Civil War itself. The word used by Parliamentarians of royalist sympathisers as well as activists, *malignants*, was one of unusual rejective force, as strong as 'wicked' – whilst the staunchest Parliamentarians were identified as 'honest'. Fletcher suggests that in the Parliament and its surroundings in 1641 and 1642 two groups of men became the prisoners of competing myths that fed upon one another, two perceptions of political reality which were fundamentally erroneous and mischievous.

One could say something similar of the assessment which Puritans had commonly made of their neighbours in the decades before 1641. Although it was theologically valid to describe mankind as divided between the elect and the reprobate, the sheep on the right hand, the goats on the left, this was an eschatological principle, a matter within the secret wisdom of God alone until the end of all things, and not a practical doctrine capable of social application. People in observable social situations do not fit neatly into one of these two categories, good and bad. At the very least there will be plausible hypocrites, about whom mistakes will be made. Richard Baxter divided his large parish of Kidderminster with its three or four thousand inhabitants not into two but into twelve categories, and he reckoned to know how many hundreds of his parishioners were in each. There were the serious and precise professors of religion, the sincere and blameless, the tractable and willing but ignorant – and so on, down to such carefully characterised types as those 'of tolerable knowledge and no drunkards or whoremongers', who nevertheless kept idle, tippling company and detested strict religious professors. Each of these groups required a different style of pastoral approach, as Baxter well knew.[44]

So why did early seventeenth-century Puritans insist on the crudest and most prejudicially damaging division of all, into *two*, as if everyone had to be the one thing or the other? There is a biblical answer to this question ('he who is not for me is against me') but the explanation also lies in the prevalent mental and rhetorical habit of addressing every proposition or topic of investigation in terms of its contrary or antithesis, the method of binary opposition, or of inversion. Thus obedience (for example, in children) was discussed in the categories of disobedience, patriarchy in terms of women on top, true religion with reference to superstition. In the words of Scripture (Ecclesiasticus 42:24) 'all things go in pairs, by opposites'. James I declared that to know God it was also necessary to know the Devil, and the practical application of this principle in part explains the so-called witch craze, a bizzare feature of early modern civilisation throughout Europe. Similarly the heightened Christocentrism of sixteenth-century Protestantism is an explanation in itself for the detailed attention paid to *Anti*christ. Far more interest was taken in Atheism than the incidence of genuine, philosophical Atheism in the seventeenth century would seem to warrant, since, as Richard Hooker defined it, Atheism is 'the most extreme opposite to true religion' and therefore requiring emphasis as a mode of establishing or commending its opposite. This may serve to explain what otherwise seems almost incomprehensible: that Thomas Nashe should insist that there was no sect in England so prevalent (his word is 'scattered') as Atheism.[45]

One peculiarly distorting consequence of what might be called the piebald mentality is that it bundled into one or other of its polar opposites all intermediate or uncertain categories, there being in effect nowhere else to put them, no halfway house between truth and error, which were both epistemological and moral absolutes. Given the existence of the Roman Catholic Church and the presence in England of a certain number of its continuing adherents, this procedure had consequences in respect of 'popery' the importance of which in English history would be very hard to exaggerate. Crypto-papists, or anyone whose religious views were in any respect suspect, were liable to be assimilated to the papists. Consequently a limited and perhaps not very threatening factor became blown up out of all proportion. It enabled John Pym or constrained him (since he seems to have been the victim of his own propaganda) to represent Arminianism as equivalent to popery and part of a grand and conspiratorial design 'to alter the kingdom both in religion and government'. And without that conviction it is unlikely that there would, could, have been a civil war. In fact in origins and theological affinity English Arminianism was closer to Lutheranism than to Roman Catholicism, but there was less polemical mileage in making that connection. Later, in 1679, similar mental habits enabled Titus Oates and Israel Tonge to convince the whole nation, from the king downwards, that it stood in the direst peril from another popish plot. And so it was that the Puritans understood their immediate world to be polarised between themselves and their religious enemies, two undifferentiated masses of good and evil. Preaching at Paul's Cross on the text 'We would have cured Babel, but she would not be healed' (Jeremiah 51:11) William Crashawe spoke of the many 'little petty Babylons' amongst his hearers, incurable sins which were 'babels, or at least daughters of Babylon'. That was to equate a shopping list of abuses from Sabbath neglect to stage plays to the impropriation of church livings with the realised principle of Satanic evil which was 'Babel'.[46]

There remains only one of those magnificently unanswerable questions: whether this characteristic mode of thought and expression arose from a deep emotional need and so reveals some inner and peculiar depths of the early modern personality; or whether as a habit of mind and discourse it was socially and culturally induced, especially by the rhetorical elements in the educational curriculum.

VI

To what extent seventeenth-century Puritans carried into the practicalities of daily existence what looks from where we stand like an extraordinary form of collective madness must remain uncertain. The degree of apartheid (so to speak) actually established and practised must have been subject to infinite variety, conditioned as it would have been by social class, family circumstance, occupation, domicile, personal character – and heaven knows what else. The details can be retrieved occasionally, when we know an individual or a community tolerably well. We know the London furniture maker Nehemiah Wallington very well indeed (he left behind 2600 pages of more or less autobiographical material in his own handwriting) and we have a sense that he did what he had to do in respect of relations, neighbours and customers. He was not 'unnatural'. But all but the more superficial and casual of his connections took place within the godly community, which extended so far as he was concerned to Massachusetts, far beyond the normal mental horizon of such a humdrum person. But Wallington cannot be considered a typical figure.

Life in the Essex village of East Hanningfield in the 1580s must have been rather unpleasant, for the puritan vicar refused communion to half of his parishioners on the grounds of ignorance and unfitness, while he met to read the Bible with the other half, who were sarcastically pilloried by their neighbours as 'saints and scripture men'. In the 1590s in Warbleton (the same Sussex village where Noah Skynner had been shot dead in the act of sawing down the maypole) rather more than half the children were baptised with such peculiar names as Much-mercy, Obedient and Zealous; whilst the others were given such ordinary names such as Richard. Presumably parental and god-parental wishes were observed in each case. Since the practice of giving names 'having some godly signification' was meant to underline the fact that baptism made a 'segregation from the world', did the two groups of children play together? Or did they constitute two groups, even fight as rival gangs, Richard and Henry versus The-Lord-Is-Near and Flee-Sin? William Kempe, schoolmaster of Plymouth where peculiar baptismal names do not seem to have been in use, nevertheless advised parents that they should keep their children apart from 'clownish playing mates and all rustical persons', ensuring that they use 'none other company than such as be both honest and civil, as well in behaviour as in language'.[47]

But generally people must have rubbed along after a fashion, or England's wars of religion would surely have broken out much earlier, and in a different and more obviously religious form. Puritans may have been thought 'singular', even 'fantastical', but it was necessary to live with them, and they for their part must have made their share of compromises with the 'carnal' and 'godless'. John Turner was a notorious figure in many Kentish parishes in the 1620s and 1630s. He was a travelling tallow chandler who ministered to a chain of puritan conventicles. But a neighbour giving evidence in court concerning his reputation (the matter was not criminal), while admitting that Turner was 'a separatist from the Church of England', nevertheless insisted that 'in his dealings' he was 'taken and reputed for an honest man'.[48]

In the Cambridgeshire village of Balsham a group of dissenters, in principle far more radically alienated from the religion of the majority than any puritan Separatist like Turner, also contrived to be taken and reputed as 'honest', or so what can be discovered about their life histories suggests. These were a group of 'Familists', adherents of the proto-Quaker sect called the Family of Love, a source of dread to the official protestant mind for the sheer enormity of their heresies, above all the notion that a man could be 'godded with God', bringing forth a fresh incarnation within himself. Some of the Balsham men had been Familists since about 1560 and they hung on tenaciously to their secret beliefs and cryptic way of life at least until 1609 and perhaps for even longer. During this time some of them continued to take their turns in the office of churchwarden and questman, they married outside the sect and they left money to general charities. This made them, in the estimation of the historian who has reconstructed their hidden world, 'respected and integrated members of local society'. When the Balsham church bells were recast in 1609 the names of some of these Familist village worthies were included in the casting, together with a motto which may have Familist implications, and the inscriptions can be seen to this day. When in the same year one member of this little cell was betrayed to the bishop, 'named upon a common fame to be of the Family of Love', the common fame was so much old hat that the presentment can only have been motivated by some private grudge.[49]

What enabled the Balsham Familists to live such normal, well-adjusted lives? Partly their wealth, for they seem to have belonged to the élite of this farming community. Partly their peculiarly cryptical practice, for Familists, unlike Puritans, were careful to conceal, even disguise their beliefs, and they lived by an elaborate casuistry which deliberately avoided demonstrative separation and witness. Both they and the 'popish sect', early seventeenth-century English Catholics, teach us that there were various ways of pitching upon what John Bossy has called 'the optimum line': 'one which would provide the maximum of self-determining capacity and the minimum of destructive isolation'. This for Catholics was equivalent to 'the degree of attendance at the parish church required to preserve the integrity of the household'.[50] However indifferent they might profess to be towards the normal social codes, Puritans too had some need to find where that 'optimum' line ran in their lives.

The principle and practice of separation in the fullest sense, including social shunning, seems to display a progressive dialectic as we move through the Reformation and post-Reformation decades. 'The first that made separation from the Church of England' were the 'freewill men', those 'congregators' who, quite unlike their Lollard progenitors, 'refused the communion' and, in Kent and Essex, made a schism against the Reformation itself in Edward's reign. Under Mary both they and the orthodox protestant 'predestinators' stood out against assimilation to the Catholicism now once again enforced, and some of them suffered for their pains. The separation of those years was drastic, as extreme as the case of Gertrude Crockhay, a member of the 'privy church' of secret London Protestants, who when told on her deathbed by the priest who came to visit her that unless she recanted and received the sacrament she could not be given Christian burial, exclaimed: 'Oh how happy am I, that I shall not rise with them, but against them'. Familism, amongst other things, was a reaction against the painful consequences of coming out and being separate. No English Familist, so far as we know, suffered execution or had to go into exile. But the principle of separation later took over in more orthodox puritan circles, both ecclesiastical separation and the social separation associated with non-separated Puritans.[51]

But street wars were not necessarily sustained for ever. Typically they erupted, as episodes of iconoclasm had erupted in the early stages of the Protestant Reformation, in demonstrations and counter-demonstrations and were resolved one way or the other. At Chester years of contention over the programme for the annual midsummer show, with anti-puritan mayors repairing the damage done by their iconoclastic predecessors, were eventually resolved in a compromise which 'for the decency of it now used' was 'thought by all both decent, fit and profitable to the city': good clean family entertainment. Elsewhere, notably at Banbury, or at Dorchester under its famous patriarch John White, the puritan ascendancy was so complete as to leave any opposition invisible and impotent. But in other towns, including Kidderminster, where Baxter's comments started us off, tensions remained, to provide tinder for the Civil War when it came. But what this argument has very deliberately not attempted is to trace in any causal, explanatory sequence the chain of events which began, as it were, with a maypole or a football and ended at Edgehill. This could be done, perhaps, but not in twenty pages.

The Civil War aside, what was the meaning and what were the consequences of these partly metaphorical, partly real 'wars of religion'? Historians who like Marx or Durkheim, or indeed Weber, begin with the premiss that religion is a mistake, false consciousness, will always look for a more or less reductionist explanation of the apparent historical importance of religious ideas and practices, outside religious phenomenonology itself. The danger is that we will follow them beyond explaining religion to explaining it away. Many social historians believe that moral and cultural conflict in early modern England was a particular expression, as it were in the language of the time, of a kind of class war between the economically secure and improving elements in society, those 'of ability' or 'of credit and reputation', and the disorderly poor. The puritan campaign against sin was not separable from the drive for order and social discipline in a society threatened with the adverse consequences of population growth and episodes of economic contraction or dislocation. For David Underdown the puritan culture of discipline is equivalent to individualism and the work ethic, and he thinks it significant that John Hole, the leading moral reformer in Jacobean Wells, a man who refused 'to go to the church ale with his neighbours', was a capitalist clothier.[52]

This is a plausible hypothesis which cannot be easily disproved empirically. Nor, by the same token, can it be proved. It involves the historian in a task not so much delicate as impossible, like dissecting a raw egg. I myself was brought up in what (before 1939) was a poor district of North London by parents who were both comfortably off and piously evangelical. I too was forbidden to play with 'clownish' mates, although my parents did not regard the plight of their families with indifference. We met at Sunday School, where my older brothers and sisters were teachers. Was it my parents' evangelicalism or their class prejudice which gave me an unnaturally cloistered upbringing in twentieth-century Islington? The sixteenth-century record is no easier to interpret. It includes the evidence of wealthy people, wealthy capitalists even, who far from standing in opposition to the festive community strongly defended it, whether as fully involved participants or, pragmatically, out of a sense of the socially conservative value of sports and pastimes. There were plenty of young people with money in their pockets who preferred dances to sermons on Sundays. Professor Peter Clark has called the seventeenth-century alehouse an establishment run by the poor for the poor, and for that reason condemned by the affluent (and godly) as a social evil. When Professor Jack Fisher heard Clark's view he remarked that perhaps the customers were poor when they came out of the alehouse but not when they went in or they would have had no money to spend on drink. Some Puritans were also poor. The point has been made that the desire of magistrates and village oligarchs to maintain social control was a constant, although it was in particular evidence at times of economic stress and distress, whereas the spirituality and marked religious zeal of Puritanism was perhaps something quite else and extra, a maverick factor. The spirit bloweth where it listeth. Keith Wrightson, in his influential study of the Essex village of Terling, is in danger of confusing with Puritanism the officious, responsible respectability of the dozen or so local farmers of substance who sat in the vestry and ran the parish. But the Terling Puritans in a more proper sense seem to have made a less influential and impressive group. After the departure of their pastor, Thomas Weld, for New England they held their conventicles in the house of the schoolmaster's widow.[53]

Professor Underdown's ingenious efforts to explain patterns of moral and cultural difference by reference to the environment are intriguing but less than compelling. There is clearly some significant correlation linking so-called open parishes, woodland and pasture communities having a mixed and partly industrialised economy with Puritanism, and manorial, corn-growing villages with the opposite, suggesting in these agrarian and pastoral environments the operation of what Weber called 'elective affinities'. Yet there are also many exceptions to the rule, to be accounted for by arbitrary, human factors. The Somerset village of Batcombe was as puritan as it was not on account of something in the water, but because of the presence of its pastor and preacher, Richard Bernard, whom we have encountered as the author of *Contemplative pictures* and *Bible battels*. And it was patronage, the somewhat exalted patronage of successive bishops of Bath and Wells, James Montague and Arthur Lake, and of an archdeacon of Taunton, which brought Bernard to Batcombe and sustained him there. To speak of Underdown's argument as the 'ecological fallacy', as some critics have done when it has been employed for other purposes, is too harsh. It is by no means wholly fallacious. But it has little explanatory power when it comes to accounting for Puritanism as a factor in the Civil War. Underdown's readers are liable to be impressed by the density of his research while asking 'so what?'[54]

VII

And what of the eventual outcome? At this point some attempt must be made, however desperate, to pull the themes of this little book together. It can hardly be said too often that the consequences of the English Reformation, like the outcome of most great and convulsive movements of the human mind and spirit which all ultimately falter, were the consequences of failure, not of success. Success would have meant the conversion of all England into one great Banbury, an England so virtuous as to exclude cakes and ale, singing nothing but the Psalms of David, reading little but the Bible and a literature pervaded with biblicism, and doing these things in a model protestant home; while protestant arms established a protestant and perhaps English ascendancy on the European and world stage. But not much of this was in the least likely to happen, and one of the things certain to frustrate total success was the protestant mind itself. For where would Protestantism have been without an antithesis, an opponent, even an all-powerful opponent?

As for the moral and cultural struggle described in this chapter, 'the war in our streets', it was not confined to England but was European in its scope, a prominent feature of Western civilisation in the early modern phase of its emergence.[55] What was almost peculiar to the English situation was the fact that the campaign for moral and cultural reform, sometimes called (with mild anachronism) 'the reformation of manners', was waged not from above by the authorities (or, as in France, by a reforming post-Tridentine episcopate) but by elements dispersed in society, enjoying at most local power, like the Whateleys of Banbury and Mayor Hardware of Chester. This in itself pointed to eventual failure. For even when the Puritans were ostensibly on top, in the aftermath of the Civil War, they found no effective means of imposing their will and ways on the population at large. Indeed, with the lapse of the ordinary procedures of ecclesiastical discipline and the closure of the church courts, the parish congregation was now in some places effectively reduced to their own small circle, demonstrating as never before just how small it was, how thinly those few grains of good wheat were scattered. At Altham in Lancashire it was decided to restrict the communion to 'serious Christians', Bible-reading Sabbath observers who had always lived by Reformation principles. These proved to be just twenty-nine persons, fourteen of them women, representing only twenty of the 150 families who made up the parish.[56]

After the Restoration in 1660 such gathered groups were often driven into a more or less permanently alienated nonconformity. That was the end of the birthpangs. By definitively formalising the division of English Protestantism it built into the succeeding centuries of English history a pluralistic diversity which English Protestantism had neither expected nor desired. Like the twins Esau and Jacob, whose contention began in the womb, the birthpangs of the English Reformation brought forth discordant triplets: Church, Dissent and Popery.

Notes

PREFACE

1. Thomas Stoughton, *A general treatise against poperie* (Cambridge, 1598) pp. 4–5.
2. Peter Clark, *English Provincial Society from the Reformation to the Revolution* (Hassocks, 1977) pp. 152–7. The Act Books of the Court of the Archdeacon of Canterbury, Cathedral Archives and Library Canterbury, are full of evidence of the cultural war of the 1570s between preachers and minstrels. A little of it is sampled in my *The Religion of Protestants: the Church in English Society, 1559–1625* (Oxford, 1982) pp. 206–7.
3. *From Iconoclasm to Iconophobia: the Cultural Impact of the Second English Reformation (The Stenton Lecture, 1985)* (Reading, 1986).

1 THE PROTESTANT NATION

1. C. A. Sneyd (ed.), *A Relation of the Island of England About the Year 1500*, O.S. XXXVII (Camden Society, 1847) pp. 20–1. John Major is quoted by Jenny Wormald in *Journal of British Studies*, XXIV (1985) 158.
2. Christopher Hill, 'The Protestant Nation', in *Collected Essays II: Religion and Politics in 17th Century England* (Brighton, 1986) pp. 28–9.
3. Michael McGiffert has drawn attention to the importance of this text for national self-consciousness in 'God's Controversy with Jacobean England', in *American Historical Review*, LXXXVIII (1983) 1151–74; with further comments, critical of his original argument, in ibid., LXXXIX (1984) 1217–18. Calvin's exposition is in J. Owen (ed.), *Commentaries on the Twelve Minor Prophets*, I (Edinburgh, 1846).
4. George H. Williams et al. (eds), *Thomas Hooker: Writings in England and Holland, 1626–1633*, Harvard Theological Studies XXVIII (Cambridge, Mass., 1975) pp. 244–8.
5. John Aylmer, *An Harborowe for faithfull and trewe subiectes* ('Strasborowe' but *recte* London, 1559) Sig. P4ᵛ; James Jones, *Londons looking-back to Jerusalem* (1635) p. 27; Latimer quoted by Hill in 'The Protestant Nation', p. 29; John Lyly, in E. Arber (ed.), *Euphues and his England* (1868) p. 456; J. Bruce (ed.), *Correspondence of Matthew Parker* (Parker Society: Cambridge, 1853) pp. 418–19.
6. Thomas Cooper, *The blessing of Japheth* (1615) Epistle.
7. John Pocock writing on England, in O. Ranum (ed.), *National Consciousness, History, and Political Culture in Early-Modern Europe* (Baltimore, 1975) pp. 98–105.

8. Patrick Wormald, 'Bede, the *Bretwaldas* and the Origins of the *Gens Anglorum*', in P. Wormald, D. Bullough and R. Collins (eds), *Ideal and Reality in Frankish and Anglo-Saxon Society: Studies Presented to J. M. Wallace-Hadrill* (Oxford, 1983) pp. 99–129.

9. John W. McKenna, 'How God Became an Englishman', in DeLloyd J. Guth and John W. McKenna (eds), *Tudor Rule and Revolution: Essays for G. R. Elton from his American Friends* (Cambridge, 1982) pp. 25–43; Joseph R. Strayer, 'France: the Holy Land, the Chosen People, and the Most Christian King', in T. K. Rabb and J. E. Seigel (eds), *Action and Conviction in Early Modern Europe: Essays in Memory of E. H. Harbison* (Princeton, 1969) pp. 15–16; John Barnie, *War in Medieval Society: Social Values and the Hundred Years War 1337–99* (1974) especially chapter 4, 'Patriots and Patriotism'; A. K. McHardy, 'Liturgy and Propaganda in the Diocese of Lincoln During the Hundred Years War', in Stuart Mews (ed.), *Religion and National Identity: Studies in Church History*, XVIII (Oxford, 1982) pp. 215–27.

10. D. Napthine and W. A. Speck, 'Clergymen and Conflict 1660–1763', in W. J. Sheils (ed.), *The Church and War: Studies in Church History*, XX (Oxford, 1983), pp. 231–62; Thomas Adams, *Englands sicknesse*, in *Workes* (1629) pp. 302–48.

11. Thomas Becon, *The polecy of warre* (1543) in J. Ayre (ed.), *Early Works* (Parker Society: Cambridge, 1843) pp. 203–61; William Whateley, *Charitable teares: or a sermon shewing how needefull a thing it is for every godly man to lament the common sinnes of our countrie* (1623) pp. 244–5.

12. Richard Cust and Peter G. Lake, 'Sir Richard Grosvenor and the Rhetoric of Magistracy', in *Bulletin of the Institute of Historical Research*, LIV (1981) 40–53; Peter Clark, 'Thomas Scot and the Growth of Urban Opposition to the Early Stuart Regime', in *Historical Journal*, XXI (1978) 1–26.

13. Richard Eedes, *Six learned and godly sermons* (1604) Sig. B; Isaac Colfe, *1588. A Sermon preached on the queenes day* (1588) Sig. B1; Maurice Kyffin, *The blessednes of Brytaine, or a celebration of the queenes holyday* (1587).

14. G. W. Bernard, 'The Pardon of the Clergy Reconsidered', in *Journal of Ecclesiastical History*, XXXVII (1986) 262; John M. King, 'The Godly Woman in Elizabethan Iconography', in *Renaissance Quarterly*, XXXVIII (1985) 41–84. C. M. D. Crowder, *Unity, Heresy and Reform 1378–1460: the Conciliar Response to the Great Schism* (1977) pp. 108–26.

15. J. Ayre (ed.), *The Sermons of Edwin Sandys* (Parker Society: Cambridge, 1841) p. 418.

16. William Burton, *Davids evidence* (1592) p. 147, quoted in Michael McGiffert, 'Covenant, Crown and Commons in Elizabethan Puritanism', in *Journal of British Studies*, XX (1980) 44.

17. David Loades, 'The Origins of English Protestant Nationalism', in *Religion and National Identity*, pp. 297–307. See also the essay in the same collection by Anthony Fletcher, 'The First Century of English Protestantism and the Growth of National Identity', pp. 309–17. Jenny

Wormald, 'Gunpowder, Treason, and Scots', in *Journal of British Studies*, XXIV (1985) pp. 141–68.

18. Patrick Collinson, 'Truth and Legend: the Veracity of John Foxe's Book of Martyrs', in A. C. Duke and C. A. Tamse (eds), *Clio's Mirror: Historiography in Britain and the Netherlands: Britain and the Netherlands*, VIII (Zutphen, 1985) pp. 31–54. See also J. F. Mozley, *John Foxe and His Book* (1940).

19. William Whateley, *A bride bush, Or, a direction for married persons* (1623), Preface.

20. William Haller, *Foxe's Book of Martyrs and the Elect Nation* (1963) is corrected by Katherine R. Firth, *The Apocalyptic Tradition in Reformation Britain 1530–1645* (Oxford, 1979), Richard Bauckham, *Tudor Apocalypse* (Appleford, 1978) and V. Norskov Olsen, *John Foxe and the Elizabethan Church* (Berkeley, 1973). Foxe's singular importance as Luther's translator is implied by the prefaces to the English editions of *A commentarie upon the epistle to the Galathians* (1575), *A commentarie upon the fiftene psalmes* (1577) and *Special and chosen sermons* (1578). See also G. R. Elton, 'Luther in England', in Bernd Moeller (ed.), *Luther in der Neuzeit* (Gutersloh, 1983) p. 126.

21. G. J. R. Parry, *A Protestant Vision: William Harrison and the Reformation of Elizabethan England* (Cambridge, 1987).

22. Albert Peel, 'Congregational Martyrs at Bury St Edmunds. How Many?', in *Transactions of the Congregational Historical Society*, XV (1946) 64–7. For Brightman on Laodicea see William S. Lamont, *Marginal Prynne 1600–1669* (1963) pp. 59–64 and his *Godly Rule: Politics and Religion, 1603–60* (1969) pp. 49–52. See also Firth, *Apocalyptic Tradition*, p. 167.

23. Becon, *Early Works*, p. 239. On England and the Calvinist international see Patrick Collinson, 'England and International Calvinism, 1558–1640', in Menna Prestwich (ed.), *International Calvinism, 1541–1715* (Oxford, 1985) pp. 197–223.

24. Thomas Cooper, *The blessing of Japheth* (1615) p. 34; Thomas Cooper, *Sathan transformed into an angell of light* (1622), Sig. A3.

25. Becon, *Early Works*, p. 353; Whateley, *Charitable teares*, Sig. O2. For the effect of national danger see Carol Z. Wiener, 'The Beleaguered Isle. A study of Elizabethan and Early Jacobean Anti-Catholicism', in *Past and Present* no. 51 (May 1971) 27–62.

26. Thomas Sutton, *Englands first and second summons* (1616), p. 30; Whateley, *Charitable teares*, Preface. See also John Stockwood, *A sermon preached at Paules crosse on Barthelmew day being the 24 of August 1578* (n.d.); Henry Leslie, *A warning for Israel in a sermon preached at Christ Church in Dublin the 30 of October 1625* (Dublin, 1626); James Cleland, *Iacobs wel and Abbots conduit* (1626) p. 6.

27. T. Twyne, *A short and pithie discourse concerning the engendring, tokens and effects of all earthquakes in generall* (1580). See also Anthony Munday, *A view of sundry examples* (1580); James Bisse, *Two sermons* (1581); Arthur Golding, *A discourse upon the earthquake* (1580). The Coventry comment will be found in R. W. Ingram (ed.), *Records of the Early English Drama*, III (Toronto, 1981) p. 294. On Halley's Comet see

Thomas Jackson, *Judah must into captivitie: six sermons* (1622) p. 25 and Preface. On the sin of swearing see Edmund Bicknell, *A swoord ageynst swearyng* (1579). Swearing was identified as 'the most odious sin' in John Fosbroke, *Englands warning by Israel and Judah* (1617), bound with *Six sermons delivered in the lecture at Kettering* (1633) p. 32.

28. Whateley, *Charitable teares*, pp. 244–5.
29. For an account of English 'Hoseads' see McGiffert, 'God's Controversy with Jacobean England' (loc. cit.).
30. Quoted in Patrick Collinson, *The Religion of Protestants: the Church in English Society 1559–1625* (Oxford, 1982) p. 230.
31. McGiffert discusses the *topos* of Nineveh and Jonah, loc. cit., pp. 1155–6. See John Hooper, *Sermons upon Jonas* (1550); T. W. [Thomas Wilcox?], *A sermon preached at Paules Crosse on Sunday the thirde of November 1577* (1578), which uses Nineveh to shame and condemn England; John King, *Lectures upon Ionas delivered at Yorke* (Oxford, 1599), which applies Jonah as a relevant type but not Nineveh; and the Lutheran Johann Brenz, translated by Thomas Tynne as *Newes from Ninive to Englande* (1570). The ballad 'A warning to England, let London begin' (Huntington Library, HEH 18269) calls 'that happy citie Ninevie' 'a goodly myrour to London'.
32. Henoch Clapham, *An epistle discoursing upon the present pestilence* (1603); *Henoch Clapham his demaunds and answers touching the pestilence* (1604); Henoch Clapham, *Doctor Andros his Prosopeia answered* (1605).
33. John Downame, *Lectures upon the foure first chapters of the prophecie of Hosea* (1608); discussed by McGiffert, loc. cit. For another energetic Jacobean engagement with Hosea see Leslie, *A warning for Israel*.
34. William Perkins, *A faithful and plain exposition upon the two first verses of the 2 chapter of Zephaniah* (postumously published by William Crashawe in 1616), in I. Breward (ed.), *The Work of William Perkins*, Courtenay Library of Reformation Classics 3 (Appleford, 1970) pp. 279–302.
35. Whateley, *Charitable teares*, p. 216.
36. Thomas Cooper, *A familiar treatise laying downe cases of conscience* (1615) p. 2.
37. Jackson, *Judah must into captivitie*, pp. 13–14, 34–5, 37, 64–5. For autobiographical details of Jackson's career see Thomas Jackson, *Davids pastorall poeme* (1603), Preface. For his anti-Puritanism see *Londons New-Yeares gift* (1609) p. 23 and *The raging of the tempest stilled* (1623) pp. 33–4. For Jackson's ambivalence in 1642 see *The razing of the record, Or, An order to forbid any thanksgiving for the Canterbury Newes published by Richard Culmer* (Oxford, 1644) p. 4.
38. McGiffert, loc. cit., p. 1169.
39. Frances Rose-Troup, *John White the Patriarch of Dorchester (Dorset) and the Founder of Massachusetts, 1575–1648* (1930) p. 424; M. McGiffert (ed.), *Gods Plot: The Paradoxes of Puritan Piety: Being the Autobiography and Journal of Thomas Shepard* (Cambridge, Mass., 1972) pp. 55–6. I owe this last reference to Dr Susan Hardman Moore.
40. John Norden, *A mirror for the multitude* (1586).

41. Cooper, *The blessing of Japheth*, p. 31; Thomas Cooper, *The cry and revenge of blood* (1620) p. 4.
42. L. B. Larking (ed.), *Proceedings in the County of Kent in Connection with the Parliaments Called in 1640* (Camden Society c, 1862) p. 21.
43. Quoted in Collinson, *The Religion of Protestants*, p. 283.

2 THE PROTESTANT TOWN

1. D. H. Sacks, 'The Demise of the Martyrs; the Feasts of St Clement and St Katherine in Bristol, 1400–1600', in *Social History*, XI (1986) 141–69; Jonathan Barry, 'Popular Culture in Seventeenth-Century Bristol', in Barry Reay (ed.), *Popular Culture in Seventeenth-Century England* (1985) pp. 59–90.
2. J. Ayre (ed.), *The Sermons of Edwin Sandys* (Parker Society: Cambridge, 1841) p. 331; James Bisse, *Two sermons* (1581), Sig. G4^v; William Birch, *A Warnyng to England, let London begin* (1565), Britwell Ballads, Huntington Library, HEH 18269; Thomas Jackson, *The converts happiness* (1609) pp. 30–5. See also verses in John Carre, *A larume belle for London* (1573):
   For thee O London, I lament,
   And wring my hands with mourning cheer
3. James Cleland, *Iacobs wel and Abbots conduit* (1626) pp. 1–2, 5–6, 42–3.
4. William Wilkinson, *A confutation of certaine articles* (1579), excerpted in John Strype, *Annals of the Reformation*, II ii (Oxford, 1824) pp. 282–3; A. J. Fletcher, 'Puritanism in Seventeenth-Century Sussex', in M. J. Kitch (ed.), *Studies in Sussex Church History* (1981) p. 154; Peter Clark, ' "The Ramoth-Gilead of the Good": Urban Change and Political Radicalism at Gloucester, 1540–1640', in P. Clark, A. G. R. Smith and N. Tyacke (eds), *The English Commonwealth 1547–1640* (Leicester, 1979) p. 184; Claire Cross, *Urban Magistrates and Ministers: Religion in Hull and Leeds, from the Reformation to the Civil War*, Borthwick Papers 67 (York, 1985) p. 1.
5. Cleland, *Iacobs wel*, p. 6; William Fulke, *A sermon proving Babylon to be Rome*, reprinted in Richard Bauckham, *Tudor Apocalypse*, Courtenay Library of Reformation Classics 8 (Appleford, 1978) p. 329; John Norden, *A mirror for the multitude* (1586) p. 73.
6. This and much other information in this chapter on the divided religious scene in Canterbury and East Kent c. 1543 is drawn from a register compiled by Archbishop Cranmer of investigations into the so-called Prebendaries Plot staged against him in his own diocese, a document preserved in Corpus Christi College, Cambridge, as MS 128. The bulk of this material, but with significant omissions, is printed as 'Cranmer and the Heretics of Kent' in *Letters and Papers of Henry VIII*, XVIII (ii), no. 546, pp. 291–378.
7. For the general history of early modern English towns the reader is referred to Peter Clark and Paul Slack (eds), *Crisis and Order in English*

Towns, 1500–1700 (1972); Peter Clark (ed.), *The Early Modern Town* (1976); Peter Clark and Paul Slack, *English Towns in Transition 1500–1700*; Peter Clark (ed.), *Country Towns in Pre-Industrial England* (Leicester, 1981); D. M. Palliser, *The Age of Elizabeth: England Under the Later Tudors 1547–1603* (1983) pp. 202–36; and Peter Clark (ed.), *The Transformation of English Provincial Towns* (1984).

8. Diarmaid MacCulloch, *Suffolk and the Tudors: Politics and Religion in an English County 1500–1600* (Oxford, 1986) pp. 44–8; J. E. Neale, *The Elizabethan House of Commons* (1949) p. 153; P. W. Hasler (ed.), *The History of Parliament. The House of Commons 1558–1603* (1981) I, pp. 223–4.

9. This event, and the response of the Ipswich magistracy to it, are recorded in the Assembly Book 6–19 Eliz. and the Chamberlain's Accounts temp. Eliz, Ipswich Borough Records, Ipswich and East Suffolk Record Office. A contemporary broadsheet was published by Timothy Granger, *A moste true and marveilous straunge wonder, the lyke hath seldome bene seene, of xvii monstrous fisches taken in Suffolke* (1568). In neither source are the 'monstrous fishes' identified as killer whales. But Granger's broadsheet is illustrated with a picture which, the day after I saw it among the Britwell Ballads in the Huntington Library, I was able to identify with the killer whales in Sea World, San Diego, California.

10. Mary Dewar (ed.), *De Republica Anglorum by Sir Thomas Smith* (Cambridge, 1982) p. 73; MacCulloch, *Suffolk and the Tudors*, pp. 321–31; Peter Clark, *English Provincial Society from the Reformation to the Revolution: Religion, Politics and Society in Kent 1500–1640* (Hassocks, 1977) pp. 82–4; *The lamentable and true tragedie of M. Arden of Feversham in Kent* (1592).

11. R. W. Scribner, 'Civic Unity and the Reformation in Erfurt', in *Past and Present*, no. 66 (1975) 29–60. See also his 'Is There a Social History of the Reformation?', in *Social History*, IV (1977) 483–505, an article critical of Bernd Moeller, *Imperial Cities and the Reformation: Three Essays* (Philadelphia, 1972) and Steven Ozment, *The Reformation in the Cities: the Appeal of Protestantism to Sixteenth-Century Germany and Switzerland* (New Haven, 1975).

12. Clark, '"The Ramoth-Gilead of the Good"', pp. 167–87.

13. Clark, *English Provincial Society*, pp. 12–13.

14. S. R. Cattley and G. Townsend (eds), *Acts and Monuments of John Foxe*, VII (1838) pp. 287–306; much information is also found in 'Cranmer and the Heretics of Kent'.

15. Cathedral Archives and Library Canterbury (hereafter CALC) MS X.10.3, fol. 57; Graham Mayhew, 'Religion, Faction and Politics in Reformation Rye: 1530–59', in *Sussex Archaeological Collections*, 120 (1982) 139–60; Jennifer C. Ward, 'The Reformation in Colchester, 1528–1558', in *Essex Archaeology and History*, 15 (1983) 84-95.

16. CALC, MS X.10.7, fol. 339.

17. Strype, *Annals*, II ii, pp. 282–3. Dickens's *bon mot* was delivered in a lecture and has not, so far as I know, appeared in print.

18. Helen Miller, 'London and Parliament in the Reign of Henry VIII', in *Bulletin of the Institute of Historical Research*, xxxv (1962)

128–49: Susan Brigden, *London and the Reformation* (Oxford, 1989) *passim*.

19. John Strype, *Ecclesiastical Memorials*, I i (Oxford, 1822) pp. 245–6; *Acts and Monuments of Foxe*, VII, pp. 477–8; BL, MS Cleopatra E. V, fol. 394^v.

20. CALC, MS X.10.2, fol. 22.

21. Borthwick Institute of Historical Research, York, HC. CP. 1567/8.

22. Susan Brigden, 'Popular Disturbance and the Fall of Thomas Cromwell and the Reformers, 1539–1540', in *Historical Journal* XXIV (1981) 273–7.

23. J. J. Scarisbrick, *The Reformation and the English People* (Oxford, 1984) may be compared with R. Whiting, ' "For the Health of my Soul": Prayers for the Dead in the Tudor South-West', in *Southern History*, V (1983) 68–94.

24. Cross, *Urban Magistrates and Ministers*, p. 1; Mervyn James, *Family, Lineage and Civil Society: A Study of Society, Politics and Mentality in the Durham Region, 1500–1642* (Oxford, 1974).

25. Claire Cross (ed.), *York Clergy Wills 1520–1600: I Minster Clergy*, Borthwick Texts and Calendars: Records of the Northern Province 10 (1984) pp. 81, 97; Patrick Collinson, *Archbishop Grindal, 1519–1583* (1979) p. 190; Claire Cross, 'Parochial Structure in the Dissemination of Protestantism in Sixteenth Century England: A Tale of Two Cities', in D. Baker (ed.), *The Church in Town and Countryside: Studies in Church History*, XVI (Oxford, 1979) pp. 269–78; D. M. Palliser, *Tudor York* (Oxford, 1979) pp. 226–59.

26. W. J. Sheils, 'Religion in Provincial Towns: Innovation and Tradition', in Felicity Heal and Rosemary O'Day (eds), *Church and Society in England Henry VIII to James I* (1977) pp. 156–76.

27. Peter Martyr, *Martyrs divine epistles*, appended to *Common places*, trans. Anthony Marten (1583) pp. 62–3.

28. Patrick Collinson, 'Episcopacy and Reform in England in the Later Sixteenth Century', in *Godly People: Essays on English Protestantism and Puritanism* (1983) pp. 154–89; Patrick Collinson, *The Religion of Protestants: the Church in English Society* (Oxford, 1982) pp. 171–3.

29. Bartimaeus Andrews, *A very short and pithie catechisme* (1586) Epistle.

30. Much of the information in this paragraph comes from the Assembly Books of Great Yarmouth 1570–98 and I am indebted for it to Miss N. M. Fuidge. The episode of Mr Mayham and the Dedham ministers is recorded in the so-called Dedham classis minute book, R. G. Usher (ed.), *The Presbyterian Movement in the Reign of Queen Elizabeth*, Camden 3rd series VII (1905) pp. 43–6. Ward's words are quoted in Collinson, *Religion of Protestants*, p. 153.

31. Ibid., pp. 171–7.

32. Patrick Collinson, *The Elizabethan Puritan Movement* (1967) pp. 168–76; Collinson, *Archbishop Grindal*, pp. 233–52.

33. Patrick Collinson, 'Lectures by Combination: Structures and Characteristics of Church Life in 17th-Century England', in Collinson, *Godly People*, pp. 467–98.

34. Information on Bacon's shopping list is kindly supplied by Professor

A. H. Smith; on Cranbrook see Patrick Collinson, 'Cranbrook and the Fletchers: Popular and Unpopular Religion in the Kentish Weald', in Collinson, *Godly People*, p. 414; on Exeter, W. G. Hoskins, 'The Elizabethan Merchants of Exeter', in S. T. Bindoff, J. Hurstfield and C. H. Williams (eds), *Elizabethan Government and Society: Essays Presented to J. E. Neale* (1961) pp. 163–87.

35. Alan Everitt, 'Country, County and Town: Patterns of Regional Evolution in England', in *Transactions of the Royal Historical Society*, 5th series, XXIX (1979) 79–108; Peter Borsay, ' "All the Town's A Stage": Urban Ritual and Ceremony 1600–1800', in *The Transformation of English Provincial Towns*, pp. 228–58.
36. Quoted in Collinson, *Religion of Protestants*, p. 171.
37. Paul Slack, *The Impact of Plague in Tudor and Stuart England* (1985) pp. 126–41.
38. Huntington Library, MS HAP Box 12, 'A note of remembrances of things in my iorney', in the hand of Sir Francis Hastings.
39. Clark, ' "Ramoth-Gilead of the Good" ', p. 172.
40. T. F. Barton (ed.), *The Registrum Vagum of Anthony Harison*, pt I, Norfolk Record Society XXXII (Norwich, 1963) pp. 98–9.
41. Peter Heath, 'Urban Piety in the Later Middle Ages: the Evidence of Hull Wills', in Barrie Dobson (ed.), *The Church, Politics and Patronage in the Fifteenth Century* (Gloucester, 1984) pp. 209–34; N. P. Tanner, *The Church in Late Medieval Norwich* (Toronto, 1984).
42. M. E. James, 'Ritual, Drama and Social Body in the Late Medieval English Town', in *Past and Present* no. 98 (1983) 3–29; MacCulloch, *Suffolk Under the Tudors*, pp. 142–3; Clark *English Provincial Society*, pp. 26–7.
43. This paragraph is based on an afternoon on site, in Lowth, followed by examination of the Louth churchwardens' accounts in the Lincolnshire County Record Office. On Louth and the Lincolnshire Rising, see Mervyn James, 'Obedience and Dissent in Henrician England: the Lincolnshire Rebellion 1536', in James, *Society, Politics and Culture: Studies in Early Modern England* (Cambridge, 1986) pp. 188–269, and Margaret Bowker, 'Lincolnshire 1536: Heresy, Schism or Religious Discontent?', in D. Baker (ed.), *Schism, Heresy and Religious Protest*, Studies in Church History, IX (Cambridge, 1972) pp. 195–212.
44. Ward, 'The Reformation in Colchester', p. 90; *Letters and Papers of Henry VIII*, XVIII (ii) no. 546, p. 308; CALC, MSS X.10.3, fol. 45, X.10.7, fol. 137fi. Borthwick Institute of Historical Research, York. MS HC.AB.6, fol. 31ʳ; CALC, MS X.1.3, fols 155ᵛ, 133ᵛ, X.10.13, fols 24–5, 32, 33ᵛ; Collinson, *Archbishop Grindal*, pp. 97–9; CALC, MS X.10.7, fol. 137ʳ.
45. C. L. Kingsford (ed.), *A Survey of London by John Stow* (Oxford, 1908) I, pp. 91–9; Keith Thomas, *The Perception of the Past in Early Modern England*, The Creighton Lecture, 1983 (1983); Peter Burke, 'Popular Culture in Seventeenth-Century London', in *Popular Culture in Seventeenth-Century England*, pp. 31–58; Michael Berlin, 'Civic Ceremony in Early Modern London', in *Urban History Yearbook* (1986) pp. 15–27.

46. A. F. Johnston and Margaret Rogerson (eds), *Records of the Early English Drama, II, York*, i (Toronto, 1979) pp. 359–62, 369–70; Sacks, 'The Demise of the Martyrs' pp. 150–1; CALC, MSS X.10.7, fol. 195, X.8.6, fol. 37ª.
47. Charles Phythian-Adams, *Desolation of a City: Coventry and the Urban Crisis of the Late Middle Ages* (Cambridge, 1979).
48. *Records of the Early English Drama, II, York*, i, p. 358; Harold Gardiner, *Mysteries' End: an Investigation of the Last Days of the Medieval Religious Stage* (New Haven, 1946) pp. 68, 87–8.
49. Lawrence M. Clopper (ed.), *Records of the Early English Drama, I, Chester* (Toronto, 1979) pp. 104–5, 109–10, 197–9, 234–8.
50. E. I. Fripp (ed.), *Minutes and Accounts of the Corporation of Stratford-upon-Avon*, 4 vols (Dugdale Society: 1921–9).
51. John Pound, *Poverty and Vagrancy in Tudor England* (1971); John Webb, *Poor Relief in Elizabethan Ipswich*, Suffolk Records Society IX (Ipswich, 1966); Paul Slack, 'Poverty and Politics in Salisbury 1597–1666', in *Crisis and Order in English Towns*, pp. 164–203; Slack, 'Religious Protest and Urban Authority: the Case of Henry Sherfield, Iconoclast, 1633', in *Schism Heresy and Religious Protest*, pp. 295–302; Frances Rose-Troup, *John White the Patriarch of Dorchester (Dorset) and the Founder of Massachusetts, 1575–1648* (New York, 1930) pp. 33–5.
52. This is argued by Peter Clark in *English Provincial Society*, pp. 38–44, and in his 'Reformation and Radicalism in Kentish Towns c. 1500–1533', in W. J. Mommsen (ed.), *Stadtbürgertum und Adel in der Reformation: The Urban Classes, the Nobility and the Reformation*, Publications of the German Historical Institute, London, 5 (1979) pp. 107–27.
53. Borthwick Institute of Historical Research, York, HC. CP. 1567/8; A. Peel (ed.), *A Seconde Parte of a Register* (Cambridge, 1915) I, p. 238.
54. Essex Record Office, MS D/B/3/3/178; George Gifford, *A briefe discourse of certaine points of the religion which is among the common sort of christians which may bee termed the countrie divinitie* (1581).
55. The question is posed and partly answered in my article 'The Church: Religion and its Manifestations', in John F. Andrews (ed.), *William Shakespeare His World, His Work His Influence* (New York, 1985), I, p. 38.
56. PRO, S.P. 12/155/11.
57. David Underdown, *Revel, Riot and Rebellion: Popular Politics and Culture in England 1603–1660* (Oxford, 1985) pp. 44–72.
58. Borsay, ' "All The Town's A Stage" '.

3 THE PROTESTANT FAMILY

1. Mary Dewar (ed.), *The De Republica Anglorum of Sir Thomas Smith* (Cambridge, 1981) p. 60.
2. Christopher Hill, *Society and Puritanism in Pre-Revolutionary England* (1966 edn) chapter 13, 'The Spiritualization of the Household'; John

Morgan, *Godly Learning: Puritan Attitudes Towards Reason, Learning and Education, 1560–1640* (Cambridge, 1986) chapter 8, 'The Godly Household'; Keith Thomas, 'Women and the Civil War Sects', in T. Aston (ed.), *Crisis in Europe 1560–1660* (1965) p. 340; S. D. Amussen, 'Gender, Family and the Social Order, 1560–1725', in Anthony Fletcher and John Stevenson (eds), *Order and Disorder in Early Modern England* (Cambridge, 1985) p. 200.

3. Hill, *Society and Puritanism*, p. 444.
4. CALC, MS X.10.2, fols 90ᵛ, 67ᵛ.
5. William Lambarde, *The duties of constables, borsholders, tithing-men, and such other low ministers of the peace* (1583) p. 18; CALC, MS X.10.8, fols 35–6ʳ.
6. Barbara A. Hanawalt, *The Ties that Bound: Peasant Families in Medieval England* (New York, 1986) p. 44.
7. H. Walter (ed.), *Doctrinal Treaties ... by William Tyndale* (Parker Society: Cambridge, 1848) p. 175; Hill, *Society and Puritanism*, p. 452.
8. Friedrich Engels, *The Origin of the Family, Private Property and the State* (Penguin Classics, 1985). I am indebted to Alan Macfarlane for the critique of Engels in his *Marriage and Love in England 1300–1840* (Oxford, 1986). See also Jack Goody, *The Development of the Family and Marriage in Europe* (Cambridge, 1983).
9. In constructing the sketch which follows of Luther's ideas on marriage and experience as a married man, I draw upon the following primary and secondary sources: Luther, 'The Estate of Marriage' (1522), 'On Marriage Matters' (1530), in *The Christian in Society* II and III, *Works* XLV and XLVI (Philadelphia 1962, 1967), *Table Talk, Works* LIV (Philadelphia, 1967); Margaret A. Currie (ed.), *The Letters of Martin Luther* (1908); Preserved Smith, *The Life and Letters of Martin Luther* (1911); R. H. Bainton, *Here I Stand: A Life of Martin Luther* (Mentor edn, 1956) pp. 223–37; Heinrich Bornkamm, *Luther in Mid-Career 1521–1530* (1983) pp. 401–15.
10. Steven Ozment, *When Fathers Ruled: Family Life in Reformation Europe* (Cambridge, Mass., 1983) p. 16.
11. For Milton's use of Bucer's *De Regno Christi* in his republication of *The Judgement of Martin Bucer concerning divorce* and the second edition of his own *Doctrine and discipline of divorce* (1644) see David Masson, *The Life of John Milton*, III (1873) pp. 255–61. William Whateley of Banbury was obliged to repudiate his allowance of divorce in *A bride bush, Or, a direction for married persons* (pp. 25–6) in a preface to *A care-cloth: or, a treatise of the cumbers and troubles of marriage* (1624), Sig. A8.
12. Bernard Vogler, *Le Clergé protestant rhenan au siècle de la Réforme (1555–1619)* (Paris, 1976) p. 211; Patrick Collinson, *The Religion of Protestants: the Church in English Society 1559–1625* (Oxford, 1982) pp. 115–16.
13. M. M. Knappen (ed.), *Two Elizabethan Puritan Diaries* (Chicago, 1933) pp. 95, 73–4.
14. CALC, MSS X.8.6, fols 52ᵛ–3ʳ, 57, X.1.15A, fol. 63ʳ, X.10.7, fols 38ᵛ–9ʳ, X.1.12, fol. 01ᵛ, X.1.13, fol. 44ᵛ.
15. Collinson, *The Religion of Protestants*, pp. 114–16. In 1576 William

Lucas of Dymchurch, Kent, was presented in the archdeacon's court for saying that if he were of the Queen's Council 'ministers should have no wives, for the goods that they have should sustain the poor, where now it doth maintaine them, their wives and children. Then at the last he said it is meet that every minister should have his wife, but then their wives should be sober, wise, discreet, ancient, and women past children.' (CALC, MS X.10.17, fol. 36^v)

16. Sir John Harington, in R. H. Miller (ed.), *A Supplie or Addicion to the Catalogue of Bishops to the Yeare 1608* (Studia Humanitatis: Madrid, 1979) p. 181; Samuel Clarke, *A Collection of the Lives of Ten Eminent Divines* (1662) p. 8.
17. PRO, S.P. 12/159/27.
18. Ralph A. Houlbrooke, *The English Family 1450–1700* (1984) p. 5; Lawrence Stone, *The Family, Sex and Marriage in England, 1500–1800* (1977) p. 141.
19. References here are to the current research of Diana O'Hara of the University of Kent; Hanawalt, *The Ties that Bound*; and J. A. Sharpe, 'Plebeian Marriage in Stuart England: Some Evidence from Popular Literature', in *Transactions of the Royal Historical Society*, 5th series, XXXVI (1986) 69–90.
20. Milton quoted by Stone, *The Family, Sex and Marriage*, p. 102; J. Ayre (ed.), *The Catechism of Thomas Becon* (Parker Society: Cambridge, 1844) pp. 302–410.
21. Clarke, *A Collection of Lives*, p. 105.
22. Thomas Fuller (ed.), *The Works of Henry Smith*, I (Edinburgh, 1866) p. 26; CALC, MS X.10.17, fol. 36^v.
23. Edward Shorter, *The Making of the Modern Family* (1977) p. 3.
24. Gawdy correspondence, British Library (BL), MS Egerton 2804; Talbot correspondence, Lambeth Palace Library and Folger Shakespeare Library, MS X.d.428.
25. BL, MS Harley 70, fol. 2.
26. Whateley, *A Bride Bush*, p. 199; William Gouge, *Of domestical duties* (1634 edn) pp. 285–6; L. B. Larking (ed.), *Proceedings in the County of Kent in Connection with the Parliaments Called in 1640* (Camden Society c, 1862) p. 55.
27. Miranda Chaytor, 'Household and Kinship: Ryton in the Late 16th and Early 17th Centuries', in *History Workshop*, 10 (1980) 25–60.
28. John Bossy, *The English Catholic Community, 1570–1850* (1976) p. 158.
29. Nicholas Guy, *Pieties pillar: or, a sermon preached at the funerall of Mistresse Elizabeth Gouge* (1626) p. 48; Collinson, *Religion of Protestants*, pp. 169–70; Richard Hooker in J. Keble (ed.), *Works* (revised R. W. Church and F. Paget, 1888) I, pp. 152–3. See Patrick Collinson, 'The Role of Women in the English Reformation Illustrated by the Life and Friendships of Anne Locke', in Collinson, *Godly People: Essays on English Protestantism and Puritanism* (1983) pp. 273–87.
30. Whateley, *A Bride Bush*, p. 84; *Works of Smith*, I, p. 29.
31. David Kunzle, 'World Turned Upside Down: the Iconography of a European Broadsheet Type', in Barbara Babcock (ed.), *The Reversible World: Symbolic Inversion in Art and Society* (Ithaca, 1978) pp. 39–94.

32. R. G. Usher (ed.), *The Presbyterian Movement in the Reign of Queen Elizabeth*, Camden 3rd series, VIII (1905) p. 35; Thomas, 'Women and the Civil War Sects'; Claire Cross, '"He-Goats Before the Flock"': A Note on the Part Played by Women in the Founding of Some Civil War Churches', in G. J. Cuming and D. Baker (eds), *Popular Belief and Practice: Studies in Church History*, VIII (Cambridge, 1972) pp. 195–202.

33. For Mary Honeywood and Dering's relations with her see Thomas Fuller, *The History of the Worthies of England* (1662) II, pp. 85–6 and my 'The Role of Women' and 'A Mirror of Elizabethan Puritanism: the Life and Letters of "Godly Master Dering"', in *Godly People*, pp. 273–324.

34. Michael Macdonald, *Mystical Bedlam* (Cambridge, 1981) pp. 217–31; Jasper Heartwell, *Trodden Down Strength* (1647). On the Drake case see G. H. Williams in *Harvard Library Bulletin* XVI (1968) 111–28; John Knox, in David Laing (ed.), *Works* (Edinburgh, 1854) III, pp. 337–402.

35. Ronald Knox, *Enthusiasm: A Chapter in the History of Religion* (Oxford, 1950).

36. W. B. Rye, *England as Seen by Foreigners in the Days of Elizabeth and James the First* (1865) p. 72.

37. N. Z. Davis, *Society and Culture in Early Modern France* (1975) pp. 65–95.

38. On the subject of early modern childhood the best account is now in Linda Pollock, *Forgotten Children: Parent–Child Relations from 1500 to 1900* (Cambridge, 1983).

39. *Works of Becon*, III, p. 607; Gouge, *Of domestical duties*, p. 546; Macdonald, *Mystical Bedlam*, p. 43; John Demos, *A Little Commonwealth: Family Life in Plymouth Colony* (New York, 1970) pp. 134–6.

40. Gouge, *Of Domestical duties*, pp. 500, 551, 432–3; Edward Hake, *A touchstone for this time present* (1574) Sigs. C7, E2, F; William Kempe, *The education of children in learning* (1588) Sig. Fᵛ; *The Catechism of Thomas Becon*, p. 350; Ozment, *When Fathers Ruled*, pp. 136–44.

41. C. John Somerville, 'English Puritans and Children: A Social-Cultural Explanation', in *Journal of Psycho-History*, VI (1978–9) 113–37; William Sloane, *Children's Books in England and America in the Seventeenth Century* (New York, 1955); Ozment, *When Fathers Ruled*, p. 163; Hanawalt, *The Ties that Bound*, p. 179.

42. BL, MS Loan 29/202, fol. 135; Paul S. Seaver, *Wallington's World: A Puritan Artisan in Seventeenth-Century London* (Stanford, 1985) p. 87.

43. Stone, *The Family, Sex and Marriage*, p. 111.

44. Edmund S. Morgan, *The Puritan Family: Religion and Domestic Relations in Seventeenth-Century New England* (New Haven, 1944) pp. 1ff, 77.

45. Hanawalt, *The Ties that Bound*, pp. 101, 185.

46. Stone, *The Family, Sex and Marriage*, pp. 109ff; D. E. Underdown, 'The Taming of the Scold: the Enforcement of Patriarchal Authority in Early Modern England', in *Order and Disorder in Early Modern England*, pp. 116–36.

47. Peter Laslett, *The World We Have Lost* (2nd edn, 1971) pp. 109–10, 119–21; E. F. Carpenter in W. R. Matthews and W. M. Atkins (eds), *A*

History of St Paul's Cathedral, (1964 edn) p. 150; W. Sparrow Simpson (ed.), *Documents Illustrating the History of S. Paul's Cathedral*, Camden n.s. XXVI (1880) p. 131; *The Catechism of Thomas Becon*, p. 349; Pollock, *Forgotten Children*, p. 264.

48. Hanawalt, *The Ties that Bound*, pp. 171ff.
49. General guidance to a vast literature is provided by Michael Anderson, *Approaches to the History of the Western Family 1500–1914* (1980), and by Michael W. Flinn, *The European Demographic System 1500–1820* (Brighton, 1981) which incorporates a bibliography of 703 items.
50. Hanawalt, *The Ties that Bound*, p. 92.
51. R. H. Helmholz, *Marriage Litigation in Medieval England* (Cambridge, 1974).
52. Huntington Library, MS EL 6162, fols 34a–36a; J.-P. Flandrin, 'Repression and Change in the Sexual Life of Young People in Medieval and Early Modern Times', in R. Wheaton and T. K. Hareven (eds), *Family and Sexuality in French History* (Philadelphia, 1980) pp. 27–48 (see also J.-L. Flandrin, *Families in Former Times: Kinship, Household and Sexuality* (Cambridge, 1979); Hanawalt, *The Ties that Bound*, pp. 34, 94, 97. The seminal article lying behind these discussions was published by J. Hajnal in 1965, 'European Marriage Patterns in Perspective', in D. V. Glass and D. E. C. Eversley (eds), *Population in History*, (1965).
53. Robert Muchembled, *Culture populaire et culture des élites dans la France moderne* (Paris, 1978); Martin Ingram, 'The Reform of Popular Culture? Sex and Marriage', in Barrie Reay (ed.), *Popular Culture in Seventeenth-Century England* (1985) pp. 125–65; R. M. Smith, 'Marriage Processes in the English Past: Some Continuities', in *The World We Have Gained: Histories of Population and Social Structure: Essays Presented to Peter Laslett on his Seventieth Birthday* (Oxford, 1986) pp. 43–99; Flandrin, 'Repression and Change'.
54. Whateley, *A care-cloth*, p. 65.
55. Chaytor, 'Household and Kinship'; Robert Wheaton in *Family and Sexuality in French History*, p. 119. On the wider issues see Richard Wall et al, (eds), *Family Forms in Historic Europe* (Cambridge, 1983), as corrective of P. Laslett and R. Wall (eds), *Household and Family in Past Time* (1972). See also David Cressy, 'Kinship and Kin Interaction in Early Modern England', in *Past and Present* no. 113 (1986) 38–69.
56. John Morris (ed.), *The Letter-Book of Sir Amias Paulet* (1874) p. 184; *Family Forms*, p. 7; Hanawalt, *The Ties that Bound*, p. 5. But Miranda Chaytor suggests that 'households were the point where kin groups, joined by marriage, shared and redistributed their resources' ('Household and Kinship', p. 39), which is a different perspective.
57. CALC, MS X.10.6, fol. 117ʳ. I owe this reference to Diana O'Hara.
58. Martin Ingram, 'Ridings, Rough Music and Mocking Rhymes in Early Modern England', in *Popular Culture in Seventeenth-Century England*, pp. 166–97; Martin Ingram, 'Ridings, Rough Music and the "Reform of Popular Culture" in Early Modern England', in *Past and Present*, no. 105 (1984) 79–113; Underdown, 'The Taming of the Scold', in *Order and Disorder in Early Modern England*, pp. 116–36.
59. Hanawalt, *The Ties that Bound*, pp. 218–19. The particular reference is to a celebrated passage in *The Boke of Margery Kempe*.

60. Ibid., p. 186.
61. Macdonald, *Mystical Bedlam*, pp. 80–5; Hanawalt, *The Ties that Bound*, pp. 177–84.
62. Ben Jonson, 'On My First Son'.
63. Kathleen M. Davies, 'Continuity and Change in Literary Advice on Marriage', in R. B. Outhwaite (ed.), *Marriage and Society: Studies in the Social History of Marriage* (1981) pp. 58–80.
64. Margo Todd, 'Humanists, Puritans and the Spiritualized Household', in *Church History*, XLIX (1980) 18–34. The argument of this article is restated more copiously in Margo Todd, *Christian Humanism and the Puritan Social Order* (Cambridge, 1989).

4   PROTESTANT CULTURE AND THE CULTURAL REVOLUTION

Further documentation for this chapter will be found in my *From Iconoclasm to Iconophobia: the Cultural Impact of the Second English Reformation (The Stenton Lecture, 1985)* (Reading, 1986).

1. This is attributed in the *corrigenda* of the *Oxford Dictionary of Quotations* to a character in the Nazi play *Schlageter* by Hanns Johst.
2. C. S. Lewis, *English Literature in the Sixteenth Century Excluding Drama* (Oxford, 1973 edn) p. 43.
3. See most recently Anthea Hume, *Edmund Spenser: Protestant Poet* (Cambridge, 1984) and her 'Spenser, Puritanism and the "Maye" Eclogue', in *Review of English Studies*, XX (1969) 155–67.
4. Donald Davie, *A Gathered Church: The Literature of the English Dissenting Interest, 1700–1930* (1978) p. 1.
5. William Tyndale, 'The Obedience of a Christian Man', in H. Walter (ed.), *Doctrinal Treatises . . . by William Tyndale* (Parker Society: Cambridge, 1848) p. 161.
6. Erasmus, 'Paraclesis', in J. C. Olin (ed.), *Christian Humanism and the Reformation* (New York, 1965) p. 97; Lily B. Campbell, *Divine Poetry and Drama in Sixteenth-Century England* (Cambridge, 1959).
7. Emanuel Le Roy Ladurie, *The Peasants of Languedoc* (Urbana, 1976) p. 271.
8. John M. King, *English Reformation Literature: The Tudor Origins of the Protestant Tradition* (Princeton, 1982) pp. 209–27; Campbell, *Divine Poetry and Drama*, pp. 18, 41–3, 49.
9. Barbara K. Lewalski, *Milton's Brief Epic: The Genre, Meaning and Art of 'Paradise Regained'* (Providence R. I., 1966); Tyndale, *Obedience*, pp. 148–9.
10. BL, MS Loan 29/202, between fols 230 and 231.
11. Barbara K. Lewalski, *Protestant Poetics and the Seventeenth-Century Religious Lyric* (Princeton, 1979) p. 3 and *passim*; King, *English Reformation Literature*, p. 141.

12. G. D. Bone, 'Tindale and the English Language', in S. L. Greenslade, *The Work of William Tindale* (1938) p. 67.
13. Lewis Wager, *A new enterlude . . . entreating of the life and repentaunce of Marie Magdalene* (1566; modern edn F. I. Carpenter: Chicago, 1940); *A newe mery and wittie comedie or enterlude newely imprinted, treating upon the historie of Jacob and Esau* (licensed 1557/8, printed 1568; Malone Society reprint 1956); *A pretie new enterlude both pithie and pleasaunt of the story of Kyng Daryus* (1565).
14. Campbell, *Divine Poetry and Drama*.
15. R. W. Scribner, *For the Sake of Simple Folk: Popular Propaganda for the German Reformation* (Cambridge, 1981) pp. 3–4.
16. Glynne Wickham, *Early English Stages 1300 to 1660*, I (1959) p. 71; C. R. Smith (ed.), *Concordia Facta Inter Regem Riccardum II et Civitatem Londinie* (Princeton University PhD dissertation, 1972); Lawrence M. Clopper (ed.), *Records of the Early English Drama, I, Chester* (Toronto, 1979) p. 75.
17. Alexander F. Johnston and Margaret Rogerson (eds), *Records of the Early English Drama, II, York*, i (Toronto, 1979) pp. 359–62.
18. R. W. Ingram (ed.), *Records of the Early English Drama, III, Coventry* (Toronto, 1981) pp. xvii, lxii, 221, 257.
19. Robert Laneham, *A Letter* (1575) pp. 33–4.
20. *Records of the Early English Drama, III, Coventry*, pp. 294, 303, 307–9.
21. Harold C. Gardiner, *Mysteries' End: an Investigation of the Last Days of the Medieval Religious Stage* (New Haven, 1946) pp. 72–83; *Records of the Early English Drama, II, York*, i, p. 353.
22. *Records of the Early English Drama, I, Chester*, pp. 197–9, 234–6, 184; David Underdown, *Revel, Riot and Rebellion: Popular Politics and Culture in England (1603–1660)* (Oxford, 1985) p. 51; E. I. Fripp (ed.), *Minutes and Accounts of Stratford-upon-Avon*, II, *1566–1577*, Dugdale Society Publications, III (1924) p. xxxvi; Ipswich and East Suffolk Record Office, Ipswich Chamberlains Accounts, temp. Elizabeth I, *passim*.
23. *Records of the Early English Drama, III, Coventry*, p. 207.
24. *Records of the Early English Drama, II, York*, i, p. 331–3.
25. T. E. Hartley (ed.), *Proceedings in the Parliaments of Elizabeth I, I, 1558–1581* (Leicester, 1981) p. 31; S. R. Cattley (ed.), *The Acts and Monuments of John Foxe*, VI (1838) p. 31; William Prynne, *Histrio-Mastix: the Players Scourge or Actors Tragedie* (1633).
26. E. J. Baskerville, 'John Ponet in Exile: a Ponet Letter to John Bale', in *Journal of Ecclesiastical History*, XXXVII (1986) 442–7. On Bale's enduring significance and influence see Rainer Pineas, *Tudor and Early Stuart Anti-Catholic Drama* (1972), King, *English Reformation Literature*, pp. 276–84, and Ritchie D. Kendall, *The Drama of Dissent: the Radical Poetics of Nonconformity, 1380–1590* (Chapel Hill, 1986) especially p. 131.
27. Ibid., p. 276.
28. CALC, MS X.10.7, fols 36^r–39^r. There are references in the Canterbury Chapter *Acta* to payments for the 'setting forth of interludes' by the scholars of the grammar school (1561) and to the 'setting forth of

tragedies, comedies and interludes' (1562) (Ibid., MS Y.11.2, fols 21, 28ᵛ). For the Whitsun Plays of New Romney see Gardiner, *Mysteries' End*, p. 68, and Peter Clark, *English Provincial Society from the Reformation to the Revolution: Religion, Politics and Society in Kent, 1500–1640* (Hassocks, 1977) pp. 153–4.

29. *A pretie new enterlude called Nice Wanton* (1560, written c. 1547–53); *An enterlude called Lusty Juventus* (1565); Thomas Inglend, *A pretie and mery new enterlude called the disobedient child* (1569, written c. 1560); W. Wager, *The longer thou livest the more foole thou art* (c. 1559–68, written c. 1559).

30. Richard Baker, *Theatrus Triumphans* (1670) pp. 30–1; John Heywood, *The play called the foure P* (1569), Sig. Ci.

31. David Bevington, *From Mankind to Marlowe* (Cambridge, Mass., 1962).

32. *Acts and Monuments of Foxe*, V pp. 404–9, 403, 445, VIII, pp. 214, 554–5, 416, 578; BL, MS Harley 421, fol. 97ʳ.

33. *Letters and Papers of Henry VIII*, XIV (ii) pp. 11–12; BL, MS Harley 425, fols 4–7; *Acts and Monuments of Foxe*, VIII, pp. 458–60; William Wilkinson, *A confutation of certaine articles* (1579), excerpted in John Strype, *Annals of the Reformation*, II ii (Oxford, 1824) pp. 282–3; CALC, MS X.8.8, fol. 349.

34. PRO, S.P. 1/99, fols 203ᵛ–4. For rites of inversion and misrule, see Martin Ingram, 'Ridings, Rough Music and the "Reform of Popular Culture" in Early Modern England', in *Past and Present*, no. 105 (1984) 79–113, and R. Eden (ed.), *Examinations and Writings of John Philpot* (Parker Society: Cambridge, 1842) p. 307.

35. Full references to what follows on the godly parodic ballad will be found in my *From Iconoclasm to Iconophobia*. The leading authority on the matters discussed here and elsewhere in this chapter is Dr Tessa Watt, author of *Cheap Print and Popular Piety 1550–1640*, to be published shortly by the Cambridge University Press.

36. Nicholas Temperley, *The Music of the English Parish Church*, 2 vols (Cambridge, 1979).

37. Campbell, *Divine Poetry and Drama*, p. 48.

38. Some Kentish evidence on the harrying of the minstrels is collected in my *The Religion of Protestants: the Church in English Society 1559–1625* (Oxford, 1982) pp. 206–7.

39. Nicholas Bownd, *The doctrine of the sabbath* (1595) pp. 241–2.

40. Hyder E. Rollins, *An Analytical Index to the Ballad-Entries in the Registers of the Company of Stationers of London*, Studies in Philology 21 i (Chapel Hill, 1924) nos 1892, 1051. Further references are in my *From Iconoclasm to Iconophobia*, notes 65–70. 'Greensleeves' is described as 'a new Courtly Sonet' in its publication in *A handefull of pleasant delites* (1584).

41. Temperley, *Music of the English Parish Church*, pp. 36, 63, 67, 34–5; H. G. Koenigsberger, 'Music and Religion in Early Modern European History', in Koenigsberger, *Politicians and Virtuosi: Essays in Early Modern History* (1986) pp. 179–210. See also H. P. Clive, 'The Calvinist Attitude to Music', in *Bibliothèque d'Humanisme et Renaissance*, XX (1958) 302–7.

42. Quoted by Sandra Clark in *The Elizabethan Pamphleteers: Popular Moralistic Pamphlets 1580–1640* (1983) p. 140. On the appearance and growth of the antitheatrical prejudice see William A. Ringler, 'The First Phase of the Elizabethan Attack on the Stage 1558–1579', in *Huntington Library Quarterly*, V (1942) 391–418; William Ringler, *Stephen Gosson: a Biographical and Critical Study* (Princeton, 1924); R. W. Chambers, *The Elizabethan Stage*, I (Oxford, 1923) pp. 242–56; Jonas Barish, *The Antitheatrical Prejudice* (Berkeley and Los Angeles, 1981); David Leverenz, *The Language of Puritan Feeling: An Exploration of Literature, Psychology and Social History* (New Brunswick, 1980) chapter 1, 'Why did Puritans hate stage plays?' I owe the point about 'the idolatrous eye' to Dr Michael O'Connell of University of California, Santa Barbara.

43. Full references to the decline of biblical and religious drama will be found in my *From Iconoclasm to Iconophobia*, notes 43–8.

44. Prynne, *Histrio-Mastix*, p. 934. Compare my *Religion of Protestants*, pp. 244–5.

45. F. S. Boas (ed.), *Five Pre-Shakespearean Comedies* (1934) (and see Robert W. Bolwell, *The Life and Works of John Heywood* [New York, 1921]); *Acts and Monuments of Foxe*, VI, p. 31; Stephen Gosson, *The Schoole of abuse* (1578), Sig. D3; H. Mutschmann and K. Wentersdorf, *Shakespeare and Catholicism* (New York, 1952) p. 102; John Awdley, *The wonders of England* (1559).

46. Scribner, *For the Sake of Simple Folk*.

47. BL, C.160.c.7.

48. N. Z. Davis, 'Printing and the People', in N. Z. Davis, *Society and Culture in Early Modern France* (1975) pp. 203–4.

49. For Godet and many other facets of this subject I am dependent upon Tessa Watt and her forthcoming study *Cheap Print and Popular Piety*, where Godot is shown to have had his successors. The standard work of reference is Arthur M. Hind, *Engraving in England in the Sixteenth and Seventeenth Centuries, I, The Tudor Age* (Cambridge, 1952) and *II, The Reign of James I* (Cambridge, 1955).

50. J. F. Mozley, *John Foxe and his Book* (1940) p. 131.

51. K. J. Höltgen, *Francis Quarles (1592–1644)* (Tübingen, 1978) p. 216.

52. K. J. Höltgen, 'The Reformation of Images and Some Jacobean Writers on Art', in U. Broich, T. Stemmler and G. Stratmann (eds), *Functions of Literature, Essays Presented to Erwin Wolff on his Sixtieth Birthday* (Tübingen, 1984) pp. 119–46.

53. *H.M.C. Calendar, Salisbury MSS*, I, p. 568; PRO, S.P. 12/167/47, 172/106, 176/16; John Morris, *The Letter-Book of Sir Amias Paulet* (1874) pp. 317–18.

54. Susan Foister, 'Paintings and Other Works of Art in Sixteenth-Century English Inventories', in *Burlington Magazine*, CXXIII (1981) 273–82.

55. John Phillips, *The Reformation of Images: Destruction of Art in England 1535–1660* (Berkeley, 1973).

56. Höltgen, 'The Reformation of Images', p. 136.

57. Hind, *Engraving in England*; information communicated by Dr Watt. Dr Watt's *Cheap Print and Popular Religion* will contain information on wall

paintings of religious topics, and especially of the Prodigal Son, which partly corrects what is said here.

58. Höltgen, 'The Reformation of Images'.
59. James Cleland, *Iacobs wel, and Abbots conduit* (1626) pp. 44, 50–2; F. E. Hutchinson (ed.), *The Works of George Herbert* (Oxford, 1941) p. 6; Nicholas Tyacke, *Anti-Calvinists: The Rise of English Arminianism c. 1590–1640* (Oxford, 1987) p. 194; L. B. Larking (ed.), *Proceedings in the county of Kent in Connection with the Parliaments called in 1640* (Camden Society c, 1862) p. 185.
60. Huntington Library, MS HA Inventories Box 1, no. 1; Egil Johanssen, 'The History of Literacy in Sweden', in H. J. Graff (ed.), *Literacy and Social Development in the West* (Cambridge, 1981) pp. 157–61.
61. Walter J. Ong, *Ramus: Method and the Decay of Dialogue* (Cambridge, Mass., 1958); Walter J. Ong, *Interfaces of the Word: Studies in the Evolution of Consciousness and Culture* (Ithaca, 1977); Frances A. Yates, *The Art of Memory* (1960). The 'She Puritan' will be found in John Earle's *Microcosmographie* (1628).
62. Philip Sidney, *The Defence of Poesie*, Cambridge English Classics (Cambridge, 1923) pp. 6–7, 9, 14.
63. Erasmus, 'Paraclesis', in *Christian Humanism and the Reformation*, p. 106.
64. Lewalski, *Protestant Poetics*.
65. R. C. Richardson, *Puritanism in North-West England: A Regional Study of the Diocese of Chester to 1642* (Manchester, 1972), p. 102.
66. Lewalski, *Protestant Poetics*, chapter 3, 'The Poetic Texture of Scripture: Tropes and Figures for the Religious Lyric'.
67. *Acts and Monuments of Foxe*, VII, p. 232. To be sure, Joyce Hales was no artisan but an educated woman.

5 WARS OF RELIGION

1. Marshall's sermon 'Meroz Cursed' can be found in *The Fast Sermons to Parliament* series of R. Jeffs (ed.), *The English Revolution, II, 1641–1642*, pp. 195–253. George Yule prints extracts with commentary in *Puritans in Politics* (Appleford, 1981) pp. 297–304.
2. H. Christmas (ed.), *The Works of Nicholas Ridley* (Parker Society: Cambridge, 1843) p. 366. Further reference could well have been made in this chapter to the use of military metaphors in the sermons preached to the Honourable Artillery Company of London in the early seventeenth century. See J. R. Hale, 'Incitement to Violence? English Divines on the Theme of War, 1578 to 1631', in Hale, *Renaissance War Studies* (1983), pp. 487–517.
3. Thomas Jackson, *Judah must into captivitie: six sermons* (1622) pp. 60–1.
4. E. G. Rupp, *Patterns of Reformation* (1969) pp. 244–5.
5. Olive Anderson, 'The Growth of Christian Militarism in Mid-Victorian England', in *English Historical Review*, LXXXVI (1971) 46–72; Edmund Gosse, *Father and Son: A Study of Two Temperaments* (1907) pp. 33–4, 41.

6. I draw here upon a conversation with the late Bishop Stephen Neill.
7. A. F. Winnington Ingram, *Into the Fighting-Line* (1912) (see his subsequent sermons *The Church in Time of War* [1915] and another book of 1915, *The Bishop of London's Visit to the Front*); Henry Newbolt, *Collected Poems 1897–1907* (1918).
8. John Aylmer, *An harborowe for faithfull and trewe subiectes* ('Strasborowe', but *recte* London, 1559) Sig. Q2.
9. Leicester's orders quoted by Simon L. Adams, 'The Protestant Cause: Religious Alliance with the West European Calvinist Communities as a Political Issue in England, 1585–1630' (Oxford DPhil thesis, 1973) pp. 57–8. For militant Christianity at Le Havre see Patrick Collinson, *The Elizabethan Puritan Movement* (1967) p. 52; and my 'Letters of Thomas Wood, Puritan, 1566–1577', in *Godly People: Essays on English Protestantism and Puritanism* (1983) p. 51; and a forthcoming study of Wood by Simon Adams. It is significant that the early puritan propagandist Anthony Gilby made the old veteran of Berwick walls 'Miles Monopodis' the hero of his *Pleasaunt dialogue betweene a souldior of Barwicke and an English chaplaine* (1581).
10. Francis Rogers, *A Sermon preached . . . at the funerall of William Proud, a lieutenant colonell, slaine at the last late siege of Mastricke* (1633) Sig. D2ᵛ.
11. See above, p. 54.
12. Quoted in Patrick Collinson, *The Religion of Protestants: the Church in English Society, 1559–1625* (Oxford, 1982) pp. 176, ix.
13. Richard Bernard, *The Bible battels. Or, the sacred art military* (1629).
14. Roy Strong, *Henry, Prince of Wales and England's Lost Renaissance* (1986) especially pp. 52, 54.
15. *The souldiers pocket Bible* (dated by Thomason 3 August 1643) has been reproduced in facsimile by John Atkins for Partizan Press, Leighon-Sea, Essex.
16. W. D. Macray (ed.), *The History of the Rebellion and Civil Wars in England . . . by Edward, Earl of Clarendon* (Oxford, 1888) I, pp. 4–5.
17. Quoted in Collinson, *The Religion of Protestants*, p. 168.
18. Jacqueline Eales, *Puritans and Roundheads: the Harleys of Brampton Bryan and the Outbreak of the English Civil War* (Cambridge, 1990).
19. William Lamont, *Richard Baxter and the Millennium: Protestant Imperialism and the English Revolution* (1979), chapter 2, 'Baxter and the Origins of the English Civil War'.
20. Anthony Fletcher, *The Outbreak of the English Civil War* (1981) pp. 417–18; John Morrill, 'The Religious Context of the English Civil War', in *Transactions of the Royal Historical Society* 5th series, XXXIV (1984) 155–78.
21. I owe this suggestion to Dr J. P. Sommerville. Christopher Hill's cautious comment on Morrill's views is in his *Collected Essays, II, Religion and Politics in 17th Century England* (Brighton, 1986) pp. vii–viii.
22. John Morrill, *The Revolt of the Provinces* (2nd edn, 1980) p. x; Ronald Hutton, *The Royalist War Effort 1642–1646* (1982) especially pp. 201–3.
23. Richard Baxter, *A Holy Commonwealth* (1659) pp. 456–7; Samuel

Clarke, *Lives of Ten Eminent Divines* (1662) p. 467.

24. David Underdown, *Revel, Riot and Rebellion: Popular Politics and Culture in England 1603–1660* (Oxford, 1986) chapter 3, 'Cultural Conflict'.
25. What follows is documented in PRO, S.P. 12/223/47, 224/54, 55, 57, 58, 61, 65, 66; *Acts of the Privy Council*, XVII, 202; PRO, Star Chamber 5 B 31/4. See also Elliot Rose, *Cases of Conscience: Alternatives Open to Recusants and Puritans Under Elizabeth I and James I* (Cambridge, 1975) pp. 169–76; Collinson, *The Religion of Protestants*, p. 145.
26. Collinson, *Godly People*, p. 70. For Cope's charitably motivated woad enterprise see Joan Thirsk, *Economic Policy and Projects: the Development of a Consumer Society in Early Modern England* (Oxford, 1978) pp. 21–2.
27. Lawrence Stone, *The Family, Sex and Marriage in England, 1550–1800* (1977) pp. 95, 98.
28. Dr Jim Sharpe has entertained both analyses. See his *Defamation and Sexual Slander in Early Modern England: the Church Courts at York*, Borthwick Papers 58 (York, 1980) and ' "Such disagreement betwyx Neighbours": Litigation and Human Relations in Early Modern England', in John Bossy (ed.), *Disputes and Settlements: Law and Human Relations in the West* (Cambridge, 1983) pp. 167–187.
29. CALC, MS X.8.8, fols 1ᵛ, 2.
30. Collinson, *The Religion of Protestants*; N. R. N. Tyacke 'Puritanism, Arminianism and Counter-Revolution', in C. Russell (ed.), *The Origins of the English Civil War* (1973) pp. 119–43; Nicholas Tyacke, *Anti-Calvinists: the Rise of English Arminianism c. 1590–1640* (Oxford, 1987).
31. Jeremy Goring, *Godly Exercises or the Devil's Dance: Puritanism and Popular Culture in Pre-Civil War England*, Friends of Dr Williams's Library 37th Lecture (1983) pp. 3, 24.
32. Keith Wrightson, 'The Puritan Reformation of Manners, With Special Reference to the Counties of Lancashire and Essex, 1640–1660' (Cambridge PhD thesis, 1974).
33. *Cal. S. P. Dom. Charles I 1633–1634*, pp. 275–6.
34. John Angier, *An helpe to better hearts for better times* (1647) pp. 75, 81–6, 415–18; CALC, MS X.10.13, fol. 129ʳ.
35. J. S. Purvis (ed.), *Tudor Parish Documents of the Diocese of York: A Selection with Introduction and Notes* (Cambridge, 1948) p. 169.
36. See above, p. 108.
37. Patrick Collinson, *English Puritanism* (1983).
38. W. H. Frere and C. E. Douglas (eds), *Puritan Manifestoes* (1954) p. 9.
39. Patrick Collinson, 'The English Conventicle', in W. J. Sheils and D. Wood (eds), *Voluntary Religion*, Studies in Church History XXIV (Oxford, 1986) pp. 223–59.
40. See above, pp. 23–4 and 27.
41. Arthur Dent, *The plaine mans path-way to Heaven* (1601), p. 287; John Darrell, *A treatise of the church written against them of the separation, commonly called Brownists* (1617) pp. 25, 28–9; M. McGiffert (ed.), *Gods Plot: the Paradoxes of Puritan Piety: Being the Autobiography and*

Journal of Thomas Shepard (Cambridge, Mass., 1972) pp. 9, 98.

42. Thomas Wilson, *Two Sermons* (1609) pp. 71–2.
43. Alan Macfarlane et al., *Reconstructing Historical Communities* (Cambridge, 1977) pp. 1–4.
44. Eamon Duffy, 'The Godly and the Multitude in Stuart England', in *The Seventeenth Century*, I (1986) 71–2.
45. Stuart Clark, 'Inversion, Misrule and the Meaning of Witchcraft', in *Past and Present*, no. 87 (1980) 98–127; Michael Hunter, 'The Problem of "Atheism" in Early Modern England', in *Transactions of the Royal Historical Society*, 5th series, XXXV (1985) 135–57.
46. William Crashawe, *A sermon preached at the Crosse Feb. 14 1607* (1608).
47. Paul S. Seaver, *Wallington's World: A Puritan Artisan in Seventeenth-Century London* (Stanford, 1985); Collinson, *Elizabethan Puritan Movement*, pp. 349–50; N. R. N. Tyacke, 'Popular Puritan Mentality in Late Elizabethan England', in P. Clark, A. G. R. Smith and N. Tyacke (eds), *The English Commonwealth 1547–1640: Essays in Politics and Society Presented to Joel Hurstfield* (Leicester, 1979) pp. 77–92; William Kempe, *The education of children in learning* (1588), Sigs. E3^v–4^r.
48. R. J. Acheson, 'Sion's Saint: John Turner of Sutton Valence', in *Archaeologia Cantiana*, 99 (1983) 183–97.
49. Christopher Marsh, '"A Gracelesse and Audacious Companie"? The Family of Love in the Parish of Balsham, 1550–1630', in *Voluntary Religion*, pp. 191–208.
50. John Bossy, *The English Catholic Community 1570–1850* (1975) p. 143; John Bossy, 'The Character of Elizabethan Catholicism' in T. Aston (ed.), *Crisis in Europe, 1560–1660* (1965) p. 226.
51. Champlin Burrage, *The Early English Dissenters* (Cambridge, 1912) II, pp. 1–6; Joseph W. Martin, '"The First that Made Separation from the Reformed Church of England"', in *Archive for Reformation History*, LXXVII (1986); J. W. Martin, 'Elizabethan Familism and English Separatism', in *Journal of British Studies* XX (1980) 53–73; J. W. Martin, 'Christopher Vitel: an Elizabethan Mechanick Preacher', in *Sixteenth-Century Journal* X (1979) 15–22.
52. Underdown, *Revel, Riot and Rebellion*, pp. 55–6.
53. Keith Wrightson and David Levine, *Poverty and Piety in an English Village: Terling 1525–1700* (1979); Peter Clark, *The English Alehouse: A Social History 1200–1830* (1983); Margaret Spufford, 'Puritanism and Social Control?', in Anthony Fletcher and John Stevenson (eds), *Order and Disorder in Early Modern England* (Cambridge, 1985) pp. 41–57. Professor Fisher's remarks were noted at an Anglo-American Conference of Historians when Professor Clark read a paper on alehouses.
54. Underdown, *Revel, Riot and Rebellion*. For Bernard and Batcombe see Collinson, *The Religion of Protestants*, pp. 85–6.
55. Peter Burke, *Popular Culture in Early Modern Europe* (1978).
56. Henry Fishwick (ed.), *The Note Book of the Rev. Thomas Jolly . . . Extracts from the Church Book of Altham and Wymondhouses*, Chetham Society n.s. 33 (Manchester, 1895) pp. 120–1, 128, 133–4.

General Index

Index of Modern Authors